*(Above)* The jackass schooner rig is splendidly shown in this fine photo of **Goldfinch** in 1930, just before she sailed out to British Guiana. Her topsail braces lead aft through blocks in the mizzen shrouds, which are pulled forward by their tension. Gaskets for stowing the headsails are made up neatly under the bowsprit. She has roller reefing, and sets her outer jib to the topmast head — two features not found in the early schooners. *(Beken)*.

*(Previous page)* By contrast, this unidentified ketch, running past Leigh, no longer carries a squaresail, but rigs a makeshift spinnaker. She also sets a somewhat reach-me-down topsail. She has a galley on deck, often preferred to the focs'le for cooking in fine weather. *(David Patient)*

# THE BIG BARGES

## The Story of Boomie and Ketch Barges

HERVEY BENHAM and ROGER FINCH

in collaboration with
PETER FERGUSON

HARRAP    LONDON

**OTHER BOOKS BY HERVEY BENHAM**

*Last Stronghold of Sail* (Harrap)
*Down Tops'l* (Harrap)
*Once Upon a Tide* (Harrap)
*Two Cheers for the Town Hall* (Hutchinson)
*Some Essex Watermills* (Essex County Newspapers)
*The Stowboaters* (Essex County Newspapers)
*The Codbangers* (Essex County Newspapers)
*The Salvagers* (Essex County Newspapers)

**OTHER BOOKS BY ROGER FINCH**

*Coals from Newcastle* (T. Dalton)
*The Ship Painters* (T. Dalton)
*From Viking Ship to 'Victory'* (HMSO)
*Sailing Craft of the British Isles* (Collins)
*A Cross in the Topsail* (Boydell Press)

*First published in Great Britain* 1983
*by* HARRAP LIMITED
19-23 Ludgate Hill, London EC4M 7PD

© *Hervey Benham* 1983

ISBN 0 245-54003-2

Designed by Michael R. Carter

Printed and bound in Great Britain
by Robert Hartnoll Ltd, Bodmin

# Contents

**Appendices**

# Introduction

This book is a collaboration between two authors who decided to pool their efforts after each had contemplated a study of the evolution and adventures of that characterful craft, the boomie barge.

Roger Finch, in addition to providing the drawings and many of the other illustrations from his own collection, has contributed the chapters on construction and on the coal trade, and has disentangled the story of the Ipswich shipyards.

Hervey Benham has undertaken most of the rest of the writing, but always based on shared knowledge, experience and opinion.

Our researches at quite an early stage attracted the interest of Peter Ferguson, editor of *Topsail,* the journal of the Society for Spritsail Barge Research, whose collaboration has extended to the provision of a great deal of the material and a revision of the whole typescript.

The result has thus proved to be a co-operative effort, with Richard Hugh Perks also contributing his wide knowledge of the Kentish scene. Our first acknowledgment must therefore be to the generous and invaluable participation of these fellow-enthusiasts.

Of making many books about sailing barges there is seemingly no end. Several of these include a chapter or two on the boomsail-rigged craft — the boomies, or ketch barges, as they were often described.

But the boomies, for all their close association with the spritsail barges, were in fact a class apart. They usually had crews of four or five, keeping four-hour watches on their longer passages, and preserving the distinction between able-bodied and ordinary seamen in the foc's'le. The skipper was very much the captain, and some expected to be addressed as 'Sir'. This contrasted with the easy-going ways of the spritties, where the skipper and mate worked as a more informal partnership, even though many spritties carried a third hand throughout the age of the boomies. As a result the boomie captains looked down on the sprittie-barge skippers — a little maritime snobbery perpetuated by the masters of the big latter-day spritsail coasters in expressing contempt for the estuary craft.

There were even degrees of superiority among the big barges. Captain Redwood of Harwich (whose father was lost in the *Mary Lyne*) always frowned on the idea of ketch barges being called boomie barges, on the grounds that a 'ketch barge is a sea-going vessel with high rails, cutwater bow, bowsprit and jibboom, martingale and a round counter — and not like those boomie barges with a square transom, and hull not much better than an ordinary barge'.

This distinction is valid, though the nomenclature is confusing, for many of the proud craft for which Captain Redwood claimed the title of ketch were registered, regarded and originally rigged as jackass schooners, while the humbler square-sterned boomies to which he denied the title were indisputably ketches!

The real distinction was, however, between boomies and spritties, both in the work they did and the way in which they did it, even though the same hull could and often did serve both purposes.

The spritsail barge was the final and ultimate development of working sail for highly specialized purposes. In the oft-quoted phrase, she would take 150 tons across the North Sea with a crew of a man and a boy, and would float wherever there had been a heavy dew. No other craft ever approached her for versatility and efficiency. Even had the internal combustion engine not ended the long reign of sail, it is doubtful if she could have been further improved; indeed, if a great tradition of human effort, endeavour and ingenuity had to end, it is some consolation that it lasted long enough to attain something like perfection.

The boomie could make no such claims. She was the last development of the traditional sailing coaster, utilitarian and in-genious, with one advantage over her spritsail sisters. She did not sacrifice certain basic qualities of seaworthiness to provide the specialized qualities of the sprittie.

The spritsail barge was sailed into her berth and out of it. She would moor up to a buoy in a tideway or come alongside a tier of moored barges without so much as touching her anchor down. The ballast barges sailed in under the chutes of the PLA dredger, filled their holds and sailed off again as a matter of routine. The skipper of a river barge once said to his mate, 'It seems a pity to bring up and go ashore with the foot boat for the shopping. This thing is so handy I swear I could check her alongside the jetty and jill around while you get a loaf of bread and a newspaper.' No other craft could perform such feats. The boomies would take a tug if one was available, or failing that anchor and warp into a berth.

*Zenobia* finished a voyage from the Rhine by 'drudging' up to St Katharine's Dock, stern first, like any river barge, as described in

Chapter 16, but the cargo books quoted in Chapter 14 show that this was the exception.

It may even be considered that boomies and spritties belonged to different worlds and different eras.

The spritties survived into the 1950s, perpetuating the age of sail into the age of advanced technology, thanks to their astonishing efficiency, which enabled them not only to shrug off such challenge as steam could offer, but even to fight a long rearguard action against that deadlier enemy, diesel.

The boomies were essentially a feature of an older world, 'the world we have lost', the world that ended with the First World War (even though a handful survived into the 1920s, and the last till 1941). Their story is part of the thrusting commercial energy of Victorian England. It was an age full of character and full of characters, epitomized by men like George Smeed, creator of Sittingbourne, who started by hawking coal from a handcart and ended with a commercial empire including eighty ships, or John Harvey of Littlehampton, who developed wooden shipbuilding into something not far short of a production line, or J. D. Foster of Emsworth, with his restless imagination and almost romantic creativity.

Many of the minor characters were hardly less colourful, such as the redoubtable Meachen family of Harwich skippers, or William Middleton, who loved a jibboom so much that he kept them in his craft long after they had gone out of fashion, or John Whitmore, who liked to jump up on a table to lead the revels, despite having a wooden leg which was liable to fall off, or Edward Garnham of Chelmondiston, near Ipswich, building up his little fleet out of his savings as an engine-driver in India.

The boomies themselves reflect the thrust of the age, some displaying the pride of builders and owners, with their clipper bows and decorative scrollwork; some more commercially conceived to load yet another fifty tons of black diamonds to meet the insatiable demands of brickworks and brewers, gasworks and maltings; some carrying the barge concept to unimaginable lengths, with barquentine and even barque rigs planted in their flat-bottomed hulls.

In line with the hard standards of the age, all had to be driven unmercifully, both on the continual slog up and down the deadly East Coast, and also on voyages as far afield as Lisbon, the Mediterranean and Christiania (Oslo). The rate of losses, though probably less than among the conventionally built sailing coasters, was appalling — a reminder (always so necessary with a subject of this sort) to avoid romanticizing the theme — and, incidentally, another contrast with the spritties, whose very vulnerability caused them to be worked within more reasonable limits, resulting in a remarkably small toll of disaster.

That the boomies were their skippers' pride and joy was proved by the number which had their portraits painted, principally by that most prolific of pierhead artists, Reuben Chappell. They were also extensively photographed, so pictorial evidence has not been hard to come by.

Their achievements and adventures, successes and misfortunes, were less recorded, though it was still possible in 1980 to talk to a few men who knew them, and a number of surviving cargo books record their daily comings and goings.

Even so, a few questions have refused to yield answers. What were the earnings of skippers and crews? Usually they relied on a share of the freight money, but how was this divided? How often was the distinction between able-bodied and ordinary seaman observed, and how were they recruited? How often were the boomies given a refit? How were freight rates fixed? (The almost derisory rate for so valuable and vulnerable a cargo as cement from Waldringfield on the Deben to Hull seems surprising.) Whether the final details in this story will ever be revealed at this distance in time remains to be seen.

Happily, the boomies attracted the interest fifty years ago of a young enthusiast on the Deben, George Doughty, who made copious notes and drawings at a time when such craft were all around him. The only child of the Rev. F. E. Doughty of Martlesham, he was much beloved by everyone on Woodbridge waterside, and perhaps the gods loved him too, for he died at the tragically early age of thirty-one in 1940. He would have liked to have compiled this book, and it is sad that he was not spared to attempt it. He spent many hours questioning old skippers and recording their memories, though his notes are so full of contradictions and confusions — often noted by him with disarming humour — that it is doubtful if he would ever have brought them to a conclusion.

About his drawings there need be no reservations. They are skilful and delightful, as well as being clearly authentic. They were, however, mostly pencil sketches, to which reproduction would not have done justice, especially after fifty years. Roger Finch has therefore redrawn some of them, with the same sense of respect for Doughty's originals that I have tried to retain when I have rewritten his words. Many were intended to illustrate his view of the evolution of the various types of boomies, which he classified into groups. This scheme we have respected and retained; it may perhaps be criticized as too simplistic, but Doughty was nearer to the scene and to the men who understood it than we can be today, and if we can be challenged over this arrangement we are at least in good company.

On Doughty's death his material passed to his friend Dr J. L. Groom of Harwich, another enthusiastic researcher and recorder, to whom I have been indebted for two previous books, *The Salvagers* and *The Codbangers,* in which a fuller biographical acknowledgment appears. Dr Groom published a little booklet, *Ketch Barges,* based on articles in the *East Anglian Magazine,* and on his death his material passed to his brother, Mr Tom Groom, who has allowed Roger Finch and myself to have access to it.

Mr Donald Sattin — himself a barge-builder and author of *Just off the Swale* — Mr Alan Cordell, Mr David Clement and Mr David Patient have been generous, particularly with the loan of illustrations, as has Mr Alf Pyner with memories and pictures of Burnham-on-Crouch. Miss Patricia O'Driscoll has contributed from her wide practical knowledge of the barging world. At the National Maritime Museum we have been helped by Mr Alan Pearsall, Mr Dennis Stonham and Mr James Lees. Down-Channel, Captain Frederick Grant of Shoreham and Mr Henry Higgs have helped us to redress the inevitable ignorance of East Coasters about South Coast affairs, while Mr Martin Bell of Exmouth has supplied details of the *Western Belle* and Captain Arthur Jemmett of the *Northdown*.

Since the time of George Doughty and Jack Groom much has of course been published, particularly in Frank Carr's *Sailing Barges* and Edgar March's *Spritsail Barges of the Thames and Medway*, both of which have accounts of Smeed's leviathans. Hervey Benham's own *Down Tops'l* has some further references to Essex and Suffolk boomies, and A. W. Roberts has written his own account of his life as the last skipper of the last boomie, *Martinet*, in *Coasting Bargemaster*.

Other books and articles are listed under Further Reading, or in some cases as footnotes, indicating the source of material used throughout the text.

Finally, both authors owe a debt of gratitude to Mr Roy Minton for his meticulous care and professional expertise in editing these chapters, to Mr Michael Carter for the design of the book, and to a number of friends who have contributed much painstaking typing, including Mrs Sandra Hopwood and Mrs Alison Woods.

HERVEY BENHAM
Feldy
West Mersea

ROGER FINCH
Ipswich
Suffolk

# Further Reading

**Hervey Benham**
*Down Tops'l* (Harrap 1951-1971)
*The Salvagers* (Essex County Newspapers, 1980)

**Arthur Bennett**
*Us Bargemen* (Meresborough Books, 1980)

**Frank Carr**
*Sailing Barges* (Conway, 1971)

**Henry Cheal**
*The Ships and Mariners of Shoreham* (Cambridge 1971)

**John Collard**
*A Maritime History of Rye* (Adams, Rye, 1978)

**Roger Finch**
*Coals from Newcastle* (Dalton, 1973)
*The Ship Painters* (Dalton, 1975)
*A Cross in the Topsail* (Boydell Press 1979)

**A. H. and R. J. Horlock**
*Mistleyman's Log* (Fisher Nautical 1977)

**Edgar March**
*Spritsail Barges of the Thames and Medway* (Percival Marshall 1948)

**Richard Hugh Perks**
*A History of Faversham Sailing Barges* (Society for Spritsail Barge Research 1967)
*George Bargebrick Esq*
(The story of George Smeed) (Meresborough Books, 1981)

**A. W. Roberts**
*Coasting Bargemaster* (Arnold, 1949)

**D. L. Sattin**
*Just off the Swale* (Meresborough Books, 1978)

**Robert Simper**
*Woodbridge and Beyond* (East Anglian Magazine, 1972)

# PART 1

# Development of the
# Big Barges

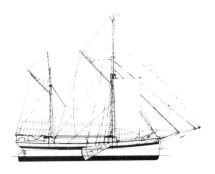

# Cutting off the Keel

During the first half of the nineteenth century the face of England was transformed as the full effects of the Industrial Revolution came to be felt. Countless trades, crafts and occupations either disappeared or were changed almost beyond recognition. Above all, the steam-engine ended the long reliance on the water-wheel and windmill, and drove the coach off the turnpike roads.

All-conquering steam took to the water, harnessed to the splashing paddle-wheel and Archimedean screw, with equally confident expectations, but with a very different outcome. Sail, developed and improved down the centuries, found new ways to increase its efficiency and adapt itself to defy the challenge. Those who could not believe the horse could ever be replaced for the movement of men and materials were proved wrong. Those who derided the idea of making a vessel go to windward by lighting a bonfire under her deck were surprisingly proved right, at least as far as the coasters and small craft of the East Coast were concerned. Though steam provided reliable and speedy passenger services, the trading coasters relegated it to the subservient role of towing them in and out of harbour, and with this new assistance went on to enjoy another half-century of prosperous activity, using the techniques of the old world to supply the demands of the new. Sail carried the coal to fuel the factories, the products the factories made, and the materials and the machinery with which they made them. Sail brought the bricks and stone with which the new towns were built, the grain to satisfy the appetites of the growing populations. For every freight the railways took away from sail they provided another, among

them the transport of the metals and sleepers for their own construction.

The sailing coasters did not shrug off the challenge of the Industrial Revolution; they responded to it. The builders of wooden sailing craft joined with the ironfounders in the restless, zestful urge towards technical improvement. Clumsy hull-forms which had evolved without critical thought, expensive to build and requiring big crews to transport small cargoes, no longer satisfied the keen scrutiny and competition of a new age. Regulations favouring depth of the hull in the calculation of tonnage were repealed in 1837. As a result there evolved craft cheaper to build and operate, specially suited to the expanding coastal trade.

The end of the Napoleonic Wars, when the reopening of the seaways stimulated a rapid expansion of trade, found the local coastal traffic dominated by the sloop; the longer coastal freights — and particularly coal from the Tyne — by brigs and schooners; and the Baltic and other foreign trades by brigantines and barques.

The sloop was a handy and universal maid-of-all-work. All-purpose, cutter-rigged smacks, useful both for fishing and for cargo-carrying, had been used for a century, and were still to be found as late as the 1920s, just before the introduction of the heavy lorry and improved roads. By this time they were chiefly employed on the East Coast for specialist seasonal trades such as fish and early potatoes, though the rig survived in the West Country estuaries for carrying bulk cargoes.

Many of these smacks had developed their stowage capacity at the expense of speed, handiness and the sea-keeping qualities required for

Predecessor of the boomie. The sloop **Good Intent,**
here seen unloading into carts at Whitstable,
demonstrates the type of deep, clumsy hull which the
barge-built sloops replaced. *(Roger Finch)*

fishing, but they were not capable of being
developed to a size which would meet the
merchants' demands for bigger 'parcels', or even
to justify the size of the crew required. Nor were
they really suitable to take the ground without
support except in soft mud, restricting their use to
harbours and quays with a reasonable depth of
water. These shortcomings applied also to
schooners and brigs, though some of these could
be laid ashore on a beach for unloading in fine
weather, as Constable's and Turner's paintings of
coast scenes show.

Moreover, none of these craft would sail
without ballast, a deficiency specially felt in the
all-important coal trade, which very frequently
involved a passage light back to the Tyne or the
Humber. Sometimes it was possible to make a
load of beach sand, shingle or chalk pay for itself,
but usually the loading of a sufficient amount to
make the vessel stable, and its jettisoning at the

end of a passage, involved unwanted delay and
expense. There was also difficulty and danger
when, to avoid the expense of discharging ballast
at the places provided, craft dumped it outside at
sea, and faced the problem of entering in a 'crank'
condition.

The flat-bottomed barge hull was free of most
of these drawbacks. It had immense cargo-
stowage capacity, it could sail without ballast, it
could make use of harbours too shallow for
round-bottomed craft, and it was well suited to
dispense with harbours altogether, loading and
unloading on any uncluttered foreshore where a
cart could come alongside at low water. It was
vulnerable on long sea passages, for leeboards
were never a real substitute for a keel, specially
when one needed to heave-to and ride out a gale.
It was thus less advantageous on deep-water
coasts, but on the shallow East Coast its suit-
ability was so great that it is somewhat surprising
that its general adoption had to wait till the mid-
nineteenth century.

The sloop was beginning to favour a barge hull

as far back as the 1820s, as is shown in many pictures of harbour scenes, and in particular in the invaluable drawings of E. W. Cooke. One may regard such craft as sloops with their bottoms cut off, but since they are usually swim-headed, or luff-bowed, it would be truer to regard them as lighters which had developed leeboards and sailing gear.

The first development of importance was the addition of a mizzen on the rudder head. This was not merely a reflection of the general tendency of sloops to develop into dandies. Among fishing smacks the 'long-boomers' decided that when a boom reached a length of around forty feet it was better to set any further canvas on a mizzen mast. These dandies were often a half-way step in the change from cutter to ketch rig. The pilots who bought old cutter yachts shortened their booms and similarly turned them into dandies for easier cruising on their stations.

The barge sloops had another purpose altogether. Their mizzens were too small to make any appreciable contribution to their propulsion, or to permit any reduction in the size of the mainsail, but mounted on the rudder they greatly assisted steering. They were in effect an extension of the rudder upward into the wind. The sail turned with the rudder, and acted as part of it.

This was particularly valuable in turning to windward with a flat-bottomed hull. A fine-lined, deep-keeled craft would carry sufficient way to luff up head to wind and then pay away on the other tack when the helm was put down, whereas the flat-bottomed hull tended to stop, and required to be twisted round its centre of lateral resistance, the leeboard.

The principle of the wind rudder was retained to the end in spritsail barges, though with the introduction of wheel steering it was found better to step the mizzen on deck, and sheet the sail to the rudder, so that instead of the whole mast and 'outligger' rotating with the rudder only the mizzen boom was pulled to windward when the helm was put down.

The sloop was thus developed into a dandy, as seen in the *Tertius* of 1844. A dozen years later

**Tertius.** A sloop with lug mizzen barge-built at Ipswich in 1844.

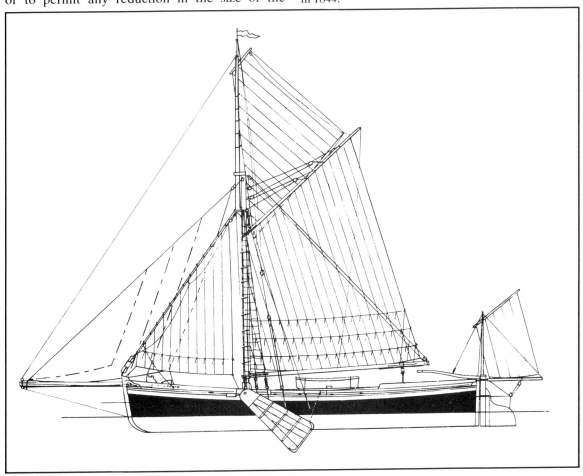

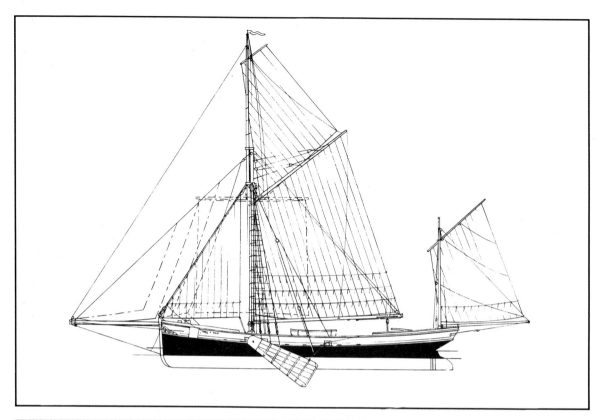

came the final refinement of the dandy with the building of the *Flower of Essex* in 1857. She would be commonly described as a ketch barge, but in her original form there was nothing of the ketch (a rig which in its modern form was unknown in the 1850s), though she was altered to this rig later.

The *Tertius* and the *Flower of Essex* represent the evolution of the ketch barge through 'the sloop with the bottom cut off'.

At the other extreme, the same treatment was

*Opposite*
**Flower of Essex.** *(Top)* Dandy built at Limehouse in 1857. *(Bottom)* After conversion from dandy to ketch rig. *(Hervey Benham)*

*Below*
The **Stour** as she was originally rigged in 1857, with jibboom, dolphin striker and whisker booms. There are three main shrouds aside, with a running backstay. The topsail is rigged on a parrel round the topmast, and if a gaff topsail was set it was a jib-header on a jackstay or 'twitching line'. The single topsail was later replaced by double topsails and by 1880 the **Stour** had wheel steering and had dispensed with mizzen topmast and wooden anchor catheads.

applied to the schooner. In the early 1850s shipbuilders, particularly on the Thames, were beginning to develop sea-going barge-built vessels capable of loading at least 200 tons, this being the 'parcel' established by the brigs that merchants were equipped and accustomed to handle and distribute.

These craft had many advantages in addition to dispensing with ballast. They were cheaper to build — perhaps half or two-thirds the cost of a round-bottomed hull. Their relative unhandiness could be compensated for by the appearance of steam towage. They could be given bigger hatches, facilitating loading and unloading, since they were not expected to make regular deep-sea voyages — unlike the schooners, whose traditional features suited them to voyages to the Mediterranean or across the Atlantic, but inhibited their commercial success on the coast. The schooner rig was, however, often retained in these early craft because it was usual and traditional in craft loading 150-200 tons.

It is impossible to determine just when and where the first really important developments of

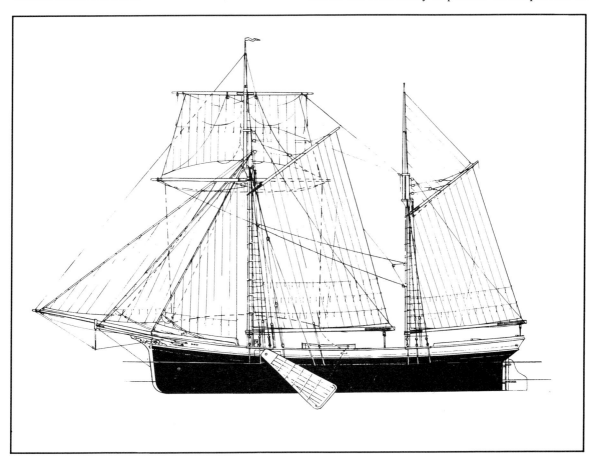

the barge hull took place, or who were the pioneers.

The *Three Brothers,* of 106 new or 72 old registered tons, was built in London as early as 1816. She was clearly of some size, but no other detail survives. The *Margaret,* built at Maidstone in 1843, was, however, registered as a schooner barge, and thus has some claim to be the first recorded example. Of 126 new, or 85 old, registered tons, she was built for T. Pybus and registered at Rochester.

Another early schooner barge, *Advance,* and the first big square-rigged barge, *Laura Shelbourne,* were both built in London in 1854, followed three years later by the *Stour* in Essex and the *General Cathcart* in Kent, and then by the *Surprise* at Ipswich in 1859.

With her jibboom, dolphin-striker and iron whiskers, her anchor catheads, her square topsails and her fidded mizzen topmast, the *Stour* was regarded by her contemporaries as a schooner. Nowadays a schooner is regarded as a vessel with the aftermast bigger than the fore mast, and a present-day observer would call the *Stour* a ketch. If one seeks a pedantic definition she was a jackass schooner, but in the context of boomie-barge evolution the qualification is unnecessary. The issue was disposed of by a Liverpool mariner who called them 'sideboard schooners'.

As originally rigged the *Stour* had no main gaff topsail, but relied entirely on one square topsail, with the upper yard on a parrel round the topmast. The single topsail was still common in deep-sea square-riggers into the 1860s, and was used in most small coasters, usually with a small topgallant sail above it. However, as the schooner barge was being conceived, the safer and more convenient double topsail was coming into fashion, despite the extra complication and expense, and before long the *Stour* was given this modification, the additional yard being rigged on a parrel round the doubling of the topmast. With this rig the upper yard could easily be dropped in a squall and set up again after it had passed. These square topsails were not merely running sails; they were designed to brace hard round on the wind, and to provide for this the topmast had to rely for support on two stays led through short crosstrees.

*Alice Watts* was one of several craft rigged with topsail braces leading forward to the bowsprit, and presumably belayed on or near the bitts, as well as aft to the mizzen. This arrangement may also be seen in portraits of several other craft, though it was not used in the *Stour.* Most have braces both forward and aft, but *Ida* rigs braces

*Alice Watts* with double topsails braced fore and aft, mizzen topsail and main gaff topsail with short headstick. *(Fred Spalding)*

forward from her upper yard and aft from her lower yard. Forward braces were used in craft which refused to allow lee braces to interfere with the proper squaring away of powerful fore-and-aft mainsails, and particularly in heavily rigged, lavishly crewed Naval and Revenue cutters,[1] but their survival or revival in a barge seems curious. Possibly they may have been useful in controlling the yards if the main braces had to be cleared away for loading.

Fore braces seem to have gone out of fashion by the time the *Record Reign* was built in 1897, and were probably quite forgotten in the 1930s, when *Goldfinch* carried her square topsails on her voyage to British Guiana. According to her boatswain, the braces of the main yard and the two topsail yards all ran through lead blocks secured to the forward swifter of the mizzen shrouds, down to a pin rail which ran round the ship inside the bulwarks.

As a further reminder of the tradition they inherited, the *Alice Watts, Lucy Richmond, Laura, Laura Shelbourne, Leading Star* and *Ellen Smeed* all sported figureheads.

The characteristics of the deep-sea schooner soon began to disappear. The barge is by nature a leewardly vessel, and it is doubtful if it was ever really suited to carrying so much lofty tophamper. Moreover, the work on the coast called for windward ability and the development of a powerful fore-and-aft rig.

The traditional trimmings soon began to go out

[1] See models of armed Naval despatch cutter in Antwerp Maritime Museum, and of Barking smack *Saucy Jack* in Doughty Museum, Grimsby; also model in Science Museum, South Kensington, illustrated along with Dutch cutter *Fly* in Keble Chatterton: *Fore and Aft.*

*Above*
**Europa** by J. Fannen (*Parker Gallery*)

*Below*
**Gippeswic** by Reuben Chappell *(Peter Ferguson)*

**Lily** of Harwich *(Richard Hugh Perks)*

**Kate and Emily,** built at Lowestoft in 1851

of fashion. Jibbooms were replaced by single-spar bowsprits, and with them went dolphin-strikers and whiskers. Wooden anchor catheads too were soon discarded.

More important, the fore-and-aft topsail asserted itself at the expense of square topsails. So long as the topmast was required chiefly for the square topsail yard, the fore-and-aft gaff topsail, if rigged at all, was no more than a jib-header, set on a jackstay or twitching line, using clips or hooks at the skipper's discretion.

Before long, however, the advantages of the fore-and-aft topsail with a headstick, used as far back as the 1820s in the smaller sloops and dandies, came to be accepted. With a headstick an extra cloth could be added to the leach, and the sail set better to windward. These new-style topsails were hooped to the topmast and stowed aloft. When they were set over a double-reefed mainsail the bottom mast-hoop was cut away.

They were generally, though not universally, adopted, as a study of the portraits and photographs in this book reveals. *Europa, Lucy Richmond* and *Record Reign* all have jib-headers, recalling their original schooner rig. (So, however, have *Gippeswic, Mazeppa, Lily* and *James Bowles,* which were always ketches.) *Nell Jess* is also remembered as setting a jib-head topsail on a

tall topmast. *Britannia* has no headstick in the photo taken in 1912 (Chapter 15), but wears one in the other photo, which was probably taken at a later date. It would thus seem that with the introduction of the headstick most skippers preferred the convenience of the hooped topsail which had to be stowed aloft, and that the minority, not content with this arrangement, did without the headstick. Yet their West Country counterparts set jackyarders on jackstays from the deck without apparent difficulty.

Some craft, including *Goldfinch* and *Nancy,* managed to combine a gaff topsail hooped to the topmast with traditional jackass schooner rig, presumably by setting the upper topsail yard on a jackstay. Others, including *Ida, Ada Gane* and *Alcyone,* solved the problem with triangular raffee topsails, *Ida* using a short headstick in hers. These sails could have been set flying, relying on the halyard to hold them to the mast, but it is more likely that some sort of jackstay was retained to keep them under control.

The need to retain some square gear is indicated by the fact that when *Goldfinch* dispensed with her double topsails her skipper-owner, J. H. Waters, found her so disappointing as a fore-and-aft ketch that he rerigged her to restore a single square topsail.

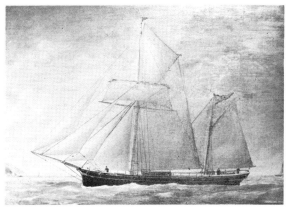

*Above*
**Ida** (1881) has rigged a main gaff topsail with headstick, hooped to the topmast, but she still retains the double topsail of the jackass schooner. The lower topsail sets on a yard mounted on the doubling of the topmast and mainmast, braced forward to the bowsprit end. The lower yard is braced aft. Since the gaff topsail hoops prevent the rigging of an upper topsail yard on the topmast, she has a short horizontal headstick in the upper topsail. This must have been set up by a special halyard, probably on a wire jackstay. In the portrait above *(left)* by Fannen — dated 1893, shortly before she was sold from Ipswich to Whitstable — this sail is set. In the other portrait *(right)* it is stowed on the upper yard. She is tiller steered and retains jibboom and old-fashioned reefing, with eyelets for a third reef in the mainsail. *(N. M. Mus.)*

*Below*
**Ida** at Stockton-on-Tees. Square topsail and flying topgallant are still rigged, with squaresail yard cockbilled, and braces still leading forward. But she now has wheel steering, and though the mainsail is concealed by a cover the mainsheet lead suggests roller reefing. The leeboard appears to have been unrigged. The size of the figures on deck (Harry Stone amidships near the load-line mark) shows what a big craft she was. *(Harry Booth)*

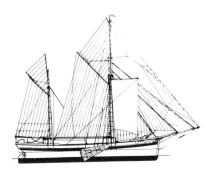

## CHAPTER 2

# Schooner into Ketch

The change from topsail jackass schooner to fore-and-aft ketch occurred in the 1860s, and from about this time a more utilitarian type began to appear.

The boomie was essentially a product of rationalization and economy, and among the smaller 'sloops with the bottom cut off' there were never any great pretensions to elegance, for the sloop itself bequeathed few such traditions. In fact, among these humbler craft it was left to the final generation of spritsail barges to show how much grace and style could be built into carriers

This unidentified ketch seen in Dover harbour probably started life as a mule-rigged sprittie. Not only does she have a steeve-up bowsprit, she also has a staysail rigged from stem to topmast head, a rig used by spritties for the sailing in close quarters seldom attempted by the traditional boomies.

While the counter-sterned ketches were usually the showiest craft, some of the smaller transom-sterned boomies were far from plain, as shown by MacLearon's splendid scroll-work on **Dannebrog,** here seen after conversion into a 'short spindle' mulie, with the wheel immediately forward of the mizzen, instead of just aft of the main horse. **Alice May** was similarly decorated. *(Roger Finch)*

of mud, mangels and haystacks.

The bigger schooners, however, as has been shown, at first adopted with enthusiasm the elaborate gear of their predecessors. The barge hull made them fully competitive, and at first there was no need to carry rationalization further. But as the steam collier increased its competitive pressure, and the influence of a commercial age came to be increasingly felt, a simpler form of boomie — minimizing cost to build and to run, and maximizing profitability in its carrying capacity — made its appearance.

The increasing demands of the general coasting trade also encouraged the building of ketches which were smaller than the big colliers and generally transom-sterned. As the spritsail barges were at the same time increasing in size, the difference between the two types of hull largely disappeared, and conversions both from sprittie to boomie and from boomie to sprittie became increasingly common.

Not that all the general-purpose boomies of the ketch era were either plain or square-sterned. Old

fashions were overtaken by new, but they did not necessarily die out. While transom sterns became the general rule, counter sterns were common to the end in boomies, though rare among spritties. *Martinet,* built in 1912, and in 1941 the last boomie at work, was counter-sterned.

Although the topsail schooner barge may seem to have been out of date by the 1870s, *Goldfinch* was built at Faversham as late as 1894, by the builder whose name she bears, and *Record Reign* at Maldon in 1890.

**Mayland** at the Skeleton Quay, Blackshore, Southwold, about 1880, with her old-fashioned square counter and hemp standing rigging.

Many of the schooner-rigged boomies no longer requiring square topsails for the long coal haul from the Tyne to Exeter, or from Saundersfoot to Southwold, were also converted to ketch — a process which usually meant no more than sending down the yards, and perhaps taking advantage of their absence to set a better main gaff topsail and improve the staying of the topmast.

The big-barge tradition was thus kept alive principally by the coal trade, and it is among these big colliers that a distinction increasingly appears between craft built simply as trading investments and those which, through the preference of the owner or the pride of the builder, retained traditional and decorative features for which there was perhaps not always a strict commercial justification.

The beautiful schooners *Lucy Richmond* and *Malvoisin* were built in 1875 and 1883 out of profits earned by motley fleets of humble craft. It is difficult not to believe that their owners — who were neighbours on the Crouch, and perhaps

rivals — were influenced by a desire to possess something of which they could be proud. On the other hand, the third major owner on that river, John Smith the coal merchant, concentrated on craft whose beauty must have been in their balance sheets. It is true that his *Rochester Castle* had her bulwarks decorated with the black and white 'painted sports' pattern that recalled the armed East Indiamen (as did *Lucy Richmond*), but this little concession to tradition cost no more than a coat of paint. Smeed of Sittingbourne was another who certainly did not live in the past; his remarkable series of huge craft were no beauties,

**Gloriana** (1871) was one of the first true ketch barges. She retains the head gear of the schooner, with jibboom, dolphin striker and catheads, but square topsails have been abandoned to provide for a hooped gaff topsail, which, however, has not yet developed a headstick. She carries a squaresail yard, kept permanently aloft and stowed cockbilled, with one end lashed to the rigging when out of use, though later craft usually lowered the yard on deck. On this was set a squaresail for running, and perhaps a jib-headed raffee topsail.

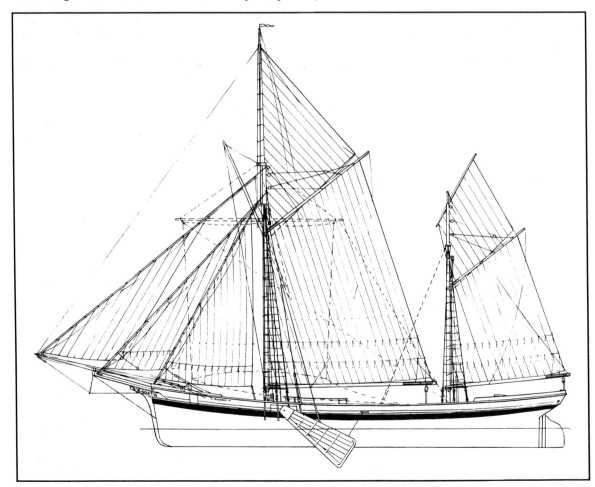

but show that for a really heavy haul square-rig never became obsolete.

The new generation of ketch barges seems to have originated in Kent with *Garibaldi* (1861) and *Adsey* and *Invicta* (1863). Barge-built craft of earlier date are to be found registered as ketches, but it is unlikely that this was their original rig.

*Gloriana,* built by Vaux in 1871, was considered the first Harwich-built ketch. Her 'clipper' bow still sports jibboom, wooden catheads and whisker booms, but she contents herself with a single fair-wind squaresail, and the topmast is entirely devoted to a gaff topsail which (at the time of her building) was still jib-headed.

With the *Osprey* of 1874 the jibboom is replaced by a single-spar standing bowsprit. The short double crosstrees are replaced by longer single spreaders, now that there is no square topsail yard to brace on the wind, and with this better support a jib topsail is introduced.

At first it was still not thought safe to take this sail's halyard to the topmast head. Instead, the sail was hanked to the topmast stay, but the halyard was taken to the mainmast head, so that the head of the sail had to depart awkwardly from the stay. This arrangement was employed to the end in some craft, though many abandoned it and set the sail to the topmast head. The same technique was employed in Severn trows. The Harwich cod smacks set their jib topsails flying to the topmast head in light weather, but kept a 'tailing tackle' rove so that in a breeze the halyard could be pulled in to the upper mast-cap, or to a point halfway up the topmast. This may have been done in some barges — indeed, it is safe to speculate that every possible alternative was tried by someone at some time.

In the 1880s the counter stern, which had usually been elliptical but was sometimes a square tuck, was increasingly discarded in the smaller boomies in favour of the transom, with the rudder outboard, or 'out of doors' as the bargemen put it.

Many of them also contented themselves with a plain straight stem, but the shapely fiddle head was lovingly maintained in others. Not many barges were built with the planks extended into the fully formed 'clipper' bow, though this refined form of construction appears to have been employed in *Record Reign* and *Cock o' the Walk*. The effect was more usually obtained with a knee, curved forward into a prow, finished sometimes with a 'pineapple' boss or occasionally with a fully carved female figurehead.

This shapely bow was a distinction denied to the spritsail barge, which rigged a bowsprit to starboard of the stem, pivoted on its heel at the bitts, so that it could be steeved up into a vertical position for close sailing in a river or in dock. The ketch barge, not having to be concerned with lightering freights from the docks, usually kept its bowsprit central, shipped through a gammon iron on the stem-head. The fiddle bow was usually retained when standing bowsprits and jibbooms gave place to running bowsprits, but a conversion to spritsail rig often included the removal of the knee to leave a straight stem. Boomies did occasionally have a steeve-up bowsprit, but this was generally a sign that they had started life as sprities.

For similar reasons the ketch barge sported quarterboards, generally painted white, above the rails or bulwarks which were supported by stanchions mortised through the covering boards, not spiked through as in sprities. These boards extended aft nearly as far as the fore horse and forward from the quarters to the mizzen rigging. Some, including *Harold*, carried them all the way round to become a topgallant rail. They kept some of the water off the deck when deep-loaded at sea, but would have been vulnerable to the swimheads of the iron lighters riding over the rails in dock — an unpleasant source of damage all too familiar to the spritsail barges.

Boomie-barges' sails were usually left white, often with the exception of a brown dressed foresail. The oil and ochre dressing always favoured by sprities would have made lowering mainsails too heavy for hoisting, and was not necessary as a protection against chafing from brails.

Boomies did not sheet their foresails to the wooden horses so familiar in spritsail barges with their very full-cut foresails, but used a shorter iron horse or a chain, sufficient for the more conventional foresail of the boomie. Possibly the vulnerability of a wooden horse when loading trees on deck also had something to do with it.

A number of square-sterned barges, such as *Harold*, still carried long bowsprits, setting two jibs and a jib topsail, but the trend in the smaller barges of the 1880s and 1890s was towards a shorter bowsprit setting only a single jib or, under suitable conditions, jib and jib topsail. In *Dannebrog* it was necessary to go out to the bowsprit end to hank on the jib, but in many of the later barges it was run out on a traveller, usually hanked to a stay. Most barges carried four sizes in addition to a fancy bit of canvas, treasured by a few skippers — a great light-weather reacher

**Record Reign**

*Opposite page*
*(Top)* at Barking creek in 1925 as an auxiliary *(Hewett collection)*:
*(Bottom)* as a topsail schooner.

*Top*
*(Left)* as an auxiliary ketch, showing the authentic schooner bow
*(Right)* the elliptical counter stern with propeller installation.

*Bottom*
*(Left)* Under way as an auxiliary. The funnel belongs to an engine installed for deck machinery.
*(Right)* Ashore at Branscome in 1935, a total loss.

which set from the bowsprit to the topmast head and sheeted aft outside the lee rigging, and could also serve as a spinnaker. A mizzen staysail was also usual.

These shorter bowsprits were often 'sliding'. They had three fid holes, and were reefed in when a smaller jib was set. Later, when fid holes were no longer provided, the bowsprit was sometimes reefed in and left with its weight on the heel-rope, which was used to haul it out, rigged to the mast-case winch.

Throughout all these phases of evolution the boat continued to be stowed on the main hatch, griped down in a cradle. Davits were not introduced till the 1890s, when they were fitted indiscriminately on either quarter, though the spritties later standardized theirs on the starboard quarter.

Tiller steering was universal till the *Alice Watts* was built with a wheel in 1875, after which there was a general move to adopt wheel steering of the chain-and-barrel pattern, rather than the sophisticated but vulnerable double-screw thread used in later spritties.

Roller reefing increasingly replaced reef points in mainsails. It was possibly used in some craft at an early date, for the *Flower of Essex* was reefing in Lowestoft Roads in 1860, when her mate was badly injured by the handle of the winch flying round. This suggests that her original dandy's sail was rolled reefed, but it is equally probable that he was working the halyard winch, setting up a sail that had been conventionally reefed. Reef points were usually retained on the mizzen, and were also used on the foresail, which was reefed in a breeze, contrary to the practice in spritties, which used their foresail reef points only to accommodate a stack on the foredeck or to give the skipper a view under the foot of the sail.

The worm-operated Appledore roller boom was seldom if ever used, the boomies being content with either a lever working on a ratchet or a wire wound round the boom and led up the mast and down to a winch on deck. With roller reefing the foot of the mainsail was laced to a batten along the boom, giving a flatter but less efficient sail than the previous loose-footed style. The need to rig the mainsheet on the after end of the boom also put extra strain on that spar. But a great advantage was that one man on deck could roll down a reef single-handed, especially if the sail had been left with the weight already on the lever or wire.

Roller reefing was also applied to some square topsails, Cunningham's Patent being a favourite

system. This enabled the topsail to be rolled on its yard without the necessity of a man going aloft. The system, introduced on single topsails, was also used on the lower topsail after double topsails were introduced.

There was also a process of evolution over anchor windlasses. The early sloop barges used hand-spikes, the style retained in small smacks to the present day. The early seagoing coasters had 'Armstrong's patents' or 'pump windlasses', as they were more usually called. A long horizontal athwart-ship lever with handles at each end rocked like a seesaw with iron drivers nearer the fulcrum engaging teeth on the windlass barrel — an arrangement which injured one skipper of the *Martinet* and was hated by his successor. Most of the later craft at least as far back as *Harold* (1900) used the geared windlass universal in the last generation of spritsail barges.

Throughout most of the boomie era peak, throat and foresail halyards were handled on winches beside the mainmast, but some of the pioneers started their lives with rope halyards, hand-cleated. Just when winches replaced 'pully-hauly' for halyards and leeboards is difficult to discover. Alfred Day, who was mate with his father in the *Stour,* and after her loss in the *Ada Gane*, recalled that the former set her sails by hand, but had crab winches for her leeboards, which were made of greenheart, while the latter had halyard winches.

Masts were stepped in the keelson or mounted on deck in tabernacles according to the owner's fancy, and no doubt the trade for which they were intended. For boomies with fixed masts, including the early schooners, there was of course no question of working above bridges, and in general most of the freights involving this were left to the spritties.

But lowering a boomie's gear was by no means

**Ada Gane** converted to yacht **Leigh Hall**.

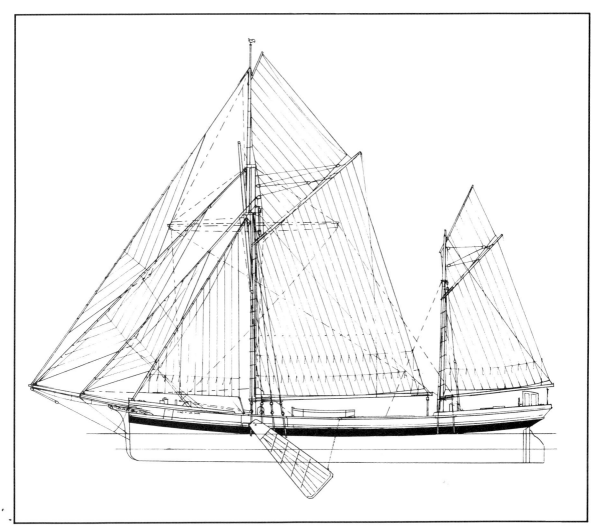

**Cock o' the Walk** (1876) has a single-spar standing bowsprit. She has a jib topsail set to the topmast head, a headstick in her topsail, diagonal cut headsails and wheel steering. She has a reaching foresail, sheeting abaft the rigging, and capable of being set under the squaresail yard, boomed out to windward. The 'schooner with the bottom cut off' has now developed into the ketch barge.

unknown, as is shown by an account of the Rhine trade in a later chapter.

*The Darnet,* an early example of the true ketch, built at Rochester in 1873, took many freights of cement from Burham, Kent, to Ymuiden for the building of the North Sea canal to Amsterdam. When it was opened in November 1876 her skipper, Samuel Scrivener, attended the ceremony, and was presented with a commemoration medal which was built into a model of the barge made by a member of the crew.

For this trade she had to face both the coasters' challenge of the North Sea passage and the river

barge's toil and frustration in river and creek, for she had to lower down for Rochester bridge, and then after a tow up the Medway had to be 'poked' up the old Burham river to the cement-works where the gear had to be hove-up again to load. The crew were of course spared the labour of heaving up sprit and mainsail, but against this they had to lower the squaresail yard on deck, run in the jibboom, and sling the boom, gaff and mainsail on deck, clear of the hatches. *The Darnet's* mizzen lowered forward, the usual practice.

Certain qualifications must be made to this necessarily truncated account of the evolution of the ketch barge.

Many craft were enlarged or converted from sloops or spritties, and even in later craft the classifications overlap, with boomies converted to sprittie rig and also vice versa, sometimes more

**Kate and Emily,** built at Lowestoft in 1851.

than once. For example, *Matilda Upton* of Ipswich was launched in 1887 as a sprittie. Sunk in a collision in Ipswich river, she was raised and bought by Cann of Harwich, who refitted her as a ketch barge. Yet when she finally ended her days on the mud at Harwich she was a mulie.

The *Rose Bud* of Harwich, a frequent trader to Woodbridge, was a boomie with a steeve-up bow-spirit, but the explanation is that she was built as a sprittie, and was not altered in this respect when converted. Apart from the alteration to bowsprit and stem-head already mentioned, the change from spritsail to boomsail rig involved little more than a new mainmast, for the short five-foot doubling at the sprittie's mainmast was not sufficient to accommodate the peak halyard and topping lift blocks of the boomie, for which a ten-foot masthead was needed.

Occasionally a barge laid down as a boomie was completed as a sprittie. This was the case with *Northdown,* which was nearly the last of the boomies. She was built on the wall at Whitstable by Anderson Rigden and Perkins, being laid down as a boomie on the outbreak of the First World War, to keep the hands employed while other work was slack. The hull was not finished and put up for sale till 1922. It was ultimately bought by Burley of Sittingbourne, who rigged it as a sprittie. *Northdown* carried this rig from 1925 till 1939, when she was sunk in dock by a PLA tug, after which she traded as a motor barge. She was re-rigged in 1972, and is still afloat.

In the end the boomie barge was not vanquished by steam, but by her near relation the sprittie. The old idea that the spritsail was an acceptable convenience in the Thames Estuary, but that a boom rig was necessary for sea work, came to be disproved — or more accurately, the superior sea-keeping qualities of the boomie came to be over-

ridden by the economy of the sprittie, which with its crew of three (and later two) outdated the boomie, just as the boomie had made her round-bottomed predecessors obsolete half a century before. The coal trade sustained the boomies, but as this traffic was increasingly taken by the rail-ways they could no longer support their crews of four or five.

The introduction of flexible steel wire rigging must have made a major contribution to the safety of the big sprittie. With wire stanliff and vang falls — not to mention the standing rigging — the gear could stand far more strain.

Even so, the acceptance of the spritsail at sea was hesitant, with the mulie at first the only acceptable concession. With this rig, if the sprit mainsail failed there was still a ketch's boom mizzen to provide a workable jury rig. One

**Lily** of Harwich (1873) after conversion to spritsail rig and registration at Faversham in 1926. Her hull form suggests her boomie origin, and she carries her boat on her port quarter, contrary to the usual practice of the spritties. (*Nautical Photo Agency*)

**Success** at Strand on the Green, a steel-built sprittie after being salvaged and boomie-rigged.

attempt to make the best of both rigs was to brail up the sails to standing gaffs, without dispensing with booms. *Pearl* was thus rigged, on both main and mizzen, in 1928 — an arrangement which must have posed its own problems when it came to setting sail in a breeze if, as I assume, the clew had to be hauled out on a wire led through a sheave in the boom with a tackle underneath it.

But mulies such as *Western Belle,* 80 tons, built in 1879 at Topsham, Devon, and *Una,* 74 tons, built in 1882 at Harwich, showed which way the prevailing wind was beginning to blow, and demonstrated that a sixty-foot sprit could be taken to sea without going overboard or through the barge's bottom. Some of the new mulies, including *Western Belle,* were soon converted to the old boomie rig, but the general trend was confirmed by the building in 1898 of the huge sprittie *Colossus,* with a tonnage of 133, followed by a number of big spritties built for Goldsmith of Grays at Papendrecht in Holland in 1903.

Four of these craft were also for a short time boomie-rigged. *Cedric, Doric* and *Norvic* were sold to South America and sailed out there as ketches, while *Cymric,* after being stranded at Ventnor, Isle of Wight, before the First World War and accepted by the insurance company as a total loss, was salvaged and rigged as a boomie at Brentford under the name *Success,* setting three jibs on a bowsprit under which a stem knee was fitted. She did not, however, carry this rig for long, but was soon sold back to Goldsmith's, who replaced her boom mainsail by a spritsail, but left her bowsprit and headsails, making her a remarkably spectacular mulie. She was still trading as a Goldsmith motor barge in 1938, and as a London and Rochester Trading Company Continental trader from 1951 to 1964. The *Solent* was similarly treated when she was given a sprit mainsail.

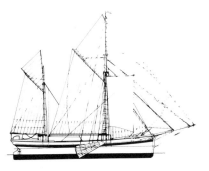

CHAPTER 3

# Flat Bottom and Square Rig

At one end of the scale it is remarkable that little sloops like *Tertius* traded everywhere between Portland and the Tyne. At the other extreme, it is no less extraordinary that flat-bottomed craft with and without leeboards were built to sizes which one would have thought quite impracticable. Yet somehow barge hulls of up to 500 tons managed to carry barquentine rig. Few of them, it is true, survived long under the arduous conditions of the

Three-masted schooner barge **Enterprise** of Yarmouth, by R. Chappell. She looks handsome in this portrait, but was not considered a success, and ended as a motor barge. *(Roger Finch)*

Launch of the **Laura Shelbourne.** From the *Illustrated London News*, 22 April 1854.

home coasting trade. The marvel is that they could be worked at all.

The three-masted schooner barge was far from uncommon. Vaux of Harwich built the 163-ton *Lymington* in 1880 and the 174-ton *Jubilee* in 1887, building both 'out of wrecks' according to Joe Mynheer, and keeping both for his own use, though whether because of their profitability or because he could not find a buyer it is difficult to say.

The *Lymington* did not last long, being wrecked on the Holm Sands in 1889, but the *Jubilee* went, after her owner's death, to Walker and Howard's fleet mentioned in Chapter 12.

It was the coal trade which provided the demand for these huge carriers. At Yarmouth, Bessey and Palmer had the 168-ton *Enterprise* built for them in 1891. She was not considered a great success, and was trading as a motor-barge by the time she was lost off the East Coast in the 1920s. Other coal merchants such as John Crampton of Portsmouth and John Smith of Burnham-on-Crouch (mentioned in later chapters) built up considerable fleets.

The three-masted schooner was by no means the ultimate development of the flat-bottomed hull, which was made to carry even the lofty top-hamper of the barque rig.

The first known example was the *Laura Shelbourne*, built at Vauxhall in 1854, the same year as the schooner barge *Advance*. Knowledge of this remarkable vessel is confined to the account of her launch in the *Illustrated London News*, which is worth quoting in full:

The *Laura Shelbourne* was built expressly for the Baltic trade and intended to ply between London and St Petersburg. She is constructed on the barge or flat-bottomed principle; she is by far the largest vessel ever built in the Thames above bridge; and though measuring 560 tons only averaged at launching a draught of 3½ feet. She is by more than 200 tons the largest vessel of the kind ever built, is adapted for the screw propeller, has accommodation for passengers, and will be barque rigged. Her dimensions are as follows: — length overall 145 feet; length on keel 119 feet, breadth 26 feet 6 inches; hold 12 feet 6 inches.

The appearance of vessels hitherto built on this plan has been an unsightliness of bow and clumsiness in general appearance; but in this vessel a much better form has been adopted and in room of the square short nose of the old plan a figurehead and cutwater with a finer bow has been substituted. The advantage obtained by the light draught and stiffness of this class of vessel under canvas may, upon the successful performance of the *Laura Shelbourne,* cause barges of larger tonnage to be more generally used for mercantile purposes.

Even allowing for the euphoria and hyperbole often to be detected in such reports, it seems clear first that the *Laura Shelbourne* was a spectacular development — a little *Great Britain* in her field — and secondly that other comparable barges had already been built, even if they were two hundred tons smaller, and a lot less elegant.

The reference can hardly be to the little sloops and dandies which are the only flat-bottomed coasters we know of before this date, for they were nearer four hundred tons than two hundred tons smaller in capacity. It could possibly be a snide sideswipe at the *Advance,* which may have been launched a few months before, but the reference clearly suggests a number of predecessors. All in all, it seems highly probable that big barges loading over three hundred tons had been built before this date, but what they were we shall now probably never know.

The expectation that big barges had a future was quickly confirmed.

The *Laura Shelbourne* was followed two years later by another barque, one size smaller but of such comparable proportions and rig as to suggest a degree of imitation.

The *Leading Star,* as she was named, was built not in a London shipyard but in the Colneside village of Fingringhoe, a place with no shipyard and no shipbuilding tradition — presumably on the ferry hard, for the simple reason that there seems no other possible site.

Her builder was Philip M. Sainty, son of that noted shipbuilder and colourful character Philip Sainty of Wivenhoe, who in 1820 was released from prison for smuggling to build for the Marquess of Anglesey the celebrated yacht *Pearl.*[1]

'Designed by the builder on an entirely new principle, with the floors perfectly flat', the *Leading Star,* like her predecessor, had a full-length female figurehead and was described as 'a handsome vessel computed to carry 400 tons... built to carry a large cargo on an easy draught of water and is expected to sail fast.' With a registered tonnage of 210, she was 130 feet long and only 23 feet 6 inches beam but with the remarkable hold depth of 13 feet.

She had an elliptic stern and 'one deck and a break' suggesting a raised quarterdeck. Whether she had leeboards is not stated; probably not with such a depth of side. In 1861 she was sold to A. P. Sidney of Hanningfield, Essex, master mariner, and three years later her registry was transferred to Folkestone, where she was employed in the coal trade, converted to brig rig.

This pioneering did not find further imitators, either in London or in Essex. It was in Kent that the development of the barge to its ultimate size was chiefly exploited — largely by one of the most remarkable characters in an age of characters, George Smeed of Sittingbourne.

Born in 1812, one of twelve children, George

George Smeed in old age: a portrait subscribed for by the townsfolk of Sittingbourne. At the unveiling ceremony in 1878 he was described as 'a man of indomitable perseverance, industry and energy, without the advantages of birth and education, who raised himself from a position of obscurity and poverty'. *Richard Hugh Perks*

---

[1]See *Last Stronghold of Sail.*

Smeed started by selling goods through the streets of the town, including coal from a handcart. Soon he was owner of a thriving coal merchant's business, buying and building colliers and barges, and he went on to own clay pits that supplied the potteries and to build a gasworks, a shipyard, a cement-works and the largest brickfield in the world.

He was described in his lifetime as a man of 'indomitable perseverance and energy' and after his death in 1881 as a man 'of strong purposes and stronger language, and the traits of character and habits of life became more accentuated in the later years of his life'. At the time of his death he owned a fleet of nearly eighty ships, and his obituary recorded that he 'may almost be said to have made Sittingbourne what it is'.

The firm which he established in 1875 in partnership with his son-in-law, Charles Hambrook Dean — Smeed, Dean and Co. Ltd — survived him for fifty years, and a spritsail barge laid down after his death and named *George Smeed* is afloat to this day.

Unlike the old-established builders at Harwich and Ipswich, Smeed thus inherited few traditions. Setting out without prejudices or preconceived ideas, he showed his perspicacity in pioneering the ketch rig with *Garibaldi* and *Invicta* in the early 1860s, and he then went on to show his ambition and imagination in producing the biggest barge of all time, the barque-rigged *Esther Smeed,* and two others scarcely less remarkable, *Eliza Smeed* and *George Smeed.*

Meanwhile at near-by Whitstable H. H. Gann turned out another example of the type, *Nellie S,* whose connection with Smeed does not seem to extend beyond her name, believed to refer to Nellie Smeed.

These extraordinary craft, along with many of their sisters, are dealt with in detail in Chapter 11, but their place in the story of the barge-built coaster must be briefly considered here.

Some of them, being round-bilged and thus perhaps not of rebated construction, were arguably not really barges at all, but all were regarded as such, and even the round-bilged craft had flat floors. Few if any had much appeal to the eye. Most of them were either lost or sold abroad, and they found few imitators. Other builders and owners continued to prefer traditional ketches and schooners.

The marvel is that they succeeded as well as they did.

A voyage to Mexico by the *Nellie S* in 1887 shows that flat-bottomed craft were quite capable of deep-sea passages. A member of her crew, Alf

Goldfinch's **Garibaldi** (built 1861) converted to a sprittie. From a painting by James Webb at Chelsea in the 1880s. Her four shrouds aside and bulky hull (contrasting with the sprittie alongside) show her origins as one of the pioneer ketch barges. *Richard Hugh Perks*

Revell, recalled[2] that she sailed from Workington under Captain Francies of Whitstable with a cargo of steel rails which gave her a freeboard of only fourteen inches amidships, with a mate, bosun, two A.B.s, two ordinary seamen and a cook.

When Alf Revell saw her he was in some doubt about the venture, and was warned against it, but they reached Progreso in nine weeks and loaded mahogany at Frontero, sailing for Fowey with two tiers on deck high above the rails. In this trim she ran safely in a westerly gale under only square foresail and lower topsail, and picked up the crew of the disabled barque *John Banfield* before reaching Plymouth safely.

In many ways the coasting trade presented even greater problems for craft which must have been terribly unhandy. Steam tugs were by this time in general use, and indeed it is probably thanks to them that these huge barges were possible at all,

[2]Told to Arthur Bennett: *Us Bargemen.*

but there must have been occasions when their assistance was not available, and then the skipper must indeed have needed nerves of iron — as well as a couple of good anchors.

Some of these giants were fitted with leeboards; others dispensed with them. The son of Captain Robert Skinner, skipper of the *Zebrina* and *Belmont* — neither of which had leeboards — said they were always sailed loaded, and so never needed them, but this cannot have been so, for *Zebrina* was sent around the coast seeking freights, and *Belmont* sailed light from her builders to Milford Haven for her first freight, and cannot always have enjoyed the luxury of a cargo after that.

There is likewise nothing to show whether John Crampton (referred to in Chapter 12) fitted leeboards to the barquentine barge *Enterprise* which he built in 1879.

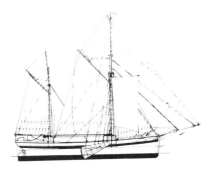

CHAPTER 4

# The Imperfect Leeboard

The usefulness and the nuisance value of leeboards in boomies is a fascinating subject, not confined to these Kentish leviathans.

The spritsail barge used her leeboards both light and loaded, and relied on them for the handiness and close-windedness essential to her river work, though some spritties with long chines would fetch along well enough at sea without them in loaded trim. The boomie could dispense with them when loaded, but used them to make the best of a bad job when light. In the bigger craft in particular the leeboard was always an

**Sarah Smeed** unloading coal at Faversham. The leeboard seems curiously far forward, under the foremast, but this was usual. (See also Chapter 11.) *(John Hunt)*

imperfect substitute for the keel in providing a 'grip of the water', as well as being dangerously vulnerable to breakage under the strains to which it was inevitably exposed in a seaway.

Four boomies, the schooner *Goldfinch* and the ketches *Kindly Light, Leading Light* and *Clymping,* were sailed out from Par to British Guiana to work sugar down the Demerara and Essequibo rivers to Booker's deep-sea steamers, as described in Chapter 16. This may seem conclusive proof of the sea-going qualities of the flat-bottomed hull, and so to some extent it was, but when these remarkable voyages were made — by the *Kindly Light* in 1926, taking forty days, by the *Clymping* in 1929, taking thirty-eight days, by the *Goldfinch* in 1930, taking fifty-five days, and by the *Leading Light* in 1933, taking forty-nine days — all four craft had their leeboards in their holds and were lightly ballasted.

When Percy Richmond owned the *Lord Nelson* he unshipped her leeboards in the Mersey for a different reason. Manchester Ship Canal dues were based on draft including extended adjustable keels. To avoid these charges the *Lord Nelson's* leeboards were hidden away out of sight, together with all gear connected with them. The point of interest is that Captain Richmond declared, 'I knew I could get her to near the German border loaded with glass bottles for Apollinaris water without leeboards.' Yet when the *Ivy P* came into the ownership of Irish schoonermen they discarded these strange contraptions — and not unnaturally found they could do nothing with her.

These examples show that when loaded a flat-bottomed ketch could get about without her leeboards if handled by men who understood her. The limitations of leeboards in sailing light are vividly shown in some of the yarns in the following chapters — particularly Captain Douse's memory of the *Friendship* being blown about all over the North Sea for a month. This sort of experience was not peculiar to flat-bottomed vessels, for brigs and schooners were occasionally driven across the North Sea to Norway in westerly gales, but craft without keels must have been particularly vulnerable. Certainly, though leeboards were fitted to all but a few of the biggest and deepest boomies, they

were accepted only as an imperfect necessity.

John Harvey, of Littlehampton, insisted that his fine craft were 'ketches, not barges', and when a photo was to be taken he would have the leeboard lowered so that it did not show. A similar reluctance to admit the existence of such contraptions may be noted in their omission from many of the ships' portraits made by pierhead artists, showing craft idealized according to their skippers' proudest and fondest dreams.

Needless to say, with the restless quest for improvement which characterized the age of the boomies attempts were made to find something better. Two contrasting novelties may be mentioned.

Down-Channel at Emsworth that most fascinating of creative innovators, J. D. Foster[1] in 1892 produced the 113-ton brigantine *Fortuna,* which was fitted with a centreboard. This gave her a draught of seventeen feet, which provided a fine grip of the water, but as well as obstructing the hold it inevitably proved leaky. Moreover, in a heavy hull constantly taking the ground a centreboard case must inevitably have become jammed with mud and stones.

Almost as odd as the *Fortuna* was the *Problem,* a 128-ton schooner built and owned by Bayley of Ipswich in 1861. She also had no leeboards, but was given three wooden keels, one under each chine and one amidships. She was rigged with jibboom and mizzen topmast, with staysails between the masts instead of a boom foresail.

A Mr Pike, who worked for Bayley, recalled:

> I don't agree that she was not a success, and I never heard that she was leewardly. Tom Hart, her skipper, always spoke very highly of her and said she was one of the handiest vessels he'd ever had. Call them what you like, but she had three proper keels. This enabled her to have a clear hold for loading machinery, also to dispense with leeboards which would have been no use pitching about in the Bay of Biscay, for she was not merely in the coasting trade; she often went to Lisbon. She had staysails between fore and main. This was useful when some awkward piece of machinery stuck out of the hold. The staysail was lowered, shifted round and hoisted on the other tack. I remember one huge piece, a steamer's stern

*Opposite*
**Clymping,** one of the barges which made the long voyage to South America. She is seen *(top)* with leeboards, loaded, and *(bottom)* with leeboards removed. Note the jib topsail set on stay to topmast head, with halyard to mainmast head, giving an awkward lead.

[1]For an account of Foster's 110-foot steam auxiliary ketch smack *Echo,* see John Leather: *Gaff Rig.*

(Top) The building of the unique flat-bottomed 'twin keel' schooner **Problem** at Ipswich in 1861 was commemorated by this plaque showing her surrounded by a remarkable variety of other types of craft. (Roger Finch)
(Bottom) A drawing by George Doughty.

frame, being carried from Lisbon stowed in the hold. One end of it projected in the air several feet above the deck.

The reference to 'staysails between fore and main' is surprising, for pictorial evidence shows she had a boomless gaff foresail, providing the same advantage. Probably the rig was altered later.

Barges quite commonly went to sea in the mid-nineteenth century without fitting the hatches on which their safety depended. The *Sextus,* a little old-timer that made a voyage from Dartmouth to London in November 1861, was chartered to carry trees from Yarmouth to Sheerness, and after delivering a number of freights finally shipped a sea off the Cutler in December, 1862, with nothing better than tarpaulins over her. The skipper's wife and two children were taken out and she was got into Harwich at a salvage cost of £200. When the owner was sued for £75 as his share he maintained that the skipper had been negligent, but this defence failed, as it was shown to be the custom to go to sea without hatches. An attempt at a meeting of the Harwich Insurance Society to stop the practice also failed on the ground that it was established custom.

Knocking about the Bay of Biscay, as the *Problem* was doing, seems the height of such folly, yet she survived and finally foundered in 1886 after striking a sunken rock between Start Point and Prawle Point.

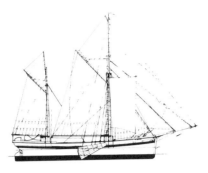

## CHAPTER 5

# Building the Boomie

The building of a big boomie barge was the unique culmination of a specialized method of wooden-ship construction. It was a technique that had very ancient roots, reaching back to an ancestry quite separate from the one which evolved into the generally accepted method of constructing a carvel-built vessel in the Northern Hemisphere.

The barge-builder's approach to building a hull had developed from a raft-building tradition, originating in prehistoric times. Its distinctive feature is a separately constructed bottom, identifying the 'raft' origin, which determines the basic shape of the vessel, and on which (when it is completed) the sides are joined. In its simplest form a vessel built in this way has ends which are devoid of differentiation, in either shape or purpose, and which merely consist of an extension of the bottom upward to a height that will accommodate to the flat sides.

The skin of the hull is made watertight by 'luting' — that is to say, inserting into the joints between adjoining planks a plastic waterproof material before fixing them permanently into position. This process is quite unlike the more widespread and equally traditional method of attempting to obtain a watertight joint by caulking — that is, driving in under pressure a sealing material between planks after they had been secured to the vessel's frames.

In Britain this barge-building technique was originally restricted to the Thames Estuary. Indeed, one of the few disadvantages associated with the method was its geographical limitations. If a boomie barge required repair outside an area bounded by the Yare and the Solent it was very difficult to discover a yard where the shipwrights could carry it out effectively. The *Kate* of Ipswich was rebuilt and lengthened at Whitby in 1869, because the shipyards in her home town were considered too expensive, but this was a rare exception to the rule.

Another exception was the *Western Belle*, launched in 1879 at Topsham, Devon, on the river Exe, but though flat-bottomed, she was built with caulked seams, on the site of Holman's old yard. It is perhaps not so surprising that a ketch barge originated so far distant from the traditional building-yards. Holman had built at least one flat-bottomed deep-sea vessel, the *Rio Grande* in 1868, and the local transom-sterned barges were a long-established tradition, although all were round-bottomed and were caulked.

The boomie-barge's ancestor, the swim-head barge of the Thames, with its overhanging 'luff' at bow and stern, was of course built in the traditional barge way, and in turn derived from an unrigged lighter. It was from this humble origin — a tradition evolved for constructing flat-bottomed, shallow-draught craft for trading on slow-moving rivers and tidal estuaries — that the boomie developed. It may perhaps seem remote from our present purpose, but it is worth noting that the identical peculiarities of construction to those of a nineteenth-century sailing barge may be found in locally constructed Roman traders whose remains have been found on the Thames, and in the surviving hull of a medieval Hanseatic cog on the Elbe estuaries. In more recent times the humble swim-headed sprittie, built at Lambeth, carrying ballast in its tarry hull to Nelson's fleet lying at Chatham, and seldom venturing beyond the Nore, was quite literally 'a sister under the skin' to such beauties of the barge-

**Kate,** an early Ipswich-built boomie, launched in 1867. *(Roger Finch)*

builder's skill as the *Record Reign* launched a century later, with a clipper bow and square topsails aloft.

The term 'barge-built', used in contemporary registers, advertisements and records, implied a number of essential factors, whether it described a thirty-ton spritsail craft or a seagoing schooner capable of loading three hundred tons. Perhaps most obvious to the eye was the sharply angled chine; the flat bottom was also important, but many conventionally constructed wooden vessels such as Severn trows or Humber keels could have a bottom almost as flat as a Thames barge. More important were the absence of any exterior keel, and the method we have already noted of attempting to produce a watertight skin by the introduction of an elastic jointing of hair and tar. This was either introduced between a double skin of planking, or used to render watertight a rabbeted joint between the planks when only a single layer was used.

We cannot, alas, at this distance of time provide irrefutable proof of exactly how the giants such as the barque-rigged *Leading Star* and the *Laura Shelbourne* were built. However, such information as we have indicates that they had all the essential characteristics of traditional barge-construction as it was understood in the mid-nineteenth century along the shores of the Thames Estuary.

They had the box-section of the barge, which is an extremely strong one, however distasteful to the eye it may appear. The unseamanlike use of 'hair and blair' (as the liquid comprising cow-hair and hot Stockholm tar was known) provided a flexible sealing for the planking of the hull, and was all-important for a vessel subjected to lying, fully loaded, on uneven mud berths. It accommodated the compressions between the joints of the planking, which forced out oakum from conventionally caulked joints or alternatively allowed it to float away if they opened up. Providing it was not tested beyond certain well-defined limits, the capacity for a barge-built hull to carry cargoes at sea, to take the ground safely, to be built cheaply and to be easily repaired, made it a sound economic proposition.

Of course, one must not overstate the case. It is rank romanticism to believe that all wooden vessels, even barges, were gems produced by

*Opposite*
Lines of **Pearl** of Ipswich (1889), taken off the vessel by W. Blake. The barge was of course built from a half-model. (*Science Museum, London*)

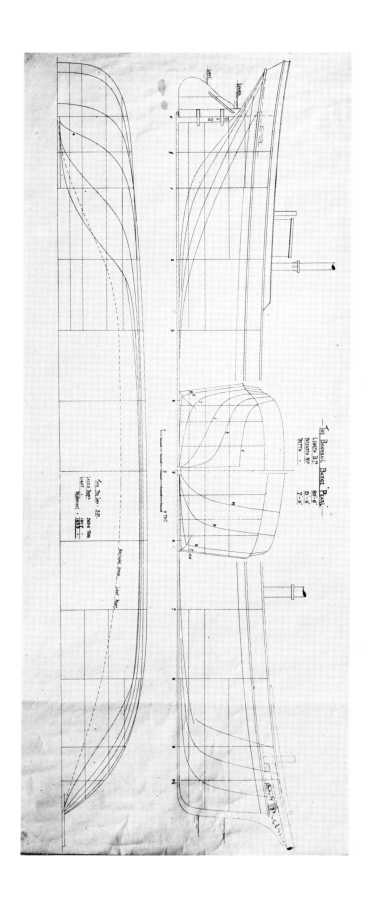

THE BOWSAIL BARGE PLAN.

LENGTH B.P.      85'-6"
BREADTH M⁹      21'-0"
DEPTH           7'-9"

skilled craftsmanship, destined to outlast their builders and owners and to sail anywhere. As we shall see when we examine in detail the building of a big barge, certain technical problems were never satisfactorily overcome. The prevention of rot in a wooden hull between layers of planking was never really understood or countered effectively. The complexities of the interlocking breast-hooks, stemson, cant frames, knight heads and in-wales at the bow were such that once severely damaged or affected by rot their renewal required weeks of skilled work to seek out the problem and then to render the vessel seaworthy. But by and large, in a field where the technology was limited and reliance had to be placed upon traditional skills and equipment, the big barge represented an outstandingly well-balanced equation between financial expenditure and potential profitability. The exploitation of the barge-building technique on a large scale also provided an unusual example of how a small, traditional industry, in one area at least, adapted itself to a rapidly changing economic climate brought about by competition from steel and steam-power.

The laying of the keel of a boomie barge could scarcely be said to invite the same sense of anticipation and ceremony as that of a conventionally built wooden round-bilged vessel. But the round-bilged trading vessel was dying out by the mid-1880s. The last of these to be built at Harwich was the *Swim*, a round-bottomed ketch, in 1883. At Ipswich the *Clementine*, a brigantine, was the last of her kind launched, in 1885. Yarmouth, Littlehampton and Rye saw a few fishing smacks built after these dates, but no round-bottomed trading vessels. As far as the East Coast was concerned the building of large wooden vessels other than barges was finished.

The shipyard-owners were therefore thankful that they could continue to employ their investment in expertise, equipment and stocks of timber in the building of wooden vessels in any manner, however humble. The keel of a ketch barge, though little more than a heavy plank, was still, according to tradition, made of elm, and in at least two or three lengths scarfed together — for it was up to ninety feet in length. The keel plank was laid in the shipyard across heavy wooden blocks, carefully lined up and high enough for a man to swing a maul accurately beneath them when working. Alongside the keel, and sometimes rabbeted into it, came the bottom planks, eight or nine on either side, and of either elm or Oregon pine, twelve inches wide or more.

If it was at all possible, building took place beneath the roof of an open-sided shed. It was quite normal for the smaller spritsail barges, most of them of about seventy feet overall, to be built under cover; work was not held up by inclement weather, which from the surveyor's point of view was good, for he knew how rain could form hidden pools in the crevices of the growing structure, providing an opportunity for rot to gain a hold. Moreover, ice was particularly dangerous for men wielding an adze, balanced on a staging, or driving home a copper bolt, so dangerous that even a Victorian ship-builder guarded against it. It was certainly dark in a building shed on winter mornings and evenings, but among the limited available sources of artificial light naphtha flares were considered an adequate illumination.

At Ipswich Gildea and Bayley built their ketch barges under cover, the former's big shed surviving until after the First World War. Yet at the same port Curtis did not build his boomies under cover, and none of the Harwich ketches were so favoured. At Maldon Howard contrived a roof under which he built his *Malvoisin* and *Record Reign*. To cover all of the 112 feet of the *Record* must have required considerable ingenuity and expense. At Littlehampton, however, John Harvey constructed all his boomies in the open air, without protection.

There was not, of course, an identical procedure in all barge yards, but to ensure a good joint between each plank it was usual to adhere to a carefully evolved method. After the pitch-pine planks had been sawn to size — and this was usually to a thickness of five inches and a width of about twelve — the edges were planed true and then hollowed slightly, with a large round-plane, along their length. Should anyone entertain rosy ideas of the work of a barge-builder he could consider the labour involved in round-planing by hand some nine hundred feet of pine, oak or elm. This done, all the boards were then drawn together with specially made bottom clamps and chains.

The shipwright then made a saw-cut along the length of each joint. Instead of the back-breaking labour of sawing through four or five inches of timber, he just cut through the edges, and since the rip-saw made a kerf of equal width throughout, a near-perfect joint was produced. The cramps were then removed and a series of holes bored at intervals of about five feet along adjoining edges so that wooden or metal dowels could be inserted. The hollowed edges were then filled with the familiar mixture of Stockholm tar and cow-hair, the cramps replaced and then tightened up. It was aimed to complete this stage

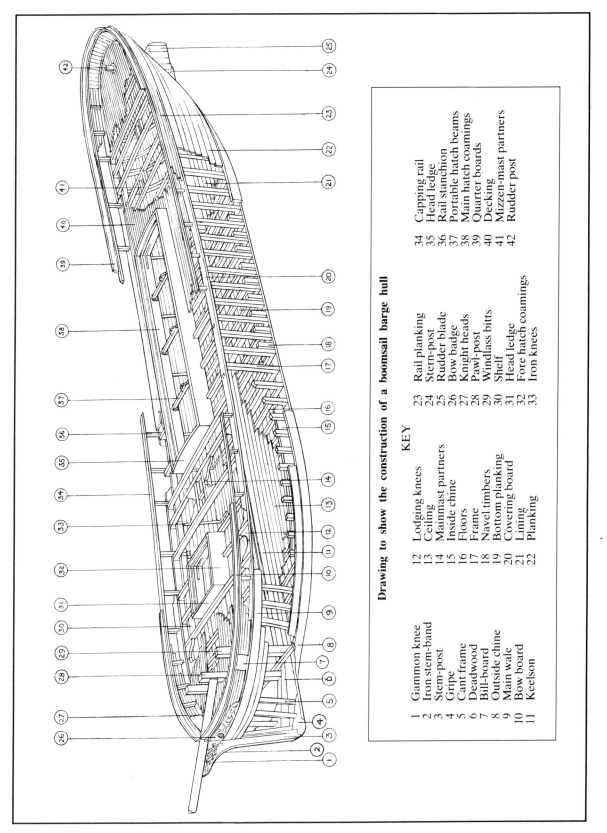

**Drawing to show the construction of a boomsail barge hull**

KEY

| | |
|---|---|
| 1 | Gammon knee |
| 2 | Iron stem-band |
| 3 | Stem-post |
| 4 | Gripe |
| 5 | Cant frame |
| 6 | Deadwood |
| 7 | Bill-board |
| 8 | Outside chine |
| 9 | Main wale |
| 10 | Bow board |
| 11 | Keelson |
| 12 | Lodging knees |
| 13 | Ceiling |
| 14 | Mainmast partners |
| 15 | Inside chine |
| 16 | Floors |
| 17 | Frame |
| 18 | Navel timbers |
| 19 | Bottom planking |
| 20 | Covering board |
| 21 | Lining |
| 22 | Planking |
| 23 | Rail planking |
| 24 | Stern-post |
| 25 | Rudder blade |
| 26 | Bow badge |
| 27 | Knight heads |
| 28 | Pawl-post |
| 29 | Windlass bitts |
| 30 | Shelf |
| 31 | Head ledge |
| 32 | Fore hatch coamings |
| 33 | Iron knees |
| 34 | Capping rail |
| 35 | Head ledge |
| 36 | Rail stanchion |
| 37 | Portable hatch beams |
| 38 | Main hatch coamings |
| 39 | Quarter boards |
| 40 | Decking |
| 41 | Mizzen-mast partners |
| 42 | Rudder post |

of the building operation in the warm summer months, when the timber was dry, and the opportunity could be taken to tighten on the clamps at intervals as the filling of tar liquefied and squeezed out in the heat of the sun.

As far as possible each bottom plank was of a single length of timber, as free from knots as possible, and the longest — those nearest the keel — could easily measure some sixty feet in length. The elm keel usually projected at least an inch below the planks which made up the barge's bottom. To accommodate this discrepancy the upper surfaces of the barge blocks were packed on either side of the keel with off-cuts of timber while the clamping together of the bottom was in progress.

When these bottom planks were securely fixed it was time for the floors to be laid across them, permanently securing the planks in readiness for the frames to be dovetailed to their outer ends. The scantling of the floors and frames and their positioning were crucial in determining the strength of the barge. Some builders, such as Fellowes at Yarmouth, preferred heavy floors, widely spaced; others placed them in pairs, and of correspondingly lighter material. Ideally it was 'space and frame', indicating that the floor of, say, twelve-inch square oak was twelve inches from its neighbour.

The frames were secured to the bottom planks by trenails, a long-established tradition, and when properly carried out a very effective one. Trenails were made from lengths of stringy oak to an octagonal section and then rounded for the greater part of their length with an iron 'mute', a monotonous job reserved for the youngest apprentice. Holes were bored for the trenails through the bottom planks by men working beneath them, between the blocks and boring each hole at a slight angle to its neighbour, canted so that a dovetailed grip was obtained. The trenails were driven home dry so that when immersed in water they swelled and ensured a secure grip.

While this was proceeding the oak stem- and stern-posts were set up. The stem was tenoned into the keel and reinforced at the joint by inset dovetailed steel plates on either side, bolted together and then strengthened by an oaken apron and deadwood. The stern-post, twelve inches in thickness and as much as eighteen in width, was similarly supported by a deadwood, and this carried the timbers which were rabbeted into them. The *Martinet* and the last of the Littlehampton and Rye-built boomies were launched with an especially wide stern-post so

that it could be used to accommodate the propeller of an auxiliary engine. The counter stern and fiddle or gammon knee at the bow which many boomies carried — particularly those built at Littlehampton and Harwich — were of little special significance in the building. But it must be said in all fairness that only a trained shipwright, skilled in the traditions of conventional wooden ship-building, could draught-out and construct a neat counter stern.

The barge's keelson gave much of the longitudinal strength usually provided in a wooden vessel by a keel, so that if at all possible it was in one length. The longest runs in a suitable timber were obtainable in the heavy pines, Oregon or pitch pine, and this was the first choice in most yards, with a preference given to pitch pine because of its highly resinous nature and greater strength. How was it possible for a team consisting of a handful of men and boys, with the minimum of mechanical assistance, to position over the floors and deadwood to within a quarter of an inch a baulk of timber, at least fifty feet long and weighing over a ton? When questioned over the matter an old shipwright pondered and replied, 'We joggled and juggled it in some 'ow.' Surely a modest recollection of days spent heaving on crowbars and tackles, winding iron jacks, driving wedges and all the while risking crushed hands or worse!

Most East Coast barge-yards were situated at ports which saw regular imports of softwoods, enabling timber to be conveniently rafted to the barge-yard's slipway. It was then stored afloat so that it did not dry out and lose its resin and elasticity, while it was also considered that the salt remaining in the timber when it dried out assisted in its preservation. When the baulks of pine were required they were manoeuvred ashore on rollers at high tide and manhandled over the yard's saw-pit and thence to the building shed. Using sheer-legs, substantial spars set up over the barge under construction, and with the help of heavy tackles the keelson — usually in two sections at least — could be juggled into position for fitting. It was then raised again and trimmed-up to accommodate the minor irregularities of the floors and to cut out the laps at its ends where it joined the deadwood, or if there was a join for the scarfs to be cut.

When the keelson was finally in position it was bolted to the floors and bottom planks with fastenings placed alternately to port and starboard down the centre line. A collar was driven over the bolt, and the end shortened by nicking on both sides with a cold chisel and then riveted over. The use of galvanized iron bolts ensured a higher classification from the Lloyd's surveyor when he made his inspection. A few ketch barges were launched with sister keelsons, fitted on either side of the main one, while the unique schooner-rigged *Problem* had a full keel and one under either bilge.

The earlier big Harwich-launched ketch barges tricked out their utilitarian lines with a gammon knee, trail board, head timbers and rails, even a figurehead, but this did not make a true clipper bow. Nevertheless, all followed the barge-builder's tradition of having an elaborately decorated bow badge, providing extra support for the chain pipes outboard, while inboard this was augmented by the knight heads to port and starboard which were substantial baulks of timber reaching down to the keelson.

The larger scale of the boomie barge compared with its sprit-rigged counterpart was particularly evident in the earlier years, during the 1860s and 1870s. At that time a barge was a big one if it loaded as little as a hundred tons of cargo, and few drew more than six feet. Such run-of-the-mill craft could be built with little more than the time-honoured formula of the barge-builder to establish the basic measurements. This stipulated that the beam should be one-quarter of the overall length (seventy feet would produce an eighty-tonner), the depth of side amidships one-third of the beam, and then with the barge-builder trusting in experience and a good eye the keel could be laid down.

But to construct a barge-built vessel, some hundred feet in length from gammon knee to the taffrail aft, and loading 250 tons, demanded something more complex.

The use of plans was extremely rare in any barge-yard. Instead, a half-model, carved from wood, provided a reference for the shipwright. A few of these survive, and lines drawn up from one that was used in the St Clement's shipyard, Ipswich, and probably employed to line-up the *Lord Hartington* is reproduced here. It does not, however, show the decorated gammon knee which gave a traditional profile to the bow, with which she was fitted before launching.

From pictorial evidence it would appear that only Howard's *Record Reign*, built at Maldon in 1890, was fitted with a genuine clipper bow, which is defined as the line of the rabbet following the forward curving shape of the cutwater, and giving a flared shape to the barge's lines. For the majority of boomie barges the stem- and the stern-post were set up plumb square with the keel, which precluded anything more shapely

than the solid and purposeful traditional barge's bow.

The shape of the curved frames and the angle of the bevel on their outboard face could be determined accurately by bow and buttock lines drawn out to full scale on the mold-loft floor from measurements taken off a half-model. The resulting shape of the timbers was therefore more likely to produce a clean-lined hull without the necessity of more time-consuming adzing and packing out of the frames. Models half an inch to the foot were used at J. & W. B. Harvey's Littlehampton yard, although a scale of a quarter-inch and three-eighths inches to the foot were used as well.

At least two variants of the half-model were used by the builders. At Ipswich a laminated half-model was carved to the scale of three-eighths of an inch to one foot. Alternating laminations of pine and mahogany were common, producing a pleasing effect, while assisting the eye in assessing any imperfections that might need modification. After the stations had been marked along the model at which the transverse measurements were to be taken, the dowels which held the half-model together were knocked out and the laminations laid out on the draughting-shed table for measuring.

It seems that at Harwich and on the Medway a solid half-model was used. When the time came for a full-sized profile drawing of the frames to be prepared from a solid model a pair of callipers was used to establish the transverse measurements along a series of water-lines, carefully scribed along the model, each line parallel to the keel, and known as the 'sunk-line'. Although requiring greater care in transposition this scheme had the advantage of allowing extra measurements to be taken at each station, particularly useful at the bow and the stern.

Whichever method was used, the scale-up measurements were recorded on the draughting floor, then connected with the aid of a thin spline of wood and drawn in by a line of tailor's chalk. These shapes were transferred to rough wood off-cuts from the saw-pits. With these patterns the foreman shipwright, accompanied by two shipyard labourers, began a search among the store of seasoning timber to find the naturally grown crooks and curves which would accommodate them. Oak was stacked either under cover or in the shade of the building-shed, and was not built into a barge until seasoned for at least three years. The dead straight frames were easily measured up and dovetailed (only halved in a poor yard) to the ends of the floors, trenailed and then temporarily strutted up to keep them at the correct flare. The curved frames were housed into the deadwood aft and bolted in position. Those immediately aft of the stem-post were fixed to the deadwood at an angle so that the sawing of the face did not produce too wide a surface.

The stern-frame, or transom — usually of English oak — was fitted to the stern-post, bolted and clenched, or alternatively should an elliptical counter stern be part of the design the counter knees and timbers were fitted, together with the stern cant frames. A few earlier boomies, such as the *Flower of Essex, The Darnet* and *Kate* of Ipswich, were launched with the older square-counter stern to be seen in the photo of the *Mayland*. Others, including *Lord Churchill*, had their counters removed. The rudder-trunk was always especially susceptible to rot, and was difficult to repair, and such wholesale surgery was often considered to be the lesser of two evils. However attractive in appearance the counter appeared, it could be a nuisance in crowded docks. While the stern was being built the frames were not only strutted, but temporary ribands of fir were fixed to them to check any irregularities, the one linking the heads determining the sheer lines. When these had been trimmed to the correct height the deck-beams could be fitted.

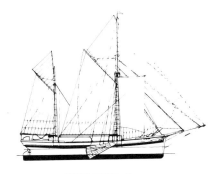

CHAPTER 6

# Framing and Planking

The deck-beams could be fitted once the keelson was in position, and were of squared oak, sawn so as to give one half-inch of camber for every foot of their length, and then halved into the timber heads. A beam joined every other pair of frames. Those in the way of the mast were especially robust, and were reinforced by lodging knees where they joined the frame, the longer side of the knee outboard and bolted to the head of an adjoining frame. In later years iron knees were substituted for reinforced grown oak crooks.

The masts of the earlier Harwich ketch barges and the later schooner-rigged craft were carried through the deck to the keelson. But in many others, such as *The Darnet,* the mast was stepped on deck in a tabernacle. In the sixties and seventies these were still of wood, reinforced with iron bands and fitted with a pin rail. The *Corinthian, Bona* and many of the 'Lord' barges were equipped with masts whose foot rested in a steel tabernacle, which, fitted with a winch, was bolted on deck with its weight distributed downward beneath the sailing beams by a massive mast prop to the keelson.

No doubt the fact that working 'above bridges' up the Rhine was possible for barges that could lower-down encouraged the change, and it must certainly have simplified the servicing of gear. However, one wonders if the builders also realized that the strains on the fabric of the hull produced when sailing with a mast taken through the deck also favoured stepping it. Certainly there were few if any disasters caused by masts carrying away from a tabernacle.

Once the deck-beams were in place the planking-up of the hull could commence. The lowest plank was of an extra depth and thickness,

up to four inches, and overlapped the outermost plank of the bottom; this was known as the outer chine. Unlike the planking of a conventional wooden vessel, there was no necessity to hollow the faces to fit curving frames, a further saving of time and money. Nevertheless, it was important that each plank should fit as snugly as possible to the one beneath it, and to ensure this, blocks of scrap timber were temporarily spiked to the frames to act as a bearing for pairs of wedges. These were driven home above each plank, forcing it downward, before it was spiked into place.

The planking was worked concurrently port and starboard, working towards the bow and stern alternately, with a team of shipwrights, apprentices and labourers each taking a side. All the planks were set with tar and hair, liberally applied so that a completed hull had a bizarre appearance. Shaggy lines of black felt outlined the seams and the uncut ends of the nails emphasized each plank.

Any butt joints along a plank were contrived to be over a frame, and were further reinforced with a lapping piece. When a barge was planked-up with a single skin, each plank was rabbeted to its neighbour, but when a double skin was used no rabbet was needed. This also had the advantage of requiring less steaming, because the thinner planks took up the contours of the hull with less persuasion. However, it was more probable that rot would gain a hold between the inaccessible faces of the two planks.

Barge-builders experienced a peculiar problem when cladding the hull. The flat bottom and flaring sides meant that the number of planks that had to be drawn up and rabbeted into the stem-post was greater than those of a conventionally constructed round-bottomed vessel. The problem was made more difficult by the relatively short stem. This led to a practice considered heretical by conventionally trained shipwrights, but tolerated in barge-building. At least one of the bottom planks was not carried forward as far as the stem, but ran out approximately under the after coaming of the fore hatch, and was notched into a neighbouring plank, ending over a frame. This 'losing' of one or more plank-ends enabled the ends of the rest to be brought up to the stem-rabbet without overmuch tapering, a process which reduced their strength and their bearing surface against the stem-post when they were spiked home.

Another intractable problem occurred at the point where the chine was extended to join the other planks in the sweep up to the stern. The scarf was difficult to make and fit satisfactorily. If it was not well made it would become a constant source of trouble, for because of the substantial dimensions of the chine — even when it was steamed before spiking into position — the joint was constantly under tension and subject to leaking.

Between each alternate floor and frame were fitted much shorter ones, known as navel timbers, to strengthen the angle of the chine. Packing pieces were introduced, particularly at the bow where the heavy windlass bitts and pawl-post were fitted. These were seated into the frames and then strutted against the stem-post.

The lining of the hold, or ceiling, was an integral part of any wooden vessel. Without it a barge was not strong enough to go to sea, and as much care was taken over the quality of the material that went into the lining, its fastening and its jointing, as over the exterior planking. Before the lining was fitted a heavy length of oak was placed directly beneath the beam-ends and carried along each side of the hull; this was termed the beam-shelf, and partnered the main wale on the exterior in binding the topsides of the hull together. Usually there were short removable lengths cut into the ceiling which were taken out when the hold was empty, and assisted in providing ventilation between the frames.

This feature also provided, incidentally, handy hiding-places for contraband. Bottles were suspended on cords between the frames and quietly retrieved at the end of a voyage from the Continent. This subterfuge was used extensively when during the wartime boom frequent voyages to France meant rich financial rewards for the crew, thus providing ready money for their illicit purchases.

But if these places provided the crew with an excellent opportunity for avoiding Customs duty they were woefully inadequate to give the necessary drying draught of fresh air a chance to penetrate the hidden recesses of the hull. Minor damage, and the everyday strains that the fabric of the hull inevitably suffered, resulted in water seepage and the subsequent risk of rot, often with fatal results. Even though the barge-builders provided a margin for this in the dimensions of the timber used, a deliberate calculation to stave off the effects of decay, it was a fact that as far as wooden vessels were concerned their end was in their beginning.

The fabric of the hull was now almost complete. It remained only to cover the space between the lining and the outer planking, sealing it at deck level with a covering board sawn from oak of three inches or more in thickness. The rail stanchions were then fitted into mortices cut in the covering board and dowelled to the frame-heads below them. The rails were particularly vulnerable to damage, so that dowels — which pulled out with the minimum of destruction to the timber-heads when an accident occurred — were preferred to bolts or spikes to fix them. Few boomies, apart from the really big examples, sported a topgallant rail, and so a simple coping rail of varnished oak covered the heads of the stanchions. This was augmented by white-painted bow-boards forward and a deep quarter rail aft, sometimes, as in the case of the *Olympia*, carried forward as far as the main hatch.

The heavy hatch coamings gave an added longitudinal strength to the relatively flat hull, particularly in the later barges, and were high enough to provide a 'breakwater' effect in a heavy sea, a welcome assistance for a vessel whose freeboard was measured in inches. The earlier boomie-barge builders retained a healthy belief that the smallest cargo hatch ensured minimum of danger from the sea, and avoided weakening the basic strength of the box section by widening them. However, to assist in cargo-handling and the carrying of awkward consignments, for which the boomies rapidly gained a reputation, the demand increased for ever wider and longer hatches. From measuring approximately one-third of the beam amidships — which was considerably wider than the traditional size for a brig or schooner of the 1860s — the main hatches were gradually widened until they exceeded one-half of the width of the deck. In earlier days the smaller main hatch was augmented by a third hatch, a few feet square, set just forward of the mizzen mast.

The deck was laid from planks of yellow or pitch pine, six inches by four, and their seams were the only ones regularly caulked with oakum and then sealed with hot pitch. Another exception to the usual 'hair and blair' sealant, also singled out for this treatment, was the important seam between the covering board and the main wale, which was particularly vulnerable to damage. The covering board of the majority of ketch barges had to be renewed at least once during their career. It suffered from the bows of other craft crushing it; pressure on the rails and the stanchions also levered it from its seating on the frame-heads and water seeped in and rotted it. If the covering board failed it meant that water could easily enter the gap between the lining and the outer planking of the hull, starting rot which could reduce the timbers to a crumbling powder.

Bilge-water was disposed of by way of four heavy-duty pumps, fitted through the deck, two forward near the main rigging and a pair aft, abreast of the mizzen mast. Slots called limber holes were cut out on the under-side of the floors before they were permanently positioned to allow water to drain fore and aft and eventually into the angle of the lee chine so that one of the two pumps on the lee side could deal with it. However well kept up, a fully loaded barge required some attention to the pumps at least once a day.

The pumps were the province of the shipyard blacksmith. He also provided iron hanging knees, forged to take up the shape of the hold, linking up beams and the beam shelf and extending down to the inner chines. They were fixed through the lining and the frames with bolts which were riveted over their collar on the outside planking; six or more of these iron knees would be fitted to each side of the barge's hold. Coping iron was fitted to protect the tops of the hatch coamings, and an iron stem-piece was forged to fit the profile of the gammon knee beneath the bowsprit, terminating in an eye for the inner jib-stay. An iron band protected the outboard edge of the covering board, and a gammon iron secured the bowsprit to the stem-head, while the leeboard winches, fitted on opposite quarters level with the mizzen mast, also required his attention. These were originally more genuinely sea-going-arrangements than the awkward crab winches of the sprittie barge. With the outboard spindle of the drum set in an especially strengthened stanchion, the substantial barrel was supported by an iron frame inboard and equipped with a pawl and handle which were operated at waist-height. The Ipswich *Pearl* carried winches of this type until the end of her days.

At regular intervals during the construction of the barge, its materials and workmanship came under the scrutiny of surveyors. These were in three main categories: firstly, the representatives of the Board of Trade, authorized by the Merchant Shipping Act; secondly, the local, more sympathetic supervision in the shape of the surveyor employed by the insurance club which would eventually underwrite the barge and her voyages in trade; and thirdly, in a few favoured cases, a gentleman from Lloyd's Chamber of Shipping. By no means all boomies were constructed under the supervision of this august body, although quite a large number will be found in 'The Big-barge Fleet' at the end of this book. The fact that merchants were more likely to take up tonnage built under Lloyd's supervision made the expense and trouble worth while.

It is frequently claimed that material was built into barges from old 'wooden walls', relics of the sailing navy which were broken up at Sheerness, Chatham or Harwich. This is unlikely, if only for the fact that few sawyers would care to risk their equipment striking hidden metal fastenings in second-hand timber; moreover, surveyors or potential owners were reluctant to accept its inclusion in a hull. The legend has its foundation in barge-builders undoubtedly taking advantage of the sale of stocks of timber, particularly well-seasoned oak and elm, which by the 1870s and 1880s were finally recognized as redundant by the Admiralty.

The dimensions of the leeboards were determined by the width of their 'fan', as the wider end was known. This measurement was equal to the barge's loaded draught, and when multiplied by three produced the appropriate overall length. The boards were generally built up of oak, but in the case of the *Stour* greenheart was used. They were reinforced at the head by an iron plate, and down their length by eight or more iron straps binding the planks together. The leeboards were secured to the hull by a pair of links which passed through the head and then through the heavy leeboard chocks, built into the bulwarks. They were secured against the hull by a loop forged into the outboard end of an iron strap, which was bolted through the deck into the deck-beam abaft the mainmast. A toggle prevented the outboard link from pulling through the head of the leeboard. It was a simple but effective device, allowing the boards to be removed easily, albeit with a great deal of heaving on tackles and winding on the dolly winch.

A dolly winch was standard equipment for all boomies, though very few spritsail barges, however large, were equipped with one. The sprittie barge-men applied this term to the light barrel mounted on top of the anchor windlass bitts, carrying a cotton line used chiefly for moving the barge in dock. The boomies' dolly winch was made of heavy oak, supported by grown oak knees bolted through to the mast partners and to a deck beam. Situated just aft of the mainmast, it provided a simple mechanical aid for sweating up halyards, shortening lines and warps when moving in dock, and handling the boat-tackles should the boat be stowed on the main hatch. The dolly winch was also useful for providing a point at which a bass spring could be heaved in and then belayed to take some of the strain off the cable when lying to an anchor in an open roadstead.

But the main duty of the dolly winch was cargo-handling. It was used for winding out coal in bushel baskets, or loading artificial manure in sacks, laboriously coaxing in iron rails, or persuading elm butts out. On barges where the main-mast lowered, the gallows across the top of the winch could be unshipped, together with the winch barrels.

Building the cargo winch on a new barge was the job of the shipwright; a ship-joiner was responsible for building and lining the cabin aft and completing the deck furniture. This work required a skill of its own, for while it did not demand the bold, creative strokes required of the shipwright, a ketch barge's cabin had few right angles, and was expected to provide an adequate substitute for a combined Victorian parlour and cottage bedroom ashore. Like them also, it was expected to be generously panelled in pine, stained and thickly varnished.

In a big barge a spiral stair gave access to the cabin, and descended from a substantial companion-way on deck into a lobby where heavy-weather clothing was hung. Entrance to the cabin proper was gained through a panelled, half-glazed door, well furnished with brass fittings. Within the cabin, against the bulkhead, a neat cast-iron fireplace, complete with over-mantel and brass fender, was flanked by wide cupboards and drawers. To port and starboard of the main cabin were miniature state-rooms, given privacy by folding doors, lit from above by deck-lights, and each fitted with a wide bunk.

Around the cabin table a horseshoe of upholstered lockers was built in, and these gave storage for coal. Here the crew sat beneath an ornate brass paraffin lamp when they ate together. In most ketch barges — during meal-times, at least — little distinction was shown between the afterguard and the fo'c'sle hands.

The meals themselves were prepared aboard the smaller ketches in the fo'c'sle, but most of the boomies of the calibre of the *Pearl*, the *Alice Watts* and *Clymping* boasted a small wooden galley on deck. Built by the joiner, it was provided with sliding doors on each side, so that ventilation was available by opening the leeward one. One may be excused for wondering how such an arrangement, vulnerable to even a moderate sea swirling aft, was tolerated for so long. The answer probably lies in the fact that the time that a boomie spent at sea, in the course of a year's trading, was less than the time spent in port. In port, cooking in the galley on deck (rather than in a cluttered fo'c'sle where a fire might be a nuisance in hot weather) certainly had an advantage.

Moreover, during the days of sail and wooden ships fire was understandably considered a serious hazard, particularly in a crowded dock. Some dock authorities strictly forbade any cabin fires to remain alight after sunset, but a galley fire on deck was exempt, as any outbreaks resulting from an untended cooking-stove could be easily identified and dealt with.

The joiner was also responsible for building the wheel-house — something of a misnomer, for it provided only the minimum of protection for the man at the wheel. Quadrant-shaped in profile, it sheltered the steering gear's mechanism, while providing lavatory accommodation on one side and a store for life-jackets and bosun's gear on the other. Some few boomies, like the *Leading Light*, extended the wheel-house to provide cover for the helmsman, while the *Martinet* had her galley built into it. But many had nothing at all except the simple steerage box of a spritsail barge, while some, such as the *Empress of India*, when first launched, had a wheel-house but were tiller steered!

Our boomie is now almost complete. The bow-sprit has been shipped, but not the mast and spars. They are being shaped from baulks of pine, first squared, then adzed to an octagon section and finally completed with a draw-knife. They can be hoisted aboard in due course; at the

Launch of the **Wellholme** at Littlehampton in 1916 from the yard of J. and W. B. Harvey. She cost £1750. The absence of the mainmast is probably due to lack of lifting gear over her building berth. (*Basil Greenhill*)

moment the blocks must be vacated, for they are required for a new keel to be laid down, and launching must take place as soon as our barge is seaworthy. The hull has been triple-painted with coal-tar from the gasworks, and her rails are enamelled black with a white band. Under the bowsprit the gammon knee has been picked out in gilt to match the bow-badges, and the carved banners on either bow and under her stern (which carry her name) have been suitably embellished.

Two iron winches have been fitted to port and starboard of the main mast and painted green, like the rest of the iron-work. The one to port will take the topsail halyard and the foresail halyard, while the starboard winch controls the roller reefing downhaul and the throat halyards.

The inside of the bulwarks are either white, or pale green with the stanchions picked out white. For her first years at sea, at least, the capping rail will be conscientiously scraped and varnished along with the windlass bitts, the dolly winch and the rest of the deck furniture. But eventually good intentions will fade away and a universal dark ochre paint will cover all, perhaps occasionally enlivened by a mate who is a self-taught master in the art of 'graining'.

The launch of a vessel, even a relatively humble ketch barge, was still accorded a certain celebration, even as the days of sail closed. Perhaps we cannot do better than to quote an account from the *East Anglian Daily Times* of 1884, recording just such an event.

Yesterday saw the launch from W. Bayley's St. Clement Shipyard, Ipswich, of a fine boomsail barge. Before entering her native element the vessel received her name, in the traditional manner, from the diminutive young lady after whom she is named *Blanche*. We understand that this vessel, of which a number have been built at Mr. Bayley's shipyard, is destined for the Continental trade. Upon the successful conclusion of the ceremony those who assisted in her construction were provided with a generous entertainment at the *Ship Launch Inn*.

# PART 2

# The Barge Coast

CHAPTER 7

# Early Days at Harwich

Let us now proceed to explore 'the barge coast,' to meet some of the owners, builders and skippers, and to discover the part they and their craft played in the life of most of the waterside towns and villages from Suffolk to Sussex.

Harwich is a good place to start, for it was the home of many skipper-owners of the early pioneering days. Here one gets a picture of the creative heyday of a small-scale enterprise and of a close-knit fraternity before the age of the commercial companies.

A typical example was John Whitmore, a deep-sea mariner who came ashore after losing a leg in an accident at sea, and became surveyor of the Harwich Barge Club, naming his mulie *Una* and his sprittie *Gladys* after his two daughters. He is remembered as a jolly old chap whose wooden leg was liable to fall off. Despite this he was fond of jumping up on the table to lead the revels. He retired from sea to keep a tailor's shop, in which trade he was followed by his son James, who had two shops in Harwich, Whitmore's and Bodgenor's.

One of James's sons, Robert, was the first skipper of the mulie *Dunkerque* when she was built in 1894. He came ashore in 1898 to set up as a ship's chandler, and the Ipswich branch of this business — carried on after his death in 1909 by his son John — continues to the present day.

The Harwich shop was bought by another character, William Middleton, who is recalled for a pleasing foible. He loved jibbooms, which his *Gloriana, Laura,* and *Era* continued to flaunt long after they had gone out of general fashion.

Middleton was ship's chandler and local coal merchant as well as ship-owner. This quite common situation encouraged the multiple ownerships which were probably more usual than the shipping registers suggest. It suited a merchant to gain an extra profit from the freights he commissioned, and it suited the other owners to have first claim on them. The chandler likewise acquired the right to supply the barge with her gear.

William Middleton died in 1906, but his son, Thomas, has left an attractive little memory of the giants (literally) of his youth, including John Vaux the shipbuilder (see Chapter 8) and William Gane the shipowner coming into his shop and seating themselves on coils of rope, to smoke churchwarden pipes and discuss their affairs. 'They all seemed to be huge men,' he recalled, and in fact Vaux and Gane each weighed over twenty stone. No doubt the young clerk behind the counter kept his ears pricked to tales of ships building and ships lost, of craft nearing completion without a sign of a buyer, of craft at sea and too long unreported (some never to be heard of again), of the latest calls on the club, as they would have described levies on the Harwich Mutual Barge Alliance to meet claims, of the iniquities of skippers who took risks and incurred damage and of skippers who avoided risks and took too long over their freights.

To have owned craft which could pay for themselves in a few years' work sounds an idyllic occupation, but personal commitment took its toll. Poor Gane, who owned cod smacks as well as the *Ada Gane* (named after his grand-daughter), ventured in 1889 on the most expensive ketch barge ever built in Harwich. The *Sunbeam*, the last boomie built by his friend Vaux, cost £8,000. Three years later she was run down by the ss

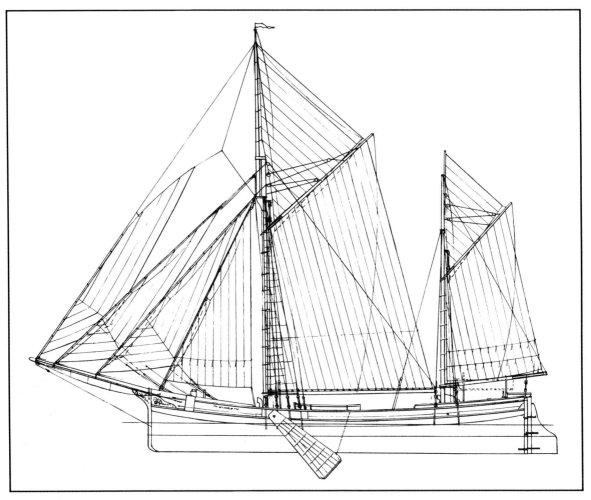

*Ariosto* off Dungeness, bound from Sunderland to Poole with coal, the crew being picked up by the steamer, including her skipper, William Whitmore, another son of the wooden-legged John Whitmore. Gane took his claim to the Admiralty High Court, where it was proved that the *Sunbeam* was not showing a stern light. The loss and the court case preyed on his mind, and after the hearing he committed suicide.

The Lewises of Harwich were best known as salvagers,[1] but John and Robert owned the *Mystery*. Robert also owned two craft named *Active* and *Sylph*. The *Sylph* was sunk in the Scheldt, and because Lewis would not pay for the cost of her salvage the *Active* was never again able to visit Belgium for fear of arrest for the debt.

Many other Harwich families owned and sailed boomies, often for several generations. Among these were the Richmonds, with ship-owning

[1]See *The Salvagers*.

**Britannia**, built in 1893.

interests back to the early years of the nineteenth century. Either Luke or Johnson Richmond owned at one time or another the *Startled Fawn*, *Fleetwing* and *Phoenix*. John Holmes, who named the *Eliza H* after his daughter, was first skipper of the *Ornate,* and bought the *Osprey* for his son, William, who became deputy harbourmaster. He had his own house flag, a white cross on a blue ground, shown in portraits of *Mazeppa* and his sprittie *Beric*. (Bayley of Ipswich was another owner with his own flag.) Charles Forster invested the profits of his sailmaker's business in the *Gem of the Ocean* and the *Emma,* and there were others too numerous to mention.

One owner must, however, be dealt with in more detail — John Watts, who gave his name to the first barge ever built in Harwich, the sprittie *John Watts,* and his daughter's to the elegant *Alice Watts.*

**Ornate**, built at Harwich in 1875, and owned there, and later at Bridgwater. (*Alan Cordell*)

His chief interest was the manufacture of 'Roman cement', a material in universal demand in the building industry before the invention of Portland cement made it obsolete. He was owner of many of the boats which dredged the raw materials from the sea, and of one of the factories, which needed half a ton of coal for every ton of cement manufactured. He had a big stake in the salvaging trade, owning salvaging smacks and the port's first steam tug, *Liverpool*. He also established the first steam ferry between Harwich and Felixstowe. He retired as one of the richest men in Harwich, but a few years afterwards his whole business was brought to ruin by the incompetence of his son, Walter Watts, made bankrupt in 1877. After being forced to sign the bankruptcy petition which destroyed all he had built up, John Watts ruined himself paying a dividend to the creditors, and died in poverty in 1897.[2]

[2] See *The Salvagers*.

This was one of several examples of the failure of Harwich enterprise to put down roots capable of developing growth. Neither John Vaux nor William Groom, owner of the boomies *Major* and *Mystery*, as well as many spritties, had sons wishing to succeed them. As a result craft were increasingly sold away to places with a more progressive mercantile outlook, and by the time the boomies reached the height of their prosperity, in the closing years of the nineteenth century, interest in them was chiefly to be found in London and in Kent.

Of the Harwich builders, Vaux and Cann were the most prominent.

John Vaux, till his death in 1874, and his son John Henry Vaux, till his death in 1894, occupied the Navy Yard, which had a long tradition of shipbuilding, from the time of Pepys's Navy up to its closure in 1928 after the failure of Vaux's successors, the McLearons, of whom there were also two generations.

The Navy Yard was an important birthplace of boomies, with twenty-three built by Vaux, father and son, and five by the McLearons. The site is today covered by the modern Navy Yard Wharf, and though the ancient treadmill crane which was still in use in the nineteenth century is preserved near by, there is now no trace of the two slipways, one a cradle on rails and the other 'hollows and rounds', which pointed out across the harbour at the extreme seaward corner of the town. Old ships were sunk in strategic positions as breakwaters to give some protection to a site otherwise totally exposed to the sea, an uncertain arrangement which lasted until the 1920s.

Both the Vauxes were men of affairs, busy with ship-owning and management, and in public life, though John Henry in particular was not above concerning himself with matters of detail.[3] The character of the *Stour* and her successors built in his yard may well have derived from two generations of foremen, William Christie (1826-1907) and his son, Tom, and also perhaps from the father of George Mynheer, the noted skipper who features in a later chapter.

The other principal Harwich yard was started by George Cann, who came from Brightlingsea and went into partnership with a boat-builder and blockmaker as Parsons and Cann. They built six ketch barges, between 1872 and 1879, when the partnership was dissolved, after which George built the *Mazeppa*. In the 1880s George's elder son, John, joined him, but in 1889 George was killed at the Harwich level-crossing while unloading timber. John continued the business and built the *Carisbrooke Castle* in 1890 with his younger brother Herbert, who was still a minor and so could not be a partner. Thereafter they traded as Cann Brothers, building a fine fleet of spritsail barges, the last being *Leofleda* in 1915, but no more boomies, till the yard closed around 1925.

In this yard it was the practice for John to make the half-models with his own hands and show them to his brother, who would make such comments as, 'She looks a thought thick here', in response to which John would take off a shaving. Due to its position up a narrow creek by the gasworks all launches at Cann's were performed at high water by tipping the barge over the edge of the quay broadside with a tremendous splash. John Cann died in 1933, but Herbert continued active into the Second World War.

The third Harwich builder, Norman, was a boatbuilder on the Bathside foreshore before that area was walled, when he moved round to share Cann's yard, near the gasworks.

From his uncle, 'Porky' Norman, a butcher, and Jonathan Brewster, a baker, Ben Norman received an order for the biggest barge at that time (1873) conceived in Harwich. He had five sons, all shipwrights, though only two of them, Isaac and Richard, were apprenticed to him. Whether the others — who were apprenticed elsewhere — joined him in this mammoth task I do not know, nor am I clear how it was accomplished, by all accounts, in a little creek in the Bathside saltings. There is no record of Norman having a slipway, but presumably some building and launching ways were laid down. The achievement is even more remarkable because this big barge of 128 tons was built entirely of oak, and she was built so well that she would take four hundred tons to sea, and even when many years later, after paying for herself over and over again, she was burned to the water's edge she was deemed worth rebuilding, as the *Crowpill* at Bridgwater, Somerset. After some years in the West Country she ended her days at Cowes owned by Samuel White.

The Normans and Brewsters were devout Wesleyans. They called the barge *John Wesley*, and to make sure of continued favour from the highest quarter they took care to find another good Wesleyan as her skipper.

---

[3]For a fuller account of J. H. Vaux, including craft owned by him, and his exploits in life-saving, see *The Salvagers*. For his interest in cod-fishing see *The Codbangers*.

CHAPTER 8

# The Shipyards of Ipswich

Ipswich was an important early centre of owner-ship and of building. Practically all the town's coal merchants either owned or had shares in boomies, as did many of their builders.

The town also claimed two of the last but finest fleets of sailing-barges — those of Cranfield's, the millers, and of R. & W. Paul, the maltsters. Cranfield's craft were exclusively spritties, but Robert and William Paul invested in one boomie for the coal trade, both to Ipswich and to the South Coast. Their *Ida* (named after William Paul's wife) was built by Bayley in 1881. Bound for Margate from Seaham with coal, she was blown across in 1890 to the French coast, driven ashore and reported a total loss, though her crew were saved. However, she was salvaged and sold to Whitstable in 1894. Paul's did not replace her, but gave her name to a new spritsail barge built by Orvis and Fuller in 1895.

It is, however, the barge-builders who are of the greater interest.

Hard-chined sailing barges had been built at Ipswich shipyards since the beginning of the nineteenth century, gradually supplanting the round-bottomed trading sloops. By the middle of the century the larger barges had shortened their long booms, for most were cutter-rigged, and shipped a small mizzen, while the smaller fry — small enough to negotiate the canalized river Gipping up to Stowmarket — remained spritsail-rigged.

The voyages of all of them invite the admira-tion of the twentieth-century yachtsman. The *Mary* 'flat' was picked up in Bangor Roads in a sinking state with her rudder washed away on 12 January 1852 — bound from Exeter to Glasgow!

As elsewhere on the shores of the Thames Estuary, and probably for the same reasons, in the 1850s the builders of these Ipswich barges decided to launch larger-scale coasters built barge-style. Almost certainly the *Surprise* of 1859 (85 reg. tons) was the first, and since at the time the ketch rig was only beginning to be seen as an economical arrangement, she was rigged as a schooner.

At the time her bottom planks were set up on the barge blocks of the St Clement's shipyard (then owned by William Bayley) three other ship and barge builders were competing for orders on the Orwell. Although barge building was gaining ground, Bayley's contemporaries were still busy launching square-riggers for the China Seas and schooners for world-wide trading and coastal work.

All these yards had benefited from the formation of the town's Wet Dock, opened in 1840. It had enclosed a bend of the river Orwell as it flowed by the old town, and its construction had forced Bayley's shipyard to move from its ancient site on Carpenter's Row, a section of the riverside which was now tideless and required for ware-houses. The new position, close by the earthen embankment sealing the old course of the river, was still affected by tidal changes, so that vessels could be easily beached for the attention of the yard's shipwrights. However, there still remained within the confines of the new Wet Dock the St Peter's Yard on its eastern bank, leased to William Read and busy with barge building.

William Read had once been a foreman ship-wright to the Bayleys when they had worked a third yard, the Halifax. This was still at work down-river, well beyond the Victorian town's

**Fearless,** built by Colchester at Ipswich in 1876 for the coal trade *(Alan Cordell)*

limits on the west bank, a little above the point where the Bourne Creek enters the main stream. The site was finally obliterated in the 1970s by dock extensions which had shortly before filled in the much older Nova Scotia shipyard, somewhat closer to the town on the same west bank. Unlike the Halifax shipyard, the one at 'Nova Scotia' had finished in the eighteenth century.

At the Halifax shipyard, thirty years before the frames of the schooner-barge *Surprise* were set up at Bayley's newly established yard, the ship-building industry of the town had reached its zenith. Here the *William Fairlee* and *David Scott,*

**Unity,** built by Curtis at Ipswich in 1885 *(Alan Cordell)*

both over 1,000 tons, had been built. But by the 1850s the centres of shipbuilding had moved to the north-east of England, and the Halifax yard was owned by Thomas Harvey and Son, who while they perpetuated a fine tradition of highly classed vessels, built on a much smaller scale and never constructed barges.

Boomie-barge building, which sustained the ancient Ipswich tradition through to the end of the age of wooden-ship construction in the 1890s, was thus confined to the St Clement's, Dock End, Cliff and St Peter's Yards.

The principal builder at the mid-century was William Colchester, who from about 1840 to about 1880 leased the Dock End yard, close by the St Clement's establishment of William Bayley. Colchester had no difficulty in reconciling his status as a ship-builder with the construction of hard-chined barges. He too had been evicted from Carpenter's Row upon the construction of the Wet Dock, and marked his first launching from the new site in 1841 by naming the barge *Primus.* A seventy-foot boomsail barge, the *Primus,* was followed the next year by the larger *Secundus,* and then the smaller *Tertius* in 1844. The series was completed in 1863 with the *Octavius.* The *Septimus,* launched in 1860, was a sloop, and was altered to a ketch in 1886. Most of them saw at least half a century of service and voyaged far afield, the *Sextus* sailing at least one

Unidentified boomie entering Ipswich dock. Note how she dwarfs the sprittie alongside her in the lock.

cargo to Dartmouth.

William Colchester lived at Little Oakley in Essex (where his house was burned down in 1857), and since his affairs became increasingly credited to V. D. Colchester he presumably had a son with these initials. He was a manure (or, as we should now say, fertilizer) merchant whose business was later developed by Wilfred Christopherson. He was also a partner with John Watts in the Harwich Roman Cement trade, and the lessee of the Orwell Oyster Fishery. With so many interests, it is perhaps no surprise that he did not concentrate very closely on his shipping concerns. This is shown by a yarn of Joe Mynheer's about the sprittie *Davenport,* later ketch-rigged but then newly built by him as a dandy:

> Jack Hooker was half-owner when she was built. Once Colchester met Hooker near the dock and Colchester said "Hullo Captain, I didn't know you were in." Hooker replied, "Yes, I have been in three weeks. I am glad I met you as I have some money to give you." Colchester answered, "You might need it so you'd better keep it." Jack Hooker thought

he did need it. This shows how much interest Colchester took in the yard.

Colchester was followed by G. P. Gildea, who, in about ten years' occupation, built three 'Lord' barges and one 'Belle' before moving to Rochester, to be succeeded by Robert Peck, a bargeman and father of R. & W. Paul's shipping manager, Robert (Ten Per Cent) Peck. His craft included *Ivy P* (named after his wife or daughter) and *Ethel Edith* (perhaps with a similar family connection).

After the time of boomie-building the Dock End was occupied for a short while (1896-1901) by Horace Shrubsall, son of R. M. Shrubsall of Milton, Kent, referred to in Chapter 11. He opened a second yard at Limehouse in 1897, but transferred both businesses to East Greenwich in 1901.

The Dock End was then taken over by R. & W. Paul, who operated it till 1978 under the management of W. H. Orvis's nephew, R. P. Orvis. Alone of all these yards it remains active to this day, one of the few surviving centres of traditional skills which seem likely to preserve sailing-barges into the twenty-first century.

The adjoining St Clement's was occupied from 1841 to about 1886 by William Bayley and Sons.

**Ethel Edith** in 1935, soon after she arrived in her last berth at Pin Mill. Her port crosstree is topped up, an arrangement universal in later spritties to avoid damage in dock or alongside a ship, but unlike most spritties she has ratlines in port as well as starboard rigging.

The brothers William and J. R. Bayley, the last of this noted family, kept St Clement's busy till around 1880, when work fell away and they retired, to be followed by Orvis and Fuller from about 1886 to the turn of the century, building the yard's last ketch barge, *Lord Tennyson,* in 1891. Thereafter the yard was owned by W. H. Orvis and Son, who 'doubled' the *Britannia* there in 1919. The yard closed in 1951.

The Cliff Yard, sited close to where Cliff Quay now begins, was taken over from John Lambert around 1870 by W. J. Curtis, who turned out half a dozen boomies before passing the yard on to his nephew, W. H. Orvis, who thus had both this and the St Clement's Yard. He was for a while in partnership with Frederick Fuller[1], an arrangement celebrated by the building first of the sprittie *Frederick William,* combining the partners' names, and then in 1883 the boomie *Eliza*

[1]Fuller was merely a financial partner, and so were two others whose names I have excluded to avoid over-complicating an already complex picture — J. Cobbold in partnership with William Bayley and Sons at St Clements in the 1860s, and Page, once a shipwright with Bayley, in partnership with William Read at Halifax. The latter partnership dissolved in 1844, a few months after Read was cleared of a sensational charge of scuttling his brig *Colina* to defraud the insurance company, for which the captain was sentenced to transportation but later pardoned.

*Patience*, linking their wives.

Hubert, who according to A. V. Robertson had the Dock End Yard before Gildea, and who according to Joe Mynheer built the *Davenport* in 1877, was in fact the yard manager in Colchester's time.

After the building of the Wet Dock, St Peter's Yard was established by William Read, who previously had the old yard below the Customs house, and also the Halifax Yard from which he moved to his new yard beside the dock, where he was a pioneer builder of iron steamships. This was on the site of the present Brown's timber-yard, beside the original entrance to the dock, abandoned when the present lock gates were built.

Here Read's nephew, Ebenezer Robertson, was apprenticed to him. The yard had a slipway into the dock, which was placed at an oblique angle. Even so, craft as they were launched fetched right across to the opposite side to a point on the site of the present Cranfield's mills.

It was a busy yard, for at the time the *Alice Watts* was being built three other craft were also on the stocks; two Lowestoft trawlers, *Velocity* and *Arethusa,* and a 64-ton composite yacht for Packard, the *Atalanta.*

Later Robertson built two small spritsail barges for his own ownership, *Ninita,* named after a Spanish dancer, and *Lilly,* named after Robertson's daughter-in-law, wife to his son Robert, who held a share in her and was her skipper. Both were converted to boomies to go down-Channel.

**Cock o' the Walk.** Built at Millwall in 1876 for Richard Cox of Weymouth with grey topsides, red bottom, black wales, with two gold ribbons, and all blocks and spars varnished. On her counter was a gilded cock with wings outspread and the words 'While I live I crow.' But she did not sail well till Captain Harry Strange took her on condition he was free to make any alterations. He shipped the mainmast three feet aft and the mizzen a foot forward, after which she no longer buried her head but sailed as well as she looked. She was sunk by German action in the First World War. *(Roger Finch)*

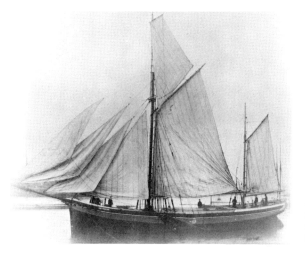

**Lord Tennyson.** A comparison with **Cock o' the Walk** is interesting. **Lord Tennyson** has only three shrouds a side and a running backstay. She also sets her jib topsail to the mainmast head. *(Roy Orvis)*

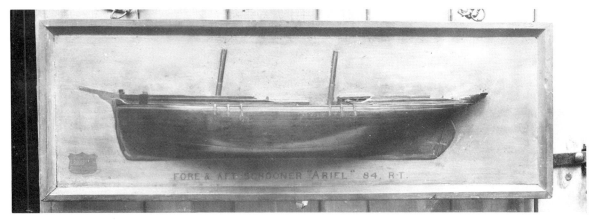

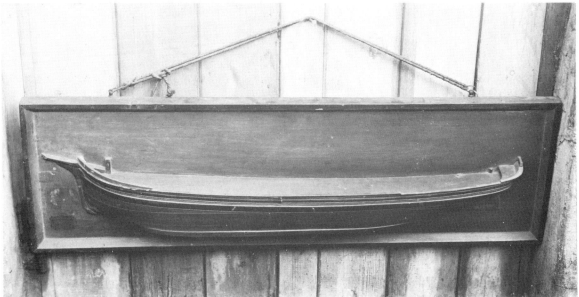

Half-models of **Lothair** *(top)* and the round-bottomed schooner **Ariel** *(bottom)* showing the distinctive sharp, hollow Robertson bow. (*J. Groom*)

Robert sailed the *Lilly* till she was lost off the Isle of Wight with a cargo of wheat. The crew were picked up in their boat by a Norwegian steamer which took them to Leith. The Norwegian skipper took a fancy to the barge's boat, offering to buy it. Robertson decided to present it to him as a gift for saving his son, but by the time the offer was sent the steamer had sailed. Robert Robertson then went into steamships.

The *Ninita* was lucky at first, paying for herself in two years, but then her luck deserted her. First she lost her rudder and blew ashore on the French coast. Then her skipper, Henry Howlett, was lost overboard in the Zuyder Zee, and Robertson sent Theo Rawson, skipper of his deep-sea three-masted schooner, *Dauntless,* to fetch her home. Rawson came out of Ostend in weather that kept the other craft in, blew away his sails and lost the barge (like the *Lilly,* uninsured), though he and his crew were saved.

Robertson's other son, A. V. ('Robbie') Robertson, after being sent to sea with Rawson in the *Dauntless* to complete his education in the hard school, moved to Woodbridge in 1888 at the age of eighteen to run the Lime Kiln Yard, which Ebenezer had bought to develop yacht-building. The patent slip was sold to a Rochester firm, and the grids for large vessels cleared away, after which both A. V. Robertson and later his son, Bert, produced many successful and popular cruising yachts up to the Second World War.

Lower down the Deben, where the present yard is located, there were also barge blocks where boomies were frequently repaired, taking advantage of the lower wage rates on the Suffolk river.

CHAPTER 9

# Woodbridge, Mistley and Pin Mill

Before leaving Suffolk three smaller centres remain to be considered, Chelmondiston and Pin Mill on the Orwell between Ipswich and Harwich, Woodbridge at the head of the Deben estuary, and Mistley, which may conveniently be included at this point, though with its neighbour Manning-tree it is in fact on the Essex side of the Stour.

In the age of the schooners Woodbridge had a vigorous maritime interest which, however, died out in the first half of the nineteenth century. The Deben was still worked by craft owned elsewhere, but local initiative did not respond.

Perhaps it was for this reason that Robert Skinner had to look as far afield as Kent to become skipper of the *Zebrina* and the *Belmont*, already referred to. Thereafter he did, however, return to his native Deben, owning the *Lord Alcester* jointly with the local coal merchant, Cox. When he reached Woodbridge with his 290 tons the word soon got about, and the customers would arrive with carts and wheelbarrows to deal direct with him.

In due course the venture was sufficiently successful for him to buy the *Lord Hartington* also, but the business failed in the depression of the 1920s, leaving the *Sussex Belle* to bring the last freight of coal to the Sun Wharf about 1923. Both the Lords were sold away, the *Alcester* being eventually lost running for Poole and the *Hartington* being run down and sunk by a German cargo liner in the Scheldt in 1928.

Robert Skinner's three sons all followed into barges. John skippered the *Lord Hartington* till he took a job ashore in North Woolwich. Wesley was mate with his father in the *Lord Alcester*, and later owned the sprittes *Martin Luther* and

*Nautilus*. George, the youngest, after a spell in the *Zebrina* returned to help his father in the coal business, but then went into steamers before reverting to barges with the sprittie *Dover Castle* and the *Lord Alcester,* in which he traded coal from the Tyne to the Biscay ports, five-handed. Finally he settled for the quieter estuary work in Cranfield's Ipswich grain barges.

Robert himself ended his days slogging shingle from the Deben Bar up to Woodbridge Quay in the tattered old sprittie *Tuesday*. He was found dead in her cabin in 1935 at the age of eighty-two — a poignantly defiant end for a man who had once carried barging to its ultimate development in the Kentish giants.

Before Skinner's return to the Deben the *Onward* was Woodbridge-owned by E. J. Passiful — a name noted along the Suffolk shore — during her short life, and had a Woodbridge crew when she was run down and sunk in 1887. But the best-remembered figure was Jimmy Lewis, a distant cousin of Robert Lewis of Harwich, with at least a part-ownership of some of the craft he skippered — *Yulan*, *Mystery*, *Justice* and *Laura*. The distinction between skipper and owner is often difficult to discern, because it is commonly recalled that a man 'had' a craft, or even that she was built for him, which may denote either capacity, but Lewis had at least a half-share with Groom of Harwich in the *Justice*.

At Mistley, where the maltings brought craft from far and near, the family whose name is almost synonymous with barging, the Horlocks, confined their interest chiefly to sprittes.

One branch of the family, under F. W. Horlock, bought the *Thalatta* in 1906 after she

Boomie with topmast housed on the blocks at Robertson's yard, Woodbridge, mentioned in the previous chapter (*Roger Finch*)

had long laid on Vaux's ways seeking a buyer. She was rigged as a sprittie, but her skipper, Jimmy Alliston, did not like this rig in a barge with flared sides — that is, with a bottom narrower than her deck. She was therefore converted to a boomie, trading with this rig as far afield as Dublin, first for Horlock and then, with an auxiliary engine and without topmast, for the Wynnfield Shipping Company. In the 1920s she was again converted to a mule-rigged sprittie by Captain Body of Southend, and ended her trading as one of Paul's Ipswich mill barges, first under sail and later as an auxiliary motor barge.

With the dispersal of Paul's fleet she was acquired to replace the sprittie *Memory* in passenger charter work. The *Memory's* lofty gear was lifted bodily into her mast-case with little

*Opposite*
At Woodbridge. *(Top)* **Sussex Belle** at the tide mill. *(Bottom)* Unidentified ketch (perhaps **Fearless**) in the Lime Kiln Dock.

alteration beyond shortening the forestay to accommodate *Thalatta's* sheering bow and high stem. To those who knew both barges the contrast was remarkable. *Memory,* a stiff beamy barge, carried her big sails upright, butting her bow through a seaway and showering her foredeck with white water, while *Thalatta,* with hardly a straight piece of wood in her shapely hull, slices her way through a sea, her deck at a steep angle but dry. Still immaculately maintained by the East Coast Sail Trust, *Thalatta* is an instructive example of the way a barge in her time can play many parts, and also of the variety in form and performance available within the seemingly circumscribed limits of the flat-bottomed hull.

The other main branch of the Horlock family, which included Alfred (Chubb) Horlock, in 1925 acquired the *Mazeppa* for £400, but only kept her a few months. Her skipper, Dick Horlock, took a freight of cement to Ostend, where he died of pneumonia. The *Mazeppa* was then sold to William Easter of Hastings, only to be run down and lost within two years by a steamer in the Thames estuary.

71

**Mazeppa** of Harwich, launched in 1887 by H. Cann. Painting by R. Chappell (*Roger Finch*)

The most prominent Mistley boomie family were the Stone brothers, Harry, Charles and Jim, sons of Charles Stone senior. A Charles Stone lost the *General Gordon* when she was run down in the 1880s, but whether this was the father or the son I have not discovered. The son traded to the Phoenix Ironworks at Lewes, importing 'long iron' from the Continent, first in a vessel named *Bucephalus* and then, when she proved awkwardly large for the bridge there, in the beautiful sprittie *Hetty* which he had built for him in Holland. The sprittie *Centaur*, today the pride of the Thames Barge Sailing Club, was also built for him.

Harry was skipper of Paul's *Ida* and then

*Opposite*
**Thalatta** *(Top)* was built as a sprittie and converted to a boomie. She then became an auxiliary motor barge, but was put back under sail as a sprittie. After another spell as a motor barge she was once again given this fine mulie spritsail rig, which she carries today. *(Bottom)* As a Wynnfield Shipping Co. auxiliary, about 1920. (*East Coast Sail Trust*)

skipper and part-owner of the *Genesta*, against which he would not hear a word spoken, though just before his death he surprised everyone by declaring she was often a pig to steer. He was one of the gentleman skippers, fond of stowing away his leeboards when coal-laden in North Country ports, to make his craft look grander. He had a flagstaff at his house at Mistley, from which he always flew an ensign when he was at home, like the Royal Family.

Jim was chiefly noted as one of the champion racing-barge skippers, but he was also skipper of the *Eliza H*, which he lost on the Longsand in 1902. She drove ashore in calm weather and later came off, but sank in deep water. Jim was in trouble for leaving her without letting go an anchor. He then had the *Harold*, which he also abandoned when she got ashore. This time the barge was salvaged, but the incident upset Harry (who had shares in her), and the partnership broke up as a result.

Another Mistley skipper-owner, John Finch, had the *Garson*, which he acquired from her original owners at Yarmouth, Garson Blake and Sons,

**Genesta** of Harwich. *(Top and centre)* A pair of portraits, with the scene centre commemorating an adventure in 1891, when she was caught in a gale bound from Snape to Dublin and towed into Penzance with a broken boom. *(Bottom)* At Rock, near Padstow, north Cornwall, as a houseboat.

brick, tile and cement merchants.

She was the first boomie built in Yarmouth in 1864, by Mills and Blake at Southtown, and one of the first with a transom stern. She was designed by George Blake, and strongly built for heavy freights of bricks and tiles from Barton-on-Humber to Yarmouth.

In 1893, during Finch's ownership, she was driven ashore on Eccles Beach near Winterton and sold where she lay, at a heavy loss, to Castle and Sons, the Yarmouth shipbuilders. (Mr A. B. Castle, who later bought her, became a director of Fellowes, which built a number of fine barges at Yarmouth.) They succeeded in getting her off and rebuilding her. In the 1920s she was again driven ashore at Landguard Point trying to enter Harwich, and once more only refloated with difficulty after several months, to be towed back to Yarmouth and converted by Fellowes into a clubhouse for the Erith Yacht Club.

**Byculla** at Wisbech quay, a destination involving the expense and delay of towage up the river Nene, but rewarded by a higher freight rate. *(Peter Ferguson)*

On the Orwell at Chelmondiston and Pin Mill the most interesting of several owners was Edward Garnham, who built up a fleet based on his savings as an engine-driver in India — surely as delightful an example of self-help as Samuel Smiles could have desired. The source of his capital may have been modest, but he ordered *Blanche* new from Bayley of Ipswich in 1884, and three years later he obtained from the same builder *Byculla,* named after a town in Southern India which was doubtless served by the railway on which he had worked. He then had *Bona* new from Harvey of Littlehampton in 1898, and *Nell Jess* from the same yard in 1902, as well as acquiring, jointly with Ruffles of Ipswich, *Harold* from Stone of Mistley.

## CHAPTER 10
# Colne, Blackwater and Crouch

So we return to Essex.

Surprisingly, in view of its long maritime tradition, Colchester had little involvement with boomies. The Hythe waterside long remembered the loss in 1880 of one of the few craft actually owned in the town, a converted dandy named *Jabez,* which capsized at sea off Withernsea, Yorks, loaded with 'big logs', a notoriously top-heavy freight, leaving a whole row of cottages inhabited by widows.

The chief activity, however, was the coal trade to the town's gasworks where the manager, Herbert Pike, was in 1893 shown as managing owner of *Startled Fawn* and of *Hesper,* whose skipper, Ralph Hatcher, was so deaf that a slate was kept on deck to communicate with him. *Alice Watts* was also so closely connected with the gasworks that when her figurehead was removed it was erected in the yard, only to be removed because it frightened the horses!

*Antelope,* a sister of *Startled Fawn,* was another regular gas collier. She was commonly called 'The Grasshopper' because an absent-minded docker so hailed her in the Humber and the name stuck. She was later owned first at Hull and then at Brixham, disappearing from the register after 1929.

While the extent of its actual ownership is not clear, the gasworks thus employed some of the fastest and smartest craft in its humble service, and relied on them up to the end of the First World War.

Farther down the river, at Brightlingsea, Aldous's busy yard, just above the present Colne Yacht Club, turned out a number of craft in the years between 1860 and the 1880s.

Robert Aldous was a notably creative builder, carrying on the traditions of Rowhedge and Wivenhoe in producing smacks famous for their speed. It is accordingly interesting to find that his *Antelope* and *Startled Fawn* were by general consent among the fastest of the boomies, and his *Harwich,* which had a narrow bottom giving her flared sides, was also considered fast.

Among Brightlingsea owners, John Sawyer — another of the leading latter-day collectors of craft of all kinds, and chairman of the Harwich Barge Club — owned the *Ethel Edith* in the 1920s. The *Britannic,* which in 1901 ran from Antwerp to Brightlingsea in twenty-four hours, was also locally owned, first by William Pannell, and for a time by her skipper, William Angier.

The *James Garfield* was not only skipper-owned by Thomas Wellum, but also crewed by his three sons. They were involved in a poignant tragedy in December 1891. They had been trying for three weeks to get down-Channel to Penzance with wheat, and were lying in the Downs when they had to seek shelter in the Swale. It was a hard beat for the entrance, but at last seventeen-year-old Leonard Wellum shouted, 'We shall fetch the Swale this time!' when the barge plunged and he went overboard.

Another Brightlingsea boomie, the *Star,* was involved in a tragedy which by chance was to influence the development of Whitby Harbour.

Built at Brightlingsea in 1868 as a sprittie, she was soon converted to ketch rig, and in the early 1900s was owned first at Lowestoft and then at Yarmouth. In November 1906 she left Hull for Sunderland with wheat, and was obliged to put into Scarborough. After nine days there she resumed her voyage, but met with a gale when

The ill-fated **Jabez.** One of the few boomies owned in Colchester, she capsized off Withernsea in 1880, drowning her crew of four and leaving a row of cottages inhabited by widows. *(Nottage Institute, Wivenhoe)*

about eleven miles north of Whitby. According to her skipper, Arthur Downes of Brightlingsea, it was 'hard going' but by 'hammering at it' all night they got within a mile and a half of the Tees entrance. Then, with sails torn, they had to give up and run before it, intending to return to Scarborough. 'But', said Captain Downes, 'with my ship in such a plight I dared not pass Whitby harbour.'

The Whitby entrance was then a notorious death-trap. The town was in decay through the decline of its shipbuilding, fishery and jet trades, and a movement to extend the harbour piers and provide a harbour of refuge had culminated in a Board of Trade inquiry only a few days before. Thus when the *Star* was seen shaping up for the entrance in such conditions an anxious crowd collected. Local seamen hoped she would not attempt to cross the bar, but would be beached on

the sands to the west of the piers, and against this prospect the rocket apparatus was got ready in front of the coastguard station.

Somehow, however, the barge was steered between the two piers, and a cheer went up as she seemed to be safe. But at that moment a great wave swept over her, carrying the mate, James White, overboard under the eyes of the spectators on the pierheads. He was kept afloat by his oilskin frock, but to no purpose, for, with the rocket apparatus now in the wrong place, efforts to launch a coble failed, and inexplicably neither of the two lifeboats was called.

The *Whitby Gazette* observed:

The occurrence of Sunday makes it plain that when our piers are built, as built they will be, the *Star* of Colchester will not be alone in seeking shelter with us. We close in the confident hope that the sea which swept James White to his doom swept also the opposition to our harbour improvement to that bourne whence no traveller returns.

*Opposite*
**Antelope** unloading at Leigh, showing the shapely bow found in craft built at Brightlingsea and Harwich, with bottoms narrower than their decks. Built by Aldous at Brightlingsea, **Antelope** was noted for her speed.
*(David Patient)*

*Below*
Schooner barge (probably **Alice Watts**) at Colchester gasworks with a fleet of spritties. Note fore braces for topsail yards led to bowsprit end.

Influenced no doubt by this dramatic tragedy, the pier extensions were in fact built a few years later.[1]

In the Blackwater, Mersea Hard and Bradwell Quay saw occasional boomies, while at Tollesbury William Frost brought his sons up to barging in the *James Bowles* (named after her original owner, whose family — numerous in Brightlingsea and Tollesbury — later followed the oyster trade to Shoreham).

One of them, Jim Frost, brought Tollesbury its coal in *The Darnet*. On his arrival the crier went round the village proclaiming '*The Darnet* is up

[1]For a fuller account see 'Death was the Great Persuader' by Peter Frank: *Coast and Country*, June 1980 (Vol. IX, No. 3).

**Harwich.** *(Top)* A portrait painted by Reuben Chappell at Goole and *(bottom)* a photo at Southwold towards the end of her career. (*Roger Finch*)

Woodrope with a cargo of coals. Give your orders to the captain, who has also brought a freight of Sunderland dishes.'

Two queer cargoes recalled by Jim Frost were a crane jib four feet longer than the barge taken

from Fambridge to Keyham (a destination I have failed to identify) with seventy tons of ballast to steady the load, and a chapel, removed from Colchester to Bursledon in Hampshire — 'pulpit and all; everything bar the parson.' He considered the worst harbours to take on the East Coast were Scarborough, Whitby and Bridlington and, down-Channel, Bridport.

At the top of the Blackwater estuary, Howard of Maldon was one of the most attractive and artistic exponents of the flat-bottomed hull, turning out a succession of spritties which were things of beauty, despite being designed for the humble trade of stack-carrying.

He also built two fine boomies. *Malvoisin* (1883) was first owned by W. T. Meeson, but she proved too large to get up to his Battlesbridge mill on most tides, and generally had to be unloaded at Hullbridge. She was sold to Kentish owners, and lasted till her loss in 1929. *Record Reign,* built seven years later for the timber merchants, Sadd's, also proved awkwardly large for her intended work into the Heybridge canal, for the lock gate could not be closed under her clipper bow when she was fully loaded. One of the most beautiful barges ever built, she had the

Unidentified ketch barge at West Mersea with the oyster smack **Unity** moored ahead of her and another under way behind. She is probably coming on to the Hard to unload coal. The creeks were less crowded then than they are today, but so big a craft must have been a handful to work through the narrow channels before the time of motor towboats.

distinction of serving as a Q-ship in the First World War.

The other chief Essex river, the Crouch, with its tributary the Roach, was a considerable centre.

Many boomies used Smith's Quay (now Prior's), Cardnell's Wharf, at the end of Belvedere Road, the Pound, on the waterfront, and the Anchor Stage, all at Burnham, as well as the Small Gains and Crouch loading on Foulness Island, where Ted Potton, Trussell and Oscar Wife managed a number of craft, among which were the regular traders *Leading Light, Kindly Light, Solent* and *Lucy Richmond*. There was also a regular trade to the mills at Battlesbridge and Rochford.

Burnham provided many skippers, including several who first traded to the town and then settled there, and though few if any boomies other than the *Triumph* were built on these rivers, their sails were made by Charrington in his thatched loft on the site of the present Royal Burnham Yacht Club.

Of the various fleets, the most colourful was

that of John Smith of Burnham (later Smith Brothers), who built up a big collection of craft ranging from collier schooners to stack barges and oyster smacks (for his interests also included the Crouch Oyster Fishery).

The first of his big 'coal carts' were a couple of schooners built by Watson at Rochester — *Russell* (1865) and *Ten Brothers* (1860). They were still owned by their builders in 1873, when they were put up for auction without success. *Ten Brothers* attracted a bid of £950, but the vendor wanted £1,000 and she was withdrawn. There were no bids for *Russell*, which at the time was in the coal and timber trade between Maidstone and Sunderland. Many boomies not built to order were kept for some years by their builders, and this is one of many occasions which make one wonder how often this was a conscious choice and how often it was impossible to find a buyer. However that may be, both were acquired by Smith a few years later. Neither lasted long in the hard trade to which he put them, *Ten Brothers* being lost in 1879 in a collision, and *Russell* being wrecked in the same year.[2]

By this time Smith had also acquired the schooners *Dauntless* (which was altered to ketch) and *Emily Lloyd* (built as *William Levitt*). He also owned the ketches *Magnet, Speedwell* and

[2]Bob Childs: 'Rochester Barges, Part 2', *River News*, Rochester, Vol. 1, No. 2.

**James Bowles.** An early (1865) ketch with single jib set flying on a traveller, smack-style. She carries a square-sail to make the most of a fair wind, as was the custom to the end, after square topsails were generally obsolete. The artist, used to painting profiles, has lost his confidence in attempting the view of her running. He has failed to draw a barge's bow, and he has shown main and mizzen sails sheeted hard in — an effect that cannot have pleased her skipper. (*Hervey Benham*)

*Rochester Castle,* but his best-remembered trio were *Friendship, Thistle* and *Vanguard,* all built for him by Taylor at Sittingbourne between 1885 and 1890.

An adventure of *Friendship,* when she was blown about the North Sea for a month, is told in Chapter 15. *Thistle* enjoyed a comparable notoriety when she was in collision off the Scottish coast. Abandoned by her crew, she finally chose to drive ashore on the golf-course at St Andrew's. After J. H. Waters of the *Goldfinch* had turned down the job (following a disagreement as to whether he or the owner should pay for the lamp-oil!) Smith sent a recovery crew in charge of Thornley King, a shipwright, who not only repaired *Thistle* but sailed her safely home.

These big 'coal-scuttles', built for profit rather than beauty, were mostly employed trading to Dover, but they would take anything anywhere if it was worth their while. *Thistle* was at Hull when the first linseed from the river Plate arrived there. Owen Parry's Colchester oil mills were out of stock, and old Henry Tunbridge (who claimed to be among the first bargemen to visit the Humber, with cement from Waldringfield in the *Ladybird,* and whose son had the *Vanguard* after she was sold by Smith Bros) took a lucrative freight from Hull to the mill. He was paid £55, with 42*s.* gratuity and a free tow by a Hull tug as far as

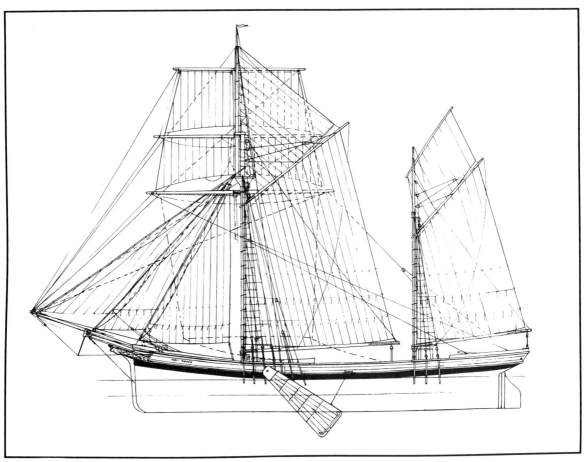

**Lucy Richmond** built at Ipswich in 1875.

Walton Naze.

Only occasionally did Smith's big colliers bring a freight to Burnham, where the coal was 'jumped out' by the crew at Smith's wharf and coal-yard. On these occasions the return freight was usually sand, loaded at Gravel Lane, Burnham, and used for glass-making in Sunderland, including the glass rolling-pins which, along with Sunderland dishes, were a favourite present for sailors' sweethearts. They also occasionally loaded sand 'over side' on the Ray and Buxey sandbanks, outside the entrance to the Crouch, an operation which, with such deep-sided vessels, must have involved building a staging alongside on to which the sand was loaded before being finally thrown overside into the hold. From Dover chalk for use on the land was a favourite return freight, often to Barton-on-Humber.

The first of the Smiths is reputed to have been a coasting skipper who settled in Burnham in the eighteenth century. A John Smith — perhaps the father of the barge-owner — included building among his activities in the 1820s, when he secured

the contract for the coastguard cottages at Tillingham. The firm continued until the early years of the First World War when it failed following the loss of a number of craft and a fire at the yard which incidentally consumed the Corinthian Yacht Club's first clubhouse.

*Friendship* was among the craft lost, off Spurn Head in 1912, but *Vanguard* and *Thistle* were sold to Alexander Moore of London. Charles Munn, an old Wynnfield Shipping Company hand, joined *Thistle* in August 1916 under W. A. Moorcraft, a Yorkshire skipper who had previously lost the Irish schooner *Glendalough* on the Shipwash. When they were taking a freight of pitch from London to Le Havre they struck a submerged object in the roadstead, and had to beach her inside the breakwater. After being patched up she returned to Rochester for repairs, but though she did another similar freight the pumps could only just keep her afloat, and this time she had to be beached at Gravesend on her return. Soon after this she was sold to the French Government, and finished as a coal hulk at Le Havre, being renamed *Jacques*.

*Vanguard* meanwhile had also been sold to

France, being lost in 1916. Smith's oyster fishery continued longer, and *Vanguard's* name was given to a dredging smack built for him by Prior.

An even larger fleet of small sprittie barges and coasting schooners was owned by the Meeson family, serving their various farms, their tide mill at Battlesbridge and the tide mill at Stambridge, owned by the Rankin family.[3]

Their only boomie was the beautiful *Malvoisin*, built for them by John Howard at Maldon in 1883. She must have been very much a queen among Meeson's motley fleet, but she had a rival as the pride of the river in another schooner barge, the *Lucy Richmond*, built by Robertson of Ipswich in 1875 for another Burnham coal merchant, Peter Richmond.

[3]For details of which see Richard Hugh Perks: 'Beyond the Shore Ends', *Journal of the Society for Spritsail Barge Research* No. 11, March 1971.

**Lucy Richmond.** By the time this portrait was painted she had dispensed with the schooner's square topsails, but she retains a fidded mizzen topmast and mizzen crosstrees. The outer jib halyard, led to the mainmast head, with lacing to topmast stay, is clearly shown. (A. Pyner)

The Richmonds (who were no connection with the Harwich family of the same name) also had interests in both the oyster fishery and barging. Peter, son of an oyster merchant of the same name, was born in 1821 and lived till 1912. By 1882 his firm had become W. T. Richmond and Co., and by the early 1890s the *Lucy Richmond* had been acquired by Edward Trussell, another Burnham merchant, who also owned the *Genesta* of Faversham. In her last years she was managed by Piper's at Greenwich. She was once missing for four days off Blyth, but was finally found and towed in with all sails gone. Piper's sailmakers got busy, and she was refitted and sailed for Guernsey within a week. She was finally hulked at Greenwich, and the huge mainmast for which she was noted was for many years to be seen built into the front of Piper's Wharf there. The hull was broken up at Cubitt Town in 1940 after sinking while at anchor as a roads barge and driving down on the ebb, waterlogged, like a submarine, to the alarm of the roadsmen in their skiffs.

The *Malvoisin* also came down in the world in her latter years. She was laid up at Whitstable in 1924, and then after eight months' idleness was given a rough refit and dispatched to Calais. She got no farther than Margate, where she brought up two anchors. The cables got foul, and after trying all day the crew failed to clear them. They finally burned flares, and the Margate lifeboat came off. With the lifeboat crew's help the anchors were cleared, but the windlass was so poor that it took the combined crews, fourteen men in all, an hour to get the port anchor and its forty-five fathoms of chain. The lifeboat cox'n also said he noted the running rigging and ship's boat were in very poor condition, with no lifebelts or lifebuoys aboard. The skipper could not make up his mind if he wanted to be assisted into Margate, but the mate and three hands made it up for him, declaring that if he did not go in 'they were finished'. The incident, which earned the lifeboatmen £75 salvage, was probably typical of many as once-proud craft eked out a final existence, ill-found and ill-manned.

*Malvoisin* continued to trade for a few years more — with the same windlass, as her owner, Mr Anderson, insisted — till she was ultimately lost off Calais in 1929.

Above Burnham, at Hullbridge, Benjamin Cackett had another fleet of aged spritties, carting chalk for the farms and lime for the Battlesbridge kilns. He also owned one well-remembered ketch barge, the *Triumph*, whose adventures and long life-story form the subject of Chapter 21.

CHAPTER 11
# Busy Times in Kent

Kent, and in particular the Medway and Swale barge country, produced in the second half of the nineteenth century not only the most extraordinary craft and the most remarkable character in George Smeed, but also the greatest number of boomies, with a recorded[1] total of one brigantine barge, one barque, three barquentines, six three-masted schooners, nine two-masted schooners and forty-two ketches.

The pioneers were probably at Faversham, where after the failure of a scheme by Telford for a canal from Hollow Shore, William Cubitt advised a selective widening of the creek 'suitable for the Billy Boy type of vessel'. Improvements were duly made, but 200-ton colliers could only reach the town on spring tides, and frequently grounded, blocking the channel.

About 1850 the cement-manufacturers Hilton and Anderson commissioned the building of three large barges, *Dido, Oak* and *Eleanor,* which may have been half-sprit rigged. In 1854 they turned to J. M. Goldfinch, at that time thirty-two years old, to build them the 'single-masted flat' *Spy,* 75.7 x 18.5 x 7, loading 120 tons. She was probably a barge hull, hoy-rigged, but she was unlucky, sinking twice. In 1861 she was unrigged and sold to Beckwith of Colchester as a lighter.

Similar vessels followed, of which the details are lost, but in 1857 Goldfinch produced the 'schooner-rigged flat' *General Cathcart.* Of 97 registered tons, loading 200 tons, she was built for Anderson and Cresswell as the cement-works collier. She may be regarded as the first big Kentish boomie barge, but she was lost within four years on the Shipwash, the gallant rescue of

her crew earning rewards from the Board of Trade and the Shipwrecked Fishermen's and Mariners Society for three smacks' crews.[2]

In forty-one years Goldfinch went on to build forty-seven barges from his yard in Faversham Creek on the south side of The Brents at the bottom of Standard Quay, opposite the end of Pollock's present yard. These included two fine schooner barges. The *Nancy* of Ramsgate was built in 1890 and owned first by J. J. Greenstreet and later by her skipper, Captain J. Smith, who lost her when she was run down in 1909 at anchor near Clayhole on a voyage from Boston to Sandwich. The *Goldfinch,* which followed four years later, was skippered for twenty-seven years by J. H. Waters of Faversham, who bought her out of his earnings in this time. He was a member of a notable family, for his father had been master of the *Eliza Smeed* and his elder brother was skipper and part-owner of the *Genesta* and *Ada Gane.* After his retirement *Goldfinch* was one of the barges sailed out to the West Indies.

Five ketches preceded these schooners — *Ann Goodhugh* (1872) and *Pioneer* (1876, lost in 1895), both for W. G. Dawson, *Bessie Hiller* (1881, lost with a defective insurance in 1893), *Cock of the Walk* (1882, which seems to have been lost before she was registered, and is not to be confused with a famous Millwall craft similarly named) and *Gem of the Ocean* (1877).

Sittingbourne and Milton Regis, however, became the most intensive centre of barge-production.

One of the finest, as well as one of the most

---

[1]By Richard Hugh Perks.

[2]See *The Salvagers.*

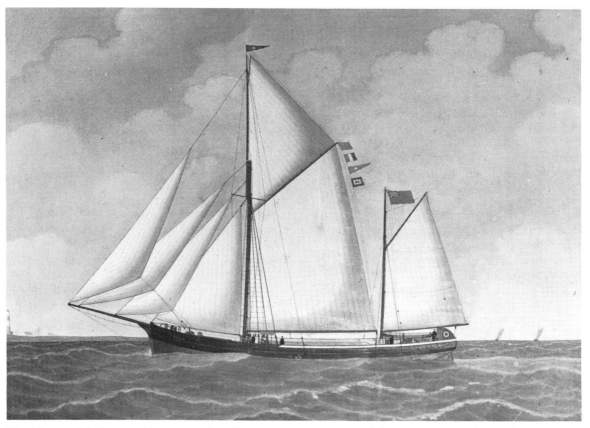

**Harold,** one of the later and best-remembered boomies. Built in 1900, she lasted till 1928.

prolific, builders, Robert Mark Shrubsall included a number of boomies among the hundred craft launched from his Milton Creek yard between 1861 and 1899. After converting the sprittie *Eclipse* into the schooner *Meteor* in 1863, he went on to build the schooner *Alpha* in 1865, the ketch *Lord Beaconsfield* of Faversham and the schooner *Agnes* in 1874 and the ketch *SJB* in 1888. His sprittie *Mystery* of Faversham (1875) also spent part of her life boomie-rigged.

At the near-by Station Brickworks Dock Alfred White turned out craft which were considered fast but somewhat lightly built, including *Teresa, Medina* and *Harold. Harold's* last owner, George Battershall, one of the great skippers in Goldsmith's huge fleet of spritties at Grays, recalled:

> She'd get along all right. Leastways she'd go to windward all right loaded. Sailed best trimmed six or seven inches by the head. But she wasn't all that wonderful running. Nor she wasn't on the wind after we carried away a leeboard off Nieuport, when all I could get

was an eighteen-foot one instead of twenty foot, same as she'd had.[3]

A less complimentary view will be found in Chapter 17. George Battershall bought *Harold* in 1924, and lost her off the Humber in 1928. He did not earn much with her, as she cost too much to run. 'Not that I skimped her,' he recalled. 'Might have done better if I had.'

Two ketch barges built at Maidstone as early as 1840 — *Isabella* (93 tons) and *Elizabeth* (64 tons) — were probably boomsail sloops or spritsail craft later converted to ketch, but at Conyer, a big centre of sprittie-barge building, J. Bird built the ketch *Eustace* in 1886 and Alfred White the *Olympia* in 1902, while at Sandwich the ketch *Pride* was built for Pordage and Co. of Ramsgate in 1857.

But it is the leviathans, very much a Kentish speciality, that are of the greatest interest. Goldfinch's lead was followed by three firms — Smeed of Sittingbourne, (already mentioned in Chapter 3), Taylor, also at Sittingbourne, and Gann at Whitstable.

[3]Arthur Bennett: *Us Bargemen.*

George Smeed's venture into mammoth barges was prompted by a strike at his shipyard, where the work force were on short time because they were unable to work ten hours a day. His answer was to engage master shipwright F. Sollitt, formerly of Chatham Dockyard, to lay down a series of big colliers to be schooner-, barquentine- and even barque-rigged, carrying up to 800 tons, yet flat-bottomed, often fitted with leeboards and all classified as barges.

The *Seven Sisters* was launched as a topsail schooner in 1862. She was converted to barquentine rig in 1881 (a reversal of the usual development, suggesting a continual quest for a manageable rig), and disappears from the register two years later. Six months later he built the pioneer ketch barge *Garibaldi* (loading 150 tons), followed in 1863 by another ketch, *Invicta*, later converted to spritsail.

*Garibaldi* had a narrow escape in December 1872. She sailed from Poole for Aylesford with 130 tons of pipeclay under Captain George Wilson, who had only a mate and third hand with him. She was off Beachy Head, with an offshore north-west wind and a rising barometer, when she was caught in a sudden gale and disabled. She finally drove ashore on the French coast at Wimereux. The skipper and third hand were washed overboard and lost, along with a French

sailor who attempted a rescue, and only the mate got ashore. The Lloyd's agent reported that she would probably go to pieces on the next high water, but Smeed sent his barge *Wave* with shipwrights and materials. They succeeded in getting her off and into Boulogne, and later towed her home with the *Wave*. She was finally lost off Saint-Malo in 1909, bound from St Helier to Rochester with slates.

Then, in 1865, Smeed produced the *Eliza Smeed*, which loaded 750 tons and was barquentine-rigged, and in 1868 the barque-rigged *Esther Smeed* which, with a registered tonnage of 494, loaded 800 tons and was the biggest barge of all time. Only one size smaller was the 477-ton barquentine *George Smeed*, built in 1866 and sold to Norway in 1879. The *Esther Smeed* disappeared from the register after 1878, but the *Emily Smeed*, built in 1872, was still owned by her skipper in Aberdeen in 1919, converted from barquentine to three-masted schooner rig, and survived as a jury-rigged lighter till 1930. Her length was 133.3 feet and her beam 25.8, and like the *Leading Star* twenty years earlier she had the extraordinary depth of 13.3 feet.

In 1872 came the 134-ton *Ellen Smeed*, which lasted till 1912, and two years later the *Sarah Smeed*, built of oak from Chatham Dockyard, and lost in 1882.

At Weymouth. **Olympia** unloading with a cargo derrick rigged on her main and peak halyards.

Near by at Crown Quay, Sittingbourne, his contemporaries John and Stephen Taylor, buil-

**Emily Smeed.** One of Smeed's legendary leviathans, she loaded 750 tons. Converted from barquentine to three-masted schooner, she traded out of Aberdeen till 1919, and was afloat as a jury-rigged lighter in 1930. (*M. R. Bouquet*)

**Europa** built in 1871 and rigged as a compromise between a topsail schooner and brigantine. She later became a ketch.

ders of the pioneer ketch *Adsey* in 1863, turned to schooners of increasing size, including *Europa*, built in 1871 with a curious, experimental rig, and *Emily Lloyd,* built in 1872, the same year as the *Ellen Smeed.*

The *Emily Lloyd* (originally named *William Levitt* after the manager of the Elmley Cement Works) was owned by Edward Lloyd Limited, and, in addition to having her bulwarks painted with black and white panels in the 'painted ports' tradition, displayed advertisements across her main and fore topsails for the Sunday newspaper *Lloyd's News* (which was presumably connected with her owners, though not with *Lloyd's Register*).

The *Emily Lloyd's* first voyages were among the most remarkable recorded. She sailed from her builder's ways straight out to the Mediterranean and back with a freight to Granton on the Firth of Forth before returning to Milton — a round voyage not far short of 5,000 miles. She then sailed again to the Mediterranean, making the passage from the Isle of Wight to Cartagena in 49 days. There she unloaded her cargo of coal and

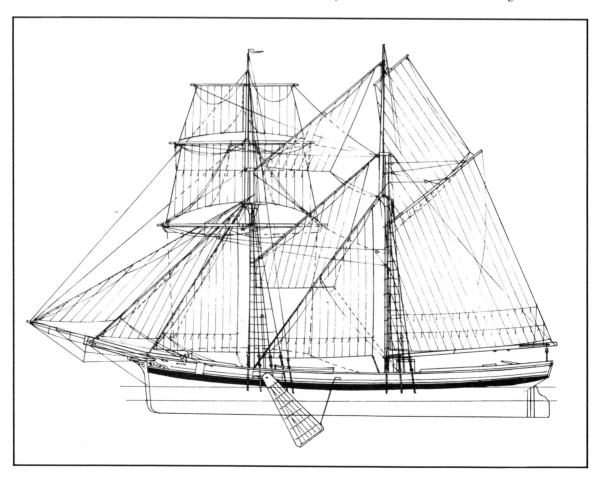

**Zebrina.** *(Top)* In Littlehampton with unidentified ketch barge behind her. *(Bottom)* At Whitstable about 1900. *(West/R. H. Perks collection)*

iron hooping, sailed round to Aguilas and again returned to Granton with iron ore in the hold and a stack of esparto grass on deck!

The Shrubsall family were bargemen as well as barge-builders, the last of them, 'Ebbie', seeing out the final days of sail and dying in 1980 at the age of ninety-two. His father, Isaiah, and his uncle (also Ebenezer) were in the *Emily Lloyd* on these remarkable voyages.[4]

[4]See Richard Hugh Perks: 'The Shrubbie Barges', *Coast and Country*, Vol. 10, No. 3, June 1981.

Isaiah then transferred to the slightly larger *Dauntless*, built by another Sittingbourne builder, W. B. Spencelaugh, in 1873, using second-hand materials. Both the *Emily Lloyd* and the *Dauntless* later passed into the ownership of Smith of Burnham, but it was Alfred and John Taylor at the Adelaide Dock to whom he turned for the rest of his fleet already mentioned in Chapter 10 — *Speedwell, Magnet, Vanguard, Thistle, Rochester Castle* and *Friendship*, built in that order between 1883 and 1890.

None of these rivalled Smeed's biggest craft, but the three-masted *Friendship*, 117 feet long and loading 490 tons, was a giant by any other standards. And it must be remembered that she was employed in the East Coast coal-trade, in many ways a more dangerous occupation than the sea-going which chiefly occupied Smeed's big square-rigged craft.

The third firm, H. H. Gann and Son of Whitstable, were considerable owners as well as builders of shipping. Their fleet in 1880 amounted to twenty-two ships, including *Nellie S*, built by them in 1876, 130 feet long by 26 feet beam, loading 500 tons on a draft of 12 feet 6 inches, the largest craft ever built in Whitstable.

The name is believed to refer to Nellie Smeed, but the connection is not clear, for she was owned

The end of the story, in Velder Creek, Portsmouth, in 1961. *(Top)* The hulk of **Zebrina,** with the remains of Crampton's little **Diamond** in the foreground. *(Bottom)* 'Camber' (ex – **Belmont**) near by. *(Joe Hines collection)*

by Gann till 1882, when she was sold to a London firm. She passed to Brazilian owners fourteen years later, and was ultimately lost on passage from Rio de Janeiro in 1905. It is not known that Smeed had any interest in Gann's business or vice versa, but there may have been some association yet to be discovered, or conceivably Gann had an eye on Smeed as a future customer.

In 1873, three years before the building of *Nellie S,* following the building of the *Eliza, Esther* and *Ellen Smeed's,* and the same year that the *George Smeed* was built, Gann produced the slightly smaller barquentine *Zebrina,* which unlike most of the big barges was knocking about in the coal trade into the 1930s.

She was no beauty, having a curious ram bow, the purpose of which it is difficult to guess, unless it was to cope with some conditions in the river Plate, for which trade she was designed. She did not, however, pay her way there, and so was sent home. She was then owned by the Whitstable Trading Company and according to her skipper, Captain Robert Skinner of Woodbridge, must have more than made up for any foreign losses.

She was concerned in one particularly gruesome incident during the First World War, when she sailed from Falmouth for a French port with coal, and was later found abandoned with all sail set and no sign of confusion aboard. Her crew of five were never heard of again; it is surmised they had been taken off by a German U-boat which was scared away before it had time to sink the *Zebrina,* and was itself destroyed with her crew aboard.

In 1932, while she was coasting as a motor-schooner for the Ajax Shipping Company, her cargo of coal caught fire. She put into Cowes so badly damaged that she was sold as scrap for £50. Apparently, however, she was found worth repairing, for she was still at work out of Bristol in 1938, fitted with a 55 h.p. auxiliary engine.

The Whitstable Shipping Company was the most notable example of the way, throughout Kent, that small owners of one or two craft — names such as Blaxland, Anderson, Holt, Camburn and Cox and Lawson and Wood — were being absorbed into, or superseded by, new commercial enterprises. Not all the new owners were exclusively concerned with shipping; in those days of adventurous capitalism quite a considerable fleet was built up at Faversham by Charles Marshall, who was by trade a draper. In addition to some round-bottomed schooners he acquired the *Malvoisin, Lucy Richmond, Ellen Smeed, SD, Kate,* and *Ellen.* These numerous small and medium-sized concerns were, however, overshadowed by the Whitstable Shipping Company, which is said to have managed at one time or another at least four hundred small ships in the coal trade and which in 1906 still owned seventeen vessels.

While many places had their own local fleet of colliers, this concentration at Whitstable was unique, serving as it did the Thames Estuary and Channel ports well into the days when steamers had taken over the London coal trade. Some of the Whitstable traders were purpose-built, but many were worn-out craft, run on the cheap. By avoiding depreciation on these old vessels and failing to insure even their new tonnage, the Whitstable Shipping Company cut its overheads and continued to pay its way long after its rivals had acknowledged defeat, much as Gustav

Erikson did in Finland with his fleet of deep-sea grain barques in the 1930s.

*Zebrina,* on her return from the river Plate, was one of this motley fleet, and out of the profits she and her sisters earned the Whitstable Shipping Company built in 1895 a slightly smaller sister, *Belmont,* the last of the giant coal-scuttles, designed on the lines of *Zebrina* but without her ugly bow.

Robert Skinner was asked to plan her rig, and chose two-masted topsail schooner. On her first voyage from Milford Haven to Ipswich with coal she discharged a cargo of no less than 317 tons, but she was always very heavily rigged for working two-masted. After narrowly escaping destruction on the rocks at Stepper Cove, Cornwall, in 1920 she was renamed *Camber* in the 1930s and registered at Portsmouth, owned by Fraser & White. Probably at this time she was rigged as a three-masted lighter. She ended her days at Portsmouth in Velder Creek, a graveyard of old wooden vessels (now filled in), lying alongside *Zebrina* and Crampton's *Diamond.*

CHAPTER 12

# London and Down-Channel

Many boomies were owned in London. Some of these owners were merely financial proprietors, with a managing owner in one of the East Coast or Kentish barge centres. There were, however, some fleets that truly belonged to London.

Of these owners the most notable were Walker and Howard of Mark Lane, who in the 1890s had a considerable fleet built for them, including a number of 'Castles' — *Carisbrooke Castle, Warwick Castle, Rochester Castle* and *Tynemouth Castle,* which was one of the few boomies built of iron. This fleet was especially respected. Bob Potton of Greenwich summed it up with the observation, 'Walker Howard's skippers were gentlemen'. It may be added that he had been one of them himself, as well as skippering his brother's *Solent.*

They also acquired a number of craft from local owners, in particular Harwich. Among these were the dandies *Dovercourt* and *Flower of Essex,* by then converted to ketch rig. The *Dovercourt* was

**Carisbrooke Castle**

owned by the Kerosine Co. Ltd., Thomas Howard managing owner, suggesting a wide range of interests under Walker and Howard's management.

They also had the three-masted *Jubilee* (formerly with Vaux), *Llama* (which at 166 tons was the biggest barge ever built at Harwich), *May Queen* (a Yarmouth-built schooner barge), *Enterprise* of Harwich (a transom-sterned craft setting her jib flying on a traveller, not to be confused with the Yarmouth three-masted schooner) and *Eustace* of Rochester, which was lost on the West Rocks, Harwich, a few years before the First World War.

Walker and Howard also managed another big fleet, that of the English & Continental Shipping Company Limited, founded by Herbert Hawkins, a Hornsey bargemaster. This comprised the 'Belles' and later the 'Lords' series, mostly built for them by Gildea of Ipswich and by Harvey of Littlehampton.

Hawkins must have been a remarkable business-man. In the 1880s he owned the *Eastern Belle, Northern Belle, Southern Belle, Western Belle,* the *Lord Beaconsfield, Lord Beresford, Lord Churchill, Lord Hartington, Lord Iddesleigh, Lord Nelson, Lord Salisbury* and *Lord Shaftesbury,* all of which were transferred to the English and Continental Shipping Company around 1890. Within a few years a number of these 'Lords' were owned as well as managed by Walker and Howard.

Some light is thrown on his methods by the registry of the *Western Belle,* which unlike her sisters was (as mentioned in Chapter 5) built by Holman of Topsham, Devon, as an early 'mulie',

**Western Belle** at West Bay, Bridport. Built as a sprittie, she is here ketch-rigged, but with wheelhouse and mizzen removed, suggesting that by this time she had been fitted with an auxiliary.

though she was later converted to boomsail ketch. She was first owned in quarter-shares by John and Richard Holman of London and Henry and Alfred Holman of Topsham. But soon after her building in 1879 all the shares were acquired by Hawkins, who over the next ten years dealt in small packets of them with fifteen individuals. Then, during December 1889 and January 1890, all the shares were bought by the English and Continental Shipping Company, of which Harold Holman was managing director.

Even with this detail, however, the relationship between Hawkins's English and Continental Shipping Company and Walker and Howard still remains obscure, as does the question why after the *Western Belle* Holman's built no more for the fleet of which Harold Holman was (at any rate for a time) managing director.

Whatever its origins and constitution, this notable fleet was not a long-lived one, for by 1901 craft were being sold off to other owners. The *Western Belle* herself went to Guernsey before being lost by fire at sea in 1922.

Down-Channel, craft built of Sussex oak were specially esteemed. Rye adapted its shipbuilding tradition to the new style, and produced three craft in particular which came to be well remembered for different reasons.

The *Sussex Belle* was universally regarded as everything a ketch barge should be; strong, capacious, seaworthy and handsome, the pride in particular of the Woodbridge river where she traded regularly.

*Sarah Colebrooke*, built by G. & T. Smith in 1913 for W. E. Colebrooke of Rye, achieved fame from serving from June 1917 to October 1918 as a Q-ship, cruising the Channel with the aim of decoying submarines. Assuming the name *Bolham* (and on one occasion borrowing the identity of the Littlehampton *Worry Not*), she exchanged shellfire with U-boats on three occasions. In one engagement off Beachy Head a shell scored a direct hit on her steel-lined leeboard, which was raised at the time, shattering it and nearly penetrating the hull — one occasion at least when a leeboard served a purpose!

Like her fellow Q-ship *Record Reign*, *Sarah Colebrooke* retained her engines and continued trading, reverting to her wartime name, *Bolham*, in 1932 and ending her days around the Mersey as a motor coaster at Connah's Quay.

**Sarah Colebrooke** *(top)* after her launch at Rye in 1913. She adopts the Dutch practice of shipping stockless anchors through hawse holes. *(Peter Ferguson)* *(bottom)* In her final years as the mb **Bolham**

William Colebrooke was a true 'Sussex worthy'. Born in 1856, the son of a master mariner of Rye, he was apprenticed to the drapery trade, but gave this up and went to sea before the mast for two years. He then settled in Southern Australia as a sheep-farmer, and later worked his passage back to Rye, where he set up as a coal merchant and ship-owner. In the 1890s he had two sailing barges bringing coal from the North for his own business, and in 1905 he went into steam trawlers, losing one trawler and one sailing barge in the First World War. He was a big farmer and land-owner, and he was twice mayor of Rye, and an alderman and JP during the 1920s and 1930s.

The third of the celebrities, *Martinet*, was also built by G. & T. Smith the year before the *Sarah Colebrooke*, with a stern-post oversized to allow for the fitting of a propeller shaft. Despite this provision she had the distinction of surviving as

the last boomie under sail, till she was lost off Orford Ness in 1941, owned by Everard's of Greenhithe and skippered by Captain A. W. (Bob) Roberts, who has told her story in his book *Coasting Bargemaster*. He was surprised to find she was as fast as a sprittie running and reaching, though she could not sail anything like so close to windward, but he disliked her 'pump' windlass, which had caused serious injury to the previous skipper.

But Rye's own local boomie story is of other craft and of an unusual venture.

In the 1880s the harbour was silting so badly that the harbourmaster had to use a plough to keep the channel open. A gale in December 1882 almost completely blocked the entrance, causing the commissioners under John Vidler to look in desperation for funds to keep it open. The town of Rye refused its help (despite the fact that Vidler was to be its mayor for the two ensuing years); the local bank, the Public Works Loan Board and private capital were no more forthcoming.

Vidler had already built and owned a fleet of flat-bottomed lug-rigged river barges for local trade. Now with a courageous faith he and some of his fellow-townsmen put up the capital to build a fleet of ketch barges to keep the Rye-based coasting trade alive. Five big barges were built by G. and T. Smith, *Enterprise* in 1888, *Surprise* in 1889, *Sunrise* and *Mountsfield* in 1890 and *Diana* in 1891.

Unlike many such stories, this one had a happy ending. Though *Enterprise* was lost in 1893 and *Sunrise* in 1902, the barges were a commercial success, taking shingle and oak bark to Scotland and bringing coal back. Some had as many as forty shareholders, and no investor who kept his shares till 1914 was the loser by it. Among these shareholders was William Rubie, a chandler and sailmaker who was later appointed harbourmaster, and who by the 1890s is shown as owner of all the craft except *Diana*, which was retained by Vidler.

The *Mountsfield* was sailed across to Norway in August 1918, and fitted with an auxiliary engine — an extraordinary voyage three months before the end of the War. What ultimately happened to her, and to *Diana* and *Surprise,* I do not know; *Enterprise* was lost in the disastrous November gale of 1893 referred to later.

Among other products of Rye shipbuilding the *Unity* (always known as 'the big *Unity*' to distinguish her from the smaller Ipswich craft of the same name) is recalled as the only boomie

**Martinet** on the London river *(M. R. Bouquet)*

needing ballast, being too tender to sail light.

Two boomies are known to have been built at Poole, where there was a big trade in clay — *Alexandra* and *Princess May*, both owned by Frederick Griffin of Salisbury — and at least one at Shoreham, *Carrie Louise*. A round-bilged ketch with elliptical stern, she was built by Thomas Stow, whose yard (chiefly concerned with yachts) was upriver about three-quarters of a mile above May and Thwaites's yard. Her owner, Edward Reeves, was a Brighton merchant who imported sugar in lumps from France to Shoreham, where it was crushed. Her predecessor in this trade was the small Rye smack *Integrity* (built there in 1858), but after a few years she was knocked out of the trade by the French steamboats *Artois*, *Béarn* and *Anjou*. After this she often traded to Ipswich. Her master, Walter Brazier, died aboard her in Le Havre, and she brought his body home to Shoreham. In September 1903 she sailed from Cherbourg for Rochester, and was never heard of again.

At Portsmouth John Crampton has some claim to be regarded as the George Smeed of the Solent. He was principally a ship-owning coal merchant, with a considerable fleet of colliers. Shipbuilding was a sideline to him, yet he built some vessels of considerable size at his Landport yard, chiefly for his own use, and experimented with the barge hull, no doubt influenced by Smeed, by producing the 275-ton barquentine barge *Enterprise* in 1879. She does not seem to have lasted long, for she is out of the register by 1893. Previous to this Crampton had built the 101-ton *Camellia* in 1876, the 169-ton brigantine *Albion* (named after his house) in 1875, and the 372-ton barquentine *Dahlia* in 1878. It is possible these colliers were barge-built, but of that there is no evidence.

More typical of the Crampton fleet were his 'jewels': *Emerald* and *Ruby*, built at Landport in 1877, *Pearl* and *Diamond*, built at Portsmouth in 1878 and 1879. They were small for colliers, all being under fifty tons, and they were probably used to distribute coal from bunkers around the area rather than to go north. It is said that their bottoms were planked athwartships instead of fore-and-aft, presumably for the economy of the short lengths of timber, and that they were the slowest things afloat. They had the ugly angular transom stern favoured at Portsmouth, and to be found also in the local 'Cowes ketches' — a near relative of the ketch barge in size and rig, but round-bilged and without leeboards (though leeboards were used in some small barges trading locally). The Emsworth-built *Annie Florence* was

**Alexandra**, one of the few Poole-built barges, at Newport, Isle of Wight. *(G. Archdale/Richard Hugh Perks collection)*

**Princess May** by R. Chappell *(Graham Hussey)*

also owned by John Crampton, who was succeeded by his son Harry.

In Chichester harbour, Emsworth was the home of two shipbuilders, Foster and Apps. William Foster (born in 1823) came to Emsworth from Southwick near Southampton, and built his first ship, the *Jane E. Foster,* in 1861. Nine years later, in 1870, he produced the 185-ton brigantine barge *Thorney Island,* owned by Ash, a Portsmouth coal merchant. She was unusual in having a raised quarterdeck, and survived as a hulk at Emsworth till after the First World War.

On William Foster's death, around 1890, his yard was taken over by Apps, whose craft do not seem to have included boomies, but in 1875 his son, John Duncan Foster, set up on his own as shellfish merchant, ship-owner and builder and timber merchant.

In addition to building smacks for the scallop and Channel oyster fisheries, which were his chief interest, he produced in 1892 the remarkable centreboard brigantine *Fortuna,* already mentioned. The Faversham schooner barge *Annie Florence* (130 tons register, owned in 1893 by S.

Payn) was also built at Emsworth in 1878, but whether by William or John Foster is not clear. The Yarmouth (IoW) ketch *Gratitude* (built in 1877, 64.32 tons, owned in 1893 by W. Prentice) may also have been a barge, but there is no record, and again the date might attribute her to either father or son.

J. D. Foster is among the most fascinating of all the characters who emerge from a study of a character-filled age. He used a collection of racing bicycles to go about his affairs, and rode a hundred miles on one of them on his eightieth birthday. He is best remembered for the beautiful and unique 120-foot ketch-rigged steam auxiliary oyster smack *Echo,* laid down in 1898, and for two white elephants — *Echo II,* an even larger smack launched in 1914 but never rigged due to the outbreak of war, and an enormous floating scallop tank known as the *Noah's Ark,* which also never saw service. When he died in 1940 — still leaving on his slipway a centreboard yacht started (probably for his own use) before the First World War and never finished — the old Emsworth he had dominated died with him, though the remains of the *Echo* and the *Noah's Ark* are to be seen in the harbour to this day.

**Carrie Louise** locking into the Wet Dock, Ipswich, with the spritties **Malvina** of Rochester (wheel steered), **Unity** of Rochester, and (with topsail set) **Victoria** of Ipswich

The most prolific builders down-Channel, and indeed anywhere in the country, were at Little-hampton, far from the main centres of the barging world.

Here in 1840 Henry Harvey came from Rye to establish a yard which in addition to building all manner of small deep-watermen, from barques and brigs to schooners, developed, under his successors, J. & W. B. Harvey, a positive production-line of ketch barges. The first of these may have been the suggestively named *Fore-runner* of Arundel, built by J. and W. Harvey in 1862 for their own use as a Southampton coaster. Given four years A1 at Lloyds, and registered as a ketch barge, she was later sold to Newport, Monmouthshire. Harvey's may well have produced other boomies during the ensuing fifteen years, but if so they are unrecorded. It is, however, known that between 1877 and 1886 they produced a series of craft, pleasantly and simply named *Annie, Susie, Sallie, Maggie, Nellie* and *Rosie,* which they themselves owned and managed.

As an owner, Harvey overcame one problem of isolation by joining the Harwich Barge Club for mutual insurance purposes, but his south coasters were evidently sometimes treated as 'furriners', as this yarn from Thomas Day shows:

> The *Susie* got into Bawdsey Haven first, followed by the *Sussex Belle* and the *Harold.* The pilots, instead of taking the first barge in, took the *Sussex Belle* and the *Harold.* We were off Methersgate Quay when Steve Leach of the *Susie* asked us to help him get up to Melton. He said he would give us anything if we would help him up.

In 1887 Harvey started a series of 'Lords' for the English and Continental Shipping Company, launching two at a time, an unequalled level of production. The first six were all around seventy-five tons, but in 1890 there was a change to a much larger size with the *Lord Dufferin, Lord Alcester* and *Lord Napier* of 132 tons.

John Harvey of Littlehampton aboard the Swedish barquentine **Bonden** after a collision, 1904-5. Near the damaged bulwark is Fred Page (shipwright). Above him is the vessel's master, while behind Harvey is Charles Mars (foreman shipwright). On the extreme right is the vessel's mate. (*Fred Grant, Brighton*)

At Littlehampton. **Charlotte Sophia**, built at Portsmouth in 1876. The vessel in the distance is **Zebrina**. (*F. W. Spry*)

**Gravelines III**, formerly **Dolgwandle**. Her name recalls her ownership under the French flag. (*Maritime Museum, Bembridge*)

Building continued without interruption up to and through the First World War. *Wessex*, built in 1918, was a pole-masted auxiliary with leeboards, but substituting an oil-engine for her topsail — the shape of things to come for the final spritties forty years later. But Harvey's last boomie, *Moultonian*, launched the following year, reverted to sail, albeit without a topsail, and spurned the ignominy of an engine for the first ten years of her life.

*Wessex* was not the first attempt to marry sail and power, for two auxiliary ketch barges had been launched on the Thames in 1912 by Edwards of Millwall, the *Traly* and *The Motoketch*. Both were built of steel with rounded bilges, a miniature quarter-deck aft over the engine-room, deck galley and wheel-house. About eighty-five feet overall, they were pole-masted, and as it was

**Wessex,** built by Harvey at Littlehampton in 1918, was given a cut-down rig and an auxiliary engine. On left she is seen at Poole *(Richard Hugh Perks)*

unlikely that they would tackle much windward work they were not fitted with leeboards. Both had long and profitable lives, the *Traly* going to augment the fleet of auxiliary ketches owned in the North Devon area after the First World War. She was registered at Barnstaple, and owned in 1938 by W. W. Petherick & Sons Ltd, Bude, Cornwall, but by the opening years of the Second World War she had been sold to Ireland.

CHAPTER 13

# Faraway Places

This was effectively the limit of 'the barge coast'.

Boomies came to be owned in places as far afield as Aberdeen, Manchester and Connah's Quay. Their regular trading took them to Saundersfoot in Wales for anthracite, and to Dublin with malt for the Guinness brewery. In 1922 to 1923 eight of the craft referred to in these chapters visited Salcombe, according to a local pilot's notebook. They were a familiar sight in the Cornish and Channel Island ports.

In none of these places did they replace the local craft to become the dominant type of coastal carrier, as they did between the Wash and the Solent, but some of those which established themselves in 'foreign' parts of the country are worth a mention.

The Ipswich-built ketch *Ivy P* spent most of her working life trading out of Liverpool and Dublin. Leeboards must have been a curiosity in the Irish Sea, for though as has been mentioned Dublin was an occasional port of call there is no other record of a barge, boomie or spritsail, visiting Liverpool, let alone being owned there. The *Ivy P*, however, had a Liverpool owner in 1919, and by 1938 she was registered in Dublin, though still managed from Liverpool.

Captain Owen Spargo recalls:

> She was bought into Wicklow by one of the schooner families, and a character called "Charlie the Dutchman" was master of her. The Irishmen dispensed with the leeboards and could not do anything with her. They sold her to Knowles, stevedores, Liverpool, who converted her to a derrick barge. They paid £110 for her. She was hit by an

The Ipswich-built **Ivy P** worked out of Liverpool and the Irish Sea. *(Above)* She is seen off New Brighton in a breeze with mizzen hastily stowed, foresail reefed and mainsail well rolled down. *(D. Clement)*
*(Opposite)* In dock at Liverpool, contrasting strangely with the Mersey craft. She now has a wheelhouse and a smart white transom *(Liverpool City Engineer)*

incendiary bomb during the blitz in 1941, burned out and sank.

This contradicts another, less convincing, account that she was lost in Wicklow Bay.

In the Bristol Channel one owner took boomies seriously. John G. Sully of Bridgwater had the *Parkend* built for him at Ipswich, and some years later bought the *Ornate* from her Harwich owner. He also bought the hulk of the *John Wesley* after she was burned out, and rebuilt her as the box trow *Crowpill*, one of several craft named like his house after the village near Bridgwater where he lived. This prominent family firm — today known

as J. and A. W. Sully & Co., Chartered Accountants, with offices throughout the West Country — was founded by a ship-owner, Thomas Sully (1767-1824), and developed as Sully & Co. Ltd, coal factors and ship-owners, by his sons Thomas Sully (1803-61) and James Wood Sully (1806-86).

The Rye ketches *Diana* and *Mountsfield* also found their way to the Bristol Channel, being owned by Sven Hanson's Haigh Hall Shipping Company at Cardiff in 1919, and Harvey's *Forerunner* was owned at Newport in the 1880s.

In general, however, the Bristol Channel remained faithful to the trow. This also developed into a flat-bottomed ketch, up to seventy-five feet long, but retained a round bilge and transom stern, and never adopted leeboards, preferring for sailing to windward to rig a portable false keel some twenty-eight feet long, two feet wide and three inches thick, which had to be worked into position and then secured by external chains. This system (also employed by a number of Norfolk wherries) seems so awkward and inefficient that to the east-coaster the rejection of leeboards

appears surprising.

North of Yarmouth the billyboy tradition also prevailed into the twentieth century, evolving from sloop into ketch much as the boomie did, though the early billyboys were clinker-built, a style only reluctantly abandoned. The billyboy ketch had much in common with the boomie, with flat bottom and usually leeboards, a mast in a tabernacle and hinged crosstrees. It was, however, round-bilged, and less capable of making a passage without ballast. The final steel-built billyboys, such as *Halcyon* and *Mavis*, retained the round stern long favoured on the Humber.

West of the Solent, the West Country trading ketch had a similar evolution, growing out of the single-masted trading smack, with some schooners also adopting the rig. The West Country ketch seen afloat was at a casual glance distinguishable from the ketch barge only by the absence of leeboards. While some were sufficiently flat-floored to unload on beaches, the type always depended on a keel, and never adopted the

101

**Parkend** (built at Ipswich in 1873) at Bridgwater, where she was owned by J. G. Sully.

The **John Wesley** was rebuilt as the box trow **Crowpill,** here seen at Bridgwater with **Parkend** alongside

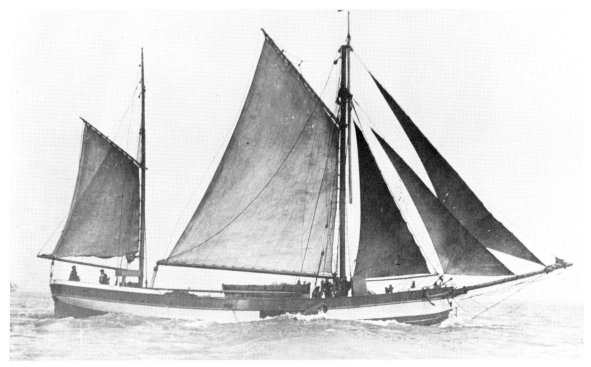

**Mavis** of Hull, a billyboy ketch built at Beverley in 1896 (*Stockton-on-Tees Ref. Lib.*)

A Dutch version of the boomie: **Ianthe** of Bristol, built at Delfzyl in 1910, and a Dutch equivalent of the ketch barge which found her way to Bristol in 1912. The substantial deckhouse and stockless anchors show her foreign origin.

tabernacle mast. It was more seaworthy than a barge and capable of occasional Atlantic voyages, but also required ballast for a sea passage.

With adoption in the early twentieth century of steel Dutch-built hulls, the klipper was also developed into a near relation to the ketch barge. The *Katherina*, built at Stadskanaal in 1910, was among the last of the Rye sailing coasters owned by Colebrooke before becoming a London motor barge, while the *Rhodesia*, built at Delfzyl in 1909 as the *Semper Spero*, was taken as a war prize and joined Abbie Anderson's Whitstable fleet, making at least one voyage to Lisbon about 1929 before ending up as a lighter on the Thames. *Ianthe*, built at Delfzyl in 1910 and re-registered at Bristol in 1912, is an interesting example of an essentially English rig in an essentially Dutch hull.

One other development must be mentioned at the end of this survey of regional activities.

Boomies — originally owned chiefly by local merchants, often for their own trade, or by their skippers, or by their builders or by some combination of all three — first came to be assembled into commercial fleets at the height of their profitability towards the end of the nineteenth century. The fleets of Walker and Howard, the English and Continental Shipping Company and the Whitstable Shipping Company have already been mentioned.

An unidentified ketch barge loads from a camouflaged First World War freighter, with a barquentine drying her sails across the harbour. This photo of Littlehampton in 1918 epitomizes how the age of the boomie spanned the two centuries.

A similar process occurred at the time of their decline, when capital was collected to buy cheap tonnage.

Among these ventures was the Vectis Shipping Company, a latter-day amalgamation of small owners in the Isle of Wight area. One of its constituents was the Wynnfield Shipping Company, based on Grimsby which later became the Williams Steam Ship Company of Southampton.

This concern developed out of a merger between the last of Harvey's Littlehampton craft, *Wessex* and *Moultonian,* with those of the Price family, whose fortunes were founded by Charles Price of Newport, Isle of Wight, owner of the Barnstaple ketch *Daring.*[1]

By an apparent paradox, the conditions which led to these amalgamations also tended in the opposite direction. The inflated earnings made during the First World War enabled a number of skippers to buy their craft, sometimes no doubt from owners who could see such conditions were likely to be short-lived.

[1] Built as a dandy at Bideford in 1863, 48 tons.

# PART 3

# The Big Barges at Sea

## CHAPTER 14

# A Freight a Month

The skipper and crew of a boomie might be paid either by the month or by the voyage.

Those serving in a ketch run as an integral part of the owner's business, provided with a steady run of cargoes, were paid by the month. A master of a 200-ton boomie, in the home trade during the 1890s, earned about £5 a month, augmented by both official and unofficial perks. The mate, who like the crew was formally signed on at the Customs House, drew £3 5s. The able seaman earned £3 if he was exceptionally reliable, or rather less on his first promotion from ordinary status, while an ordinary seaman (usually a lad in his teens) got £2 or a little more if he was physically tough and experienced. The cook — usually a boy, but nevertheless expected to help at trimming the cargo and working it out, only knocking off an hour before the rest to prepare meals — was paid thirty shillings. His other duties ranged from tending the lamps to cleaning the master's boots.

Should the barge have to seek its own cargoes, the skipper meeting brokers to arrange freights, and the owner relying upon his known integrity and professional ability, both he and the crew, with the exception of the cook, were paid by the voyage. His wage would then be as much as £6, and the crew's money would be raised in proportion. This provided an incentive to 'get about', the hallmark of a good skipper and a well-found boomie.

When assessing these figures it is worth recording that the ship fed the crew — and as far as one can judge, quite well — and that at this time ship's biscuits were 5s. 6d. per cwt, and a Suffolk farmworker, with a tied cottage and firewood free, had to manage on 13s. a week.

Quite a detailed picture of the way the money was earned can be reconstructed from surviving records.

An account book of the *Gloriana* shows that as a new craft in 1872 she made what may have been her first freight from Ipswich to Eu with wheat. This destination, which was evidently a common one over a number of years, is explained in a later memory of Joe Mynheer, whose experiences both with the *Gloriana* and with the *Pearl* are described in Chapter 18.

I once took 150 tons of grindstones in the *Pearl* from Fillingshore on the Tyne to Ville de Eu, above Tréport. That is up a canal. The river ran alongside the canal. The biggest weighed about eighteen hundredweight and they weren't ground with a lathe, but cut out with a chisel. The smallest were the size of cheeses. I took this cargo several times as the sides of my hold were very square and the grindstones could fit in well.

The *Gloriana*'s visit was in February 1872. In March she took oats from Abbeville to Newhaven, in April barley from Abbeville to Schiedam, in May coals from Sunderland to Woodbridge with a lightering freight of gasworks bog ore to Ipswich, in June wheat from Ipswich to Eu, in July oats from Eu to Ipswich, in August coal from Sunderland to Trouville, in September rye from Rouen to Schiedam, in October coal from Sunderland to Abbeville, in November seed and spelter from Abbeville to London and in December pitch from London to Antwerp.

Considering the length of the voyages and the number of passages light, this freight a month was

A boomie was sufficiently important (and unhandy) to 'take steam' in places where a sprittie would have to sail, 'poke' or be manhandled into her berth by her crew. This unidentified ketch is being towed by the **Pioneer** in Faversham creek. The tug, which belonged to the Commissioners of Faversham Navigation, was seventy-one feet long, so this was evidently a big ketch barge *(John Hunt)*

a splendid year's work. It was profitable, too, for with freights between £50 and £120 she grossed £974 and made 'clear earnings' of £661 after deducting sailing expenses £213 and presumably some other costs not shown.

The earnings were divided between crew and owners, giving £330 to the former and £260 to the latter, after deducting £70 for 'bills, club and wages'. These items refer to such expenses as by custom or agreement were accepted by the owner, including the premium for the mutual insurance society, and the wages for the boy, who at this time seems usually to have been provided by the owners and not by the skipper.

Within a few years the *Gloriana* was turning increasingly to the home coasting trade, and by the end of the century, under Herbert Meachen, she was entirely employed shuttling back and forth between the Tyne and Colchester gasworks. In this trade also she averaged nearly a freight a

month from 1898 to 1903, and with freights at 6s. 6d. a ton (the same as twenty years before, showing the steady decline in earnings, even in those relatively non-inflationary days) she was grossing around £700 a year, with a regular annual profit. Her ten freights in 1903, averaging around 200 tons, yielded £637 gross.

The expenses of the year were, however, heavy, including £23 for sixty fathoms of chain (34½ cwt), and in addition to two half-yearly 'club calls' for £3 10s. (presumably the basic mutual insurance premium) the *Gloriana* had to pay a £6 call for *Eliza H* and another £6 call for *Eliza Patience*, both these *Eliza*s being lost at this time.

One may also note that the *Gloriana* required new leeboards in 1898, 1899 and 1900, though as a board was then supplied by McLearon for about £15, the annual breakage was not so serious as it would be today, when such a replacement would involve nearer £250. New sail-covers were bought in 1903, and a new squaresail in 1898. A new foresail and main jib were supplied in the same year for £10, and a new mast the following year for £24.

A clearer picture of the actual trading is to be found in the boomies' cargo books, which were kept aboard and entered up by the skipper, unlike the account book already mentioned which was the work of an owner's clerk.

In the *Eliza Patience* in 1897, Joe Mynheer made the following freights, being either lucky or well served, for on almost every occasion he had a return freight ready for him.

In May and June he took old rails from Newhaven to Dunkirk and returned with slates to London. In July he took teak planking from London to Newcastle. In September he took cement from Waldringfield to Hull, returning in October with deals to London. From London he took wheat to the Isle of Wight, returning with sleepers to London, and in January 1898 he took fertilizer to Dunkirk.

He then left the *Eliza Patience* for the *Pearl*, and in March took slates from London to St Helens, Isle of Wight, in April timber from St Helens to Newcastle, and in May firebricks back from Newcastle to London.

Very comparable performances were recorded by *Mazeppa* in the 1890s, and by *Justice* ten years later.

In 1894 *Mazeppa* carried fourteen freights, working mostly down-Channel to Portland and the Channel Islands for stone, and across to

Dunkirk, with one voyage to Barrow-on-Humber (taking timber and returning with tiles) and only a single coal freight, from Hull to Salcombe. In all this voyaging she only made three passages light, from Southampton to Portland, from Salcombe to the Channel Islands and from Yarmouth to Hull. She filled in a few days in February lightering from Harwich to Ipswich.

The following two years saw her equally busy. In 1895 she carried fourteen freights, twice having to return from Portsmouth to London light, and in 1896 she managed sixteen freights, including trips to Cherbourg, Antwerp and Terneuzen to load stone, slates and glass.

Robert Ruffles took over the *Justice* at Truro in April 1906. His first freight was clay to Antwerp, whence he returned to Heybridge with stone. He then took 170 tons of stone from Nieuport to Sandwich, returned for a similar freight to Whitstable, and made five more freights before the end of the year, three between Ipswich and Dunkirk, and then down to Hull and back to Heybridge.

In 1907 he carried seventeen freights, including visits to Antwerp and Dieppe, with two passages light, one from Hull to Ipswich and one from Erwarton Quay, near Harwich (where he had delivered 157 tons of coal) back to Seaham for another load for Ipswich.

The regularity of this trading is a reminder that the freak passages often remembered were the exceptions which did not prove the rule. For instance, it was often recalled that the *Alice Watts* once left Colchester light, loaded coal at Newcastle and was back within a week, and that on another occasion the *Gloriana* took seventeen weeks over the same voyage. But the cargo books quoted show that year after year the freights averaged out at rather better than one a month.

Payments for demurrage are not itemized in these books, but a charter agreement made by the London Granite Company with Ralph King, skipper of the *Sussex Belle,* shows that when she took 155 tons of stone from Bruges to Southwold in 1927, at 8s. 3d. per ton, the vessel was to be unloaded within six working days, after which demurrage was payable at 1s. per gross ton per day. This agreement also included a two-guinea gratuity for the captain, an extra so customary that it forms part of the printed terms in the contract.

When Mynheer took the *Pearl* a good freight was worth around £60, less expenses of around £18. The nett freight of £42 was divided between owner and crew, the owner paying special ex-

penses including the boy's wages (say £3), to leave around £16.

Some of the return freights were, however, barely profitable. Cement from Waldringfield to Hull was worth only 3s. 3d. a ton, yielding £18 for 120 tons, and chalk from London to Hull only 2s. 3d. a ton. But evidently anything was better than nothing, for rather than return from London to Ipswich light Mynheer loaded 100 tons of loam (moulding sand) at two shillings a ton, giving the crew £4 4s. 7d. for their share, and the owners (after allowing ten shillings for the boy) £3 14s. 7d.

*Justice* in 1907 similarly found it worth loading 145 tons of shingle from Shoreham to Hull at 3s. 9d. a ton. Scrap iron and iron rails were also poorly paid, with *Justice* taking 153 tons of scrap from Yarmouth to Hull at 3s. a ton and 154 tons of rails from Ipswich to Middlesbrough at 3s. 9d. She was also content with 3s. a ton for 160 tons of phosphates from Ipswich to Dunkirk, but this was a return freight, as she was then bringing locust beans from Dunkirk to Ipswich, loading up to 690 quarters at 1s. 1d. a quarter.

Mynheer usually took a tow into dock or up to London above Gravesend. Besides the inescapable pilotage over the Haven Bar, he would pay

*Justice* working at the end of her days as a motor barge, here seen laid up and patched up.

£1 for 'help down from Waldringfield'. He would employ a pilot (or, as he always spelled it, 'polit') from Harwich up to Mistley, and a tidesman to help on the way down. And while he and his crew doubtless worked loading and unloading, there is usually an expense for hiring labour on both operations.

If we are trying to reconstruct the life of a coasting skipper in the days of the boomies, let Joe Mynheer have the last word, and touch in his own picture of the little frustrations and vexations which were in fact so much more familiar and conspicuous than the dramas and adventures.

The *Pearl* was classed at Lloyd's.[1] Her certificate ran out in ten years. Orvis, her part-owner, said he could get her re-classed at a small cost. I, however, said I didn't think it was worth the expense. I then suggested having her passed by the Board of Trade. Orvis said that doesn't matter. I replied "Hold on, I have a small wife and large family." But Orvis said "If they say anything refer them to me." He liked to think he was above everyone.

Nothing happened till after he died and I became sole owner. Then at Newcastle while loading for a French port the Board of Trade official walked across the schooner *Girl of the Period* and the ketch barge *Lord Hartington* to see me. He asked to see my Lloyd's certificate. I showed it to him. He told me it was no good as it had run out. He telephoned Lloyd's to this effect and they told me to send them back their certificate.

The Board of Trade official then said as my Lloyd's loadline was now one foot and half an inch it must be two inches more as an unclassified vessel. That is, the freeboard amidships must be fourteen and a half inches. I was also to wait till I had been surveyed. I said, "What about the *Lord Hartington?* She has only a loadline of six and a half inches." The official replied, "She is only going to London." So I said, "Oh! So there isn't enough water to get drowned in in the North Sea? You have to go down Channel to do that. You stop me with a load line of twelve and a half inches while you let another barge go which is damn nearly

The round counter stern favoured by so many boomies is well shown in this unidentified photo. The mainsail is cut back at the tack to allow it to roll on the boom without fouling the reefing gear. The patching on the mainsail shows why the topping lift was often protected against chafing with 'baggywrinkle'.

sunk." Fortunately I only had to wait five days before I was remeasured and I was then given a loadline of nine and a half inches — three inches less than what Lloyd's had previously given me.

In the course of a long life at sea it is unbelievable some of the things I have had to put up with.

Thus, one inspector condemned my life-jackets. They were of good material. He wrenched off the tapes which go around the body. I went and bought a set of secondhand jackets not nearly as good as mine and these were passed. I then sewed fresh tapes onto the old ones so that I then had two sets.

Another official said I had to have a compass with a binnacle lamp for the barge's boat. Who could go lighting lamps in such an emergency? One inspector condemned the rudder and tiller. I must use an oar for steering. Five oars must be kept in the barge's boat and the fifth oar must be painted green. Who could see what colour an oar is in the dark?

[1]Classification at Lloyd's, a distinction enjoyed by only a minority of boomies, enabled them to secure valuable cargoes. It was awarded at his discretion by a Lloyd's surveyor who watched the building, examining the timber used and giving a certificate for the number of years he considered it merited.

CHAPTER 15

# Fair Winds and Foul

The boomies ventured everywhere, from the Shetlands to the Mediterranean. A trip to Lisbon, Scotland or Dublin was nothing out of the way. The *Emily Lloyd*'s maiden voyages to the Mediterranean have already been mentioned — including returning to the Firth of Forth with a stack of grass on deck. In the *Arundel Castle* Walter Ward also loaded a six-foot stack of timber in Christiania. The *Mountsfield* sailed to Norway to have an engine fitted. The *Edith Wood* took a cargo of tobacco from Spain to Belgium.

Little sloops that were hardly fit to trade out of the estuary found their way down-Channel to Southampton and Dartmouth, as well as taking their chance on open beaches all round the coast. Ketches with lowering masts braved the North Sea to turn themselves at Dordrecht into lighters and be towed far up the Rhine into the heart of Germany.

Many of the craft were wrecked. The cliffs of Withernsea in Yorkshire and the beaches of

On the Seine near Rouen about 1900. Unidentified boomie (perhaps **Davenport**) lying alongside sprittie **Lord Warden** (*R. H. Perks collection*)

Unidentified boomie in Amsterdam, 1893. She is waiting with Dutch craft for the Westerkanaal railway bridge to open to reach the Noordzeekanaal, so she is probably homeward-bound, light, having taken a cargo to Holland. *(Historisch Topografische Atlas Gemeentelijke Archiefdienst, Amsterdam/Robert Simper collection)*

Norfolk claimed a specially heavy toll. Others disappeared, often down-Channel, swamped by seas which swept over craft loaded down to a few inches of freeboard. Remarkably few, I think, were lost through ignorance or gross error; at any rate, a study of the terrible toll of the Thames Estuary reveals very few boomies in the weekly lists of major casualties.

Indeed, it is surprising that so many craft survived as long as they did, bearing in mind that their East Coast voyages took them through some of the most difficult and dangerous waters, exposing them to risks greater in many ways than those experienced by the big square-riggers on their deep-sea passages. For while the barge hull provided great benefits in economy and convenience, its only advantage at sea was that if it came to the worst a shoal-draught craft had more

chance of driving up ashore close enough to be reached by a life-saving rocket, and with a greater prospect of being salvaged after the gale was over.

The crews were thought large by sprittie sailormen, but with only two men to a watch the boomies were far from heavily manned when it came to an emergency.

The hardships and frustrations of sea-going in small craft under sail, as helpless when there was too little wind as when there was too much, can never really be comprehended by those who take power for granted. The memories which follow, however, will conjure up some vivid pictures, particularly to today's yachtsmen, who can be thankful that they are seldom exposed to such ordeals in their weatherly, snug-rigged cruisers.

Perhaps the most terrible couple of days in the history of the boomies was 18-19 November 1893, when no less than five ketch barges were lost — *Bessie Hiller, Enterprise* of Rye, *Masonic, Tynemouth Castle* and *Winifred Mary*. A glimpse of that dreadful blow may be obtained from the memories of the mate of the *Emma,* who experienced it and survived.

She came out of the Backwaters at Walton, bound for Hartlepool, on a Thursday, falling in with a fleet from Harwich, which included the ill-fated *Masonic.* They were well on the way, double-reefed, when they were struck by a wind like a hurricane which stripped the *Emma* of every stitch of canvas. Driving helpless, they set a jib in an effort to keep clear of a billyboy, but that sail too blew away.

They picked up the Humber lights at 9 p.m. on the Saturday and let go their anchor in seven fathoms on the Inner Dowsing. Soon they parted from the anchor and at 6 a.m. they were driven ashore at Hunstanton. By a stroke of fortune the *Emma* found a safe berth and was got off on the Tuesday. After it was all over the mate produced a letter which he had already put in a bottle. 'But', he said, 'I didn't need it, thank God.'

In addition to craft actually wrecked, every winter blow saw the salvaging yawls and smacks, and later the lifeboats, struggling to assist craft dismasted or leaky, with sails gone or anchors lost.

To quote but one example at random, the Margate lifeboat *Quiver* was called out on 30 November 1897, in a north-westerly gale to go to four ketches — *Flower of Essex, Lord Beresford, Eustace* and *Enterprise* (of Harwich) — all brought up near the Hook Sand. She finally got back to Margate with fourteen men and three dogs — a surprisingly small average of human crew and a remarkably high canine complement.

All the barges survived — a reminder that for every one of the many losses recorded there were several such narrow escapes, all in the day's work. A high proportion of boomie-barge men got first-hand acquaintance with lifeboats, and a high proportion of boomies had nine lives.

Down-Channel, Portland Stone was a notoriously nasty freight. A light cargo was ideal; with the weight of a few lumps carefully stowed on her bottom, a boomie was 'like a little lifeboat', but if it was a full cargo stone was, in the words of one old skipper, 'funny stuff'. Apart from the dangers of overloading, the heavy concentration of weight in great two-ton pieces strained the hulls, both in loading and at sea, and must account for many unexplained disappearances.

The risks of beach work, in which the smaller, early flat-bottomed craft were so freely employed, are obvious. A barge would lie on an open shore only for one tide, but in that short time there was always the chance of a sea getting

up, making it impossible to haul off, and leaving only the desperate expedient of pulling out the plugs to prevent the barge floating and knocking her bottom out in the surf.

Another important cargo in earlier days was 'big logs'. This was not the sawn-timber trade familiar to later sprittie sailormen, but great trunks of elm and oak. These had to be loaded using the barge's gear, which was a factor in the popularity and survival of the sloop rig. The later ketches generally rigged a cargo derrick on their main and peak halyards, but the early sloops often used the long main boom, which could be swung out over a quay or seawall to negotiate great weights from a considerable distance.

The loading of trees was one reason why the crews of the sloops and dandies had to put up with booms of excessive length. The *Emma's* was forty-eight feet, which might have been acceptable for a fish-carrier, lightly loaded and heavily crewed, but must have been excessive for the hard slog of the coasting trade. As Joe Mynheer said:

> Dandies went north, even though the mainsail was too big. We could always reef it. My first voyage in the *Flower of Essex* was with round timber. We loaded at Ferry Dock, Woodbridge, the old iron crane being used, and we took the timber to Newcastle. She then had her big mainsail and lug mizzen with fixed boom.

On this occasion I think one must respect Joe Mynheer's spirit more than his judgment.

The boomies' much-vaunted ability to sail light without ballast was not always effective, as is proved by a memory of Captain Douse in the three-masted schooner *Friendship.* She was bound for Seaham, light, when she got caught in a gale off Cromer and was blown right out into the North Sea. She was only drawing three foot six, and was like a bladder on the water. The close-reefed mainsail blew away, and she was driving about for thirty-two days, hove-to but making sail whenever it was possible to gain any westing.

Captain Douse had plenty of food aboard but very little water. When he finally made the land it was at Kinnaird Head. He had no charts of the area, and at sunset he saw a light flashing which he did not recognize. He got out his almanack, and a yellow page caught his eye. It was a Notice to Mariners announcing a light that would begin to operate from a certain date. This was that very day and that very light; in fact, Captain Douse reckoned he was the first vessel ever to pick it up.

However, that night they had another westerly gale and he was blown out to sea again. Altogether he had four different gales, west or south-west, before he finally made the land again at Whitby. After he had refused one tug another came alongside and insisted on towing him without payment. The *Friendship* had been given up as lost, and the relatives of some of the crew had already put in claims for insurance. His father, skipper of the *Empress of India,* was among those who joined in the welcome.

Afterwards Captain Douse said that while hove-to and driving about in the North Sea the *Friendship* was as dry and comfortable as a house. Then he added, 'I ought to have let go both anchors on the Dowsing, though if I had lost them I'd have looked sillier still.'

The boomie captains were fond of jeering at the spritties with their brailing mainsails, saying that 'they were like bloody women; when they were in trouble all they could do was lift up their skirts and run'.

But a memory of Ned Goodman and the *Britannia* — less dramatic but more typical than Captain Douse's — is a reminder of the limitations even of the boomie in standing up to a breeze of wind.[1]

[1]Told by A. H. Horlock: *Mistleyman's Log.*

He was bound from London to Sunderland, and after three days and nights out was off Redcar with a nice westerly wind. In the next hour there came a gale from the north, and *Britannia* could make no headway against the wind and the now flooding tide. He had no choice but to run the hundred miles back to the Humber for shelter.

After a terrifying eight-hour run, with the sea licking at his heels, he was off Spurn Head when the wind backed to the north-west, straight out of the Humber. Again the tide was against him, and he decided to run to the Wash, hoping for a change of wind. But the change was into the north-east, and off Cromer Ned realized his only refuge was Harwich, where he ultimately ended up, 200 miles from his destination.

Under such conditions many a deep-keel schooner or brig would have done little better. But most of them could keep plugging to windward longer than a barge, and when conditions finally got too bad most of them were able to heave-to.

This was an uneasy manoeuvre in a barge, especially when light, and it was seldom attempted, though when Walter Ward brought his timber stack across the North Sea in the *Arundel Castle* he was hove-to with it for three days on the

**Friendship.** *(Below)* As the portrait-painter saw her. *(Opposite)* Two photos under tow leaving Dover. *(Roger Finch)*

Dogger Bank. He declared afterwards that he was quite happy down in the cabin, playing cards!

Alf Taylor recalled:

> I was only hove-to once and that was for two or three days in the *Gem of the Ocean*. We were under storm jib, one-reef foresail and two-reefed mizzen. Mainsail was stowed. Helm lashed by tiller ropes. The helm was hard a-port or hard a-starboard according to which tack we were on. Keep helm up, that is helm hard a-weather. Sometimes she would ride off and then would have to be hove-to again. She was light and like a bloody old bladder flopping about. I was glad when I was out of it.

Lashing the helm hard up sounds strange advice, but it is what Captain Taylor is recorded as saying. Even assuming he was correctly understood, Captain Mynheer's version is more convincing:

> To heave to, stow fores'l. Set inner jib and put the sheet to the forestay. Make it fast to windward and to leeward. The mainsail is set and reefed. The vessel falls off and the mainsail will draw a little. Lash the helm to the best advantage; a little down as a rule.

**Britannia.** A fine example of a transom-sterned ketch. She is seen (*top*) off Orford Ness bound from the Humber to Pin Mill with coal. Her forestay sets inboard abaft her stem (*Roger Finch*)

The photo (*bottom*) was taken off the Farne Islands from the yacht **Sunbeam** on 10 August 1912, when she was bound to Berwick-on-Tweed with meal and barley from King's Lynn (*Roger Finch*)

CHAPTER 16

# Across the Atlantic and up the Rhine

The voyages of *Goldfinch* and *Leading Light* to British Guiana in the 1930s throw some interesting light on the ability of the barge hull under extreme conditions.

Both craft were lightly ballasted with firebricks and had their leeboards in their holds, but in other respects they faced the Atlantic with conventional boomie gear. Both had galleys on deck — an arrangement favoured by a number of boomies even in the home trade, for in fine weather it was pleasanter to cook on deck. These galleys had two doors, so the leeward one could be opened. But on her Atlantic voyage *Goldfinch*'s was washed overboard by a sea. Their crews comprised skipper, mate, bosun, two ABs and one OS.[1]

*Goldfinch* sailed in September 1930, straight into a succession of equinoctial gales. She was rigged with her old gear, including double topsails, just as she came off the coast, and kept her crew busy pumping, repairing running rigging, and above all taking up her rope lanyards, which could not cope with the continual rolling and pitching. She carried away her mainbrace (giving them the difficult task of replacing it with the squaresail yard aloft), sprung the mast-cap to which the lower topsail yard was fixed (replaced by a figure-of-eight wire lashing), and damaged her upper rudder pintle (involving some hazardous work under the counter in the boat to make it good with wires and spikes). She proved undercanvassed for windward work, but 'ran like a scalded cat before the north-east trades'.

When it came to *Leading Light's* turn she was properly refitted with new sails and gear.

This fine ketch was unusual — perhaps unique — in that she had one skipper in all her twenty-eight years in home waters, Albert Vince, who for much of this time was also her owner. With his nephew George Vince as mate he carried on the tradition of passage-making to the very end of the days of sail, as her freights between 1930 and 1934 show.

She took coal from Goole to Salcombe and returned from Bridport to Grimsby with shingle. Then she loaded coal at Keadby for Rye gasworks, again returning with shingle to Grimsby. Next it was down-Channel with basic slag to Plymouth, and on to Penzance to load stone for Yarmouth, Isle of Wight. Then back to Teignmouth to load china clay for Leith, and across the Firth of Forth for coal at Burntisland for Rye.

Her most frequent voyages were to Rye gasworks, Salcombe and Plymouth from Goole and Keadby, but she also visited Helford and Truro, loading stone back from Newlyn to Poole.

These voyages involved some adventures. In 1932, after loading at the little Scottish colliery village of St David's, they met bad weather and sheltered under the lee of the Bass Rock for a week. By the time they reached Rye after a month at sea the coal had overheated and they had to call the fire brigade to spray the cargo as the hatches came off.

On another occasion, unable to enter Rye owing to the weather, they had to run back to the Downs for shelter, breaking the boom and splitting the mainsail, after which they lay in Ramsgate weather-bound for two weeks.

When Albert Vince decided to sell the *Leading*

[1] 'Deep Water Boomie Passages' by Stan Hugill, who sailed on both occasions as bosun, under Captain Thomas Orford. Published in the *Journal of the Thames Barge Sailing Club*, Winter 1970-1.

**Goldfinch** at Falmouth lying to two anchors in a gale with leeboards lowered. She has double topsails with gaff topsail stowed in the rigging. Later her skipper-owner, J. H. Waters, reduced her to ketch, but found it worth while to restore a single square topsail. *(Richard Hugh Perks)*

*Light* to Booker Brothers her deep-sea refit included wire lanyards (into which they somehow succeeded in working the traditional Matthew Walker stopper knots) and newly coppered bottom (which frightened away the flying-fish so welcome aboard *Goldfinch*). She carried a big flying squaresail which was set throughout much of the voyage, and the only reefing they did was to roll down the mizzen to ease steering with a fair wind. With better gear and kinder weather they suffered much less damage, though they carried away the clew of the mainsail, and when they were twenty days out the mizzen peak parted, sending the gear down on top of the lifebelts, which were washed overboard, making the sea a blaze of light as the calcium flares reacted in the water.

They were also lucky to save the topmast, first when the crosstrees broke, and again when the ketch gybed, parting the lee backstay from its chain pennant and leaving the weight of the boom on the weather backstay.

Both barges averaged 5-7 knots, covering 100-120 miles a day with fair winds. Thanks chiefly to better conditions, *Leading Light* made Madeira in a time ten days better than *Goldfinch*. On 8 June she logged 174 miles.

*Leading Light* was used to carry sugar in bags from the Berbice Estates to Georgetown. She was later converted to a dumb barge, sold to a Mr Van Sluytman, and ultimately sank in the Berbice river. *Goldfinch* lasted till 1947, when she was hulked, being then owned by J. Sibley of New Amsterdam.

There was a curious little epilogue to these, the most notable of boomie voyages. When *Leading Light* arrived a Negro captain insisted that the crew visit his vessel, which proved to be an exact copy of *Goldfinch*, topsail yards and all, named *Raima*. She was built of greenheart, and in view of the durability of this material it would be interesting to know how long she lasted. At any rate, she must be accepted as the last of the boomies — built in South America.

A more modest voyage, but one more typical of a boomie's working life, was that of *Zenobia* up the

Rhine to fetch a cargo of Apollinaris water in 1912.

This trade was then a considerable source of employment. Apollinaris, a mineral water rich in carbonic acid gas, takes its name from the Apollinaris spring in the Ahr valley. This spring was discovered in 1857 — in the course of an endeavour to trace the fumes that were destroying the local vineyard! It soon became popular in Great Britain as an ideal blend for whisky — Vesta Tilley was singing about 'Scotch and Polly' and Conan Doyle did not omit to mention it — and by 1875 six million bottles were being shipped to London in spritties and such boomies as could lower their masts. The empty bottles provided a return freight. When the *Empress of India* was wrecked at Caister in 1910 it was said that the breaking of bottles made a noise like a shooting gallery at a fair.

Two ketches loading at the primitive staging, from a postcard published in 1907. The craft in the foreground has the old-fashioned loose-footed main sail, and has a stay-fall for lowering her mast, with wooden blocks near the hounds. The craft behind is loaded, and is lowering her mast for the tow under the bridge down to Dordrecht, using a similar tackle on her mainsail. Her mizzen is being lowered forward, without removing the boom, gaff and sail, which are cocked up in the air, suggesting that the mizzen sheet was used to take the weight of the descending mast.
*(McKnight Photography)*

The trade was killed by the outbreak of war in 1914, when one sprittie, Whitmore's *Dunkerque*, was caught up the Rhine and used by the Germans while her crew endured internment. It revived between the wars, only to be similarly extinguished again in 1939.

*Zenobia's* voyage was recalled by Harry Keeble, one of five Maldon brothers who all followed their father's example and became barge-skippers. This voyage was his only excursion into boomies, for after it was over he returned to spritties before coming ashore to work at Maldon and with Marconi's at Chelmsford, and starting the Maldon Sea Scouts with his son Bert. He retired in 1950, and died in 1975 at the age of eighty-three.

His vivid story, based on his detailed log, clearly shows the pride of a young man in sharing responsibility for a fine craft with a skipper he clearly respected, Jimmy Alliston.[2]

*Zenobia,* which carried four hands and a cook-boy, was lying in Poole in June 1912, having unloaded superphosphates from Ipswich. Harry Keeble had been her mate for three months. After waiting two weeks for a freight, they received orders to load white clay for Bonn, and were towed the few miles to the loading berth at

[2]*Journal of the Thames Barge Sailing Club*, 1971-2, and Winter 1972. For details of the Keebles, see *Topsail* No. 19 (Winter 1980).

REMAGEN,
BLICK AUF DIE ERPELER LEY.

Harry Keeble in later life as skipper of a spritsail barge

Goats Head, where the young mate enjoyed himself chasing squirrels up trees.

After loading 145 tons they lashed the boat in its chocks and sailed on Friday afternoon (defying one sailorman's superstition!) with a fair wind and east-going tide. Leaving Christchurch Ledge to starboard, they ran through the Inner Shingles and sailed through the Solent in the night. In the morning they got a fix on the Warner light-vessel and took the Looe Channel, cutting off eight or ten miles. Here the young mate was in charge, for the skipper turned in from 10 a.m. till 2 p.m.

At 4 p.m. on Saturday they were off Beachy

The Rhine trade. At Remagen, where Apollinaris water was loaded.
(Below) An English boomie alongside a foreign barge

*Opposite*
(*Top*) The product advertised on a boomie's mainsail. Ahead of her lies an English sprittie. (The advertisement is possibly only scratched on the negative.)
(*Bottom*) Unloading the bottles in London

Head, when the wind veered into the north and they made little progress till they got a new south-westerly wind on the Sunday evening. After a breakfast of cold beef, hot coffee and hard biscuit Harry Keeble had his watch below from 6 a.m. to 10 a.m., and at dusk they picked up the Belgian coast.

The French pilot cutter told them to sail eight miles to the north-west to find a pilot. This they thought 'a bit rough', so they hailed a fishing-boat and a fisherman came aboard, making a five-foot leap, to pilot them to 'Zurrick Zee' where they would clear Customs and pick up a river pilot. Passing West Kapelle, they entered the Maas, sailed past Veere and, having been sealed by the Customs at Zierickzee, ran on to reach Dordrecht at 2 a.m. on the Tuesday. Here the pilot left for home, while Keeble stayed on watch till 6 a.m.

That day was spent lowering down the gear and getting *Zenobia* ready for the week-long tow against the relentless current of the Rhine through Holland and up into the heart of Germany. After tea they got an evening ashore, marvelling at the strange costumes, the carts pulled by dogs and the houses 'much nicer and cleaner' than at home. Next morning as they waited for their tug they watched the shipping 'the like of which you never see in home waters', from great trains of lighters carrying 3,000 tons down to little flat-bottomed boats selling everything from cigars and groceries to sweets and slippers.

Away they went after dinner and towed till the tug rang its bell at 8 p.m., when they anchored for the night. The bell rang again at 4 a.m. and they were off once more. With all hands bar cook taking two hours at the wheel there was nothing to do for six hours but watch the countryside go by, the flat landscape giving place to hills after they passed the German frontier at Emmerich.

After towing under the stone bridge at Cologne they had to pass through a bridge of boats. 'They haul some one way and some another and we passed through one of the queerest bridges I have ever seen,' Harry observed. For eight days they were sixteen hours under tow with eight at rest, till they reached the jetty where the clay was unloaded by Germans using the long-handled Continental shovels they had never seen before.

They finished unloading on the Saturday, and after a three-hour tow reached Remagen to load Apollinaris water, but found three or four English vessels already waiting, so they had ten days of enjoyable sightseeing.

The tow down with the current was, of course, much quicker. The first evening they were at Cologne, and the next back at Emmerich. Another day saw them at Dordrecht, where they hove the gear up again, provisioned the ship, took a pilot and sailed in the evening. With a fair wind they ran all night to reach Zierickzee at dawn.

There they said goodbye to the pilot and reached Veere Gat in the afternoon with hopes of a quick run home. But when they turned out in the morning it was blowing hard from the south-west, and they had to lie at anchor for a week. Their trips ashore included a visit to a windmill.

On the Friday afternoon before August Bank Holiday the wind came south-east and they were away at dawn on Saturday, hoping for the holiday at home. But off the Belgian coast it fell calm, with the skipper prophesying rough weather next day. It came in north-east in the night and freshened, but by this time they had picked up the North Foreland. Off Sheerness a storm did some damage to other shipping, but they were well reefed down and made their high water in a calm without damage.

On the Bank Holiday they had a quiet run, clearing Customs at Gravesend and making Limehouse Reach that tide. Next day, after breakfast, as if to acknowledge they were home from foreign parts and back in the bargeman's river, they tripped the anchor and let *Zenobia* 'drudge' up stern first to St Katharine's Dock.

Harry Keeble has left an idyllic memory of his little three-month odyssey. It was summer. It was long ago, and he was young. Not many freights can have been so much like a yachtsman's holiday. But it is agreeable to be reminded of the rewarding moments in a hard life.

CHAPTER 17

# Random Recollections

Fifty years ago old men could recall not only the life-span of the boomies, but also the last days of their predecessors.

In 1937 Joe Culf, of Manningtree, which like Woodbridge was a busy shipping centre in the first half of the nineteenth century, told Dr J. L. Groom:

Joe Culf

> I am now 83 and the first vessel I went to sea in was the *Economy* brigantine of Mistley when I was a boy of about thirteen. We took corn to the North, and came back with coal. I was in the *Vecta,* a schooner in the same trade. Her skipper was William Green of Manningtree. The larger vessels went to the Baltic for timber. I went there in the *Mistley Park* brigantine. Later she was used as a lighter for Paul, being towed backwards and forwards between Ipswich and Butterman's Bay. Then I went as a deep-sea sailor before the mast in the tea clipper *Agnes Muir.* [All square-riggers were tea-clippers in the memories of their crews!]
>
> When I first went to sea there were very few ketch barges about. The vessels which brought the coal were nearly all billyboys. I never saw a flat-bottom sloop without a mizzen, but saw deep-keeled sloops with one mast. The *Alice,* belonging to Chissell, was a clinker-built billyboy with only one mast.[1]
>
> In 1890 there was a very severe winter. I took 73 days from London to Antwerp in the *Garibaldi.* We lay in Faversham Swale. There were over 100 barges there. We froze up for five or six weeks. Some barges drove

[1]*Alice* of Harwich, sloop, built Burton Stather 1835, 41 tons, owned by Joseph Chissell.

high and dry on the mud. In 1904 or 1905 I was frozen in the Thames off Woolwich. Traffic was stopped for weeks and weeks. We do not have these severe winters now like we used to do. When I was a boy we used to be pleased to be frozen up at Mistley Quay for six weeks or a couple of months.

The memories of Jimmy Lewis of Woodbridge also included the schooners which dominated the trade before the development of the boomies.

He recalled the *Rudolph*, lost by Captain Norton at Orford Haven while entering the river with coal. Another schooner, *Ariel*, under Captain Whyard, brought coal to Orford for Rope, a coal merchant who also had maltings and the Jolly Sailor pub, and in partnership with Mingay owned a small fleet of traditional coasters. Skipper Lewis recalled that:

her masts were raked aft like the schooner

**Mystery** wrecked on the pier at Dover in December 1929 after dragging her anchor. (*N. M. Mus.*)

*English Rose* which my father had. The *English Rose* was 130 tons and drew ten feet. The *Rudolph* was about 230 tons. She was the biggest schooner coming into Orford. The *Ariel* was a little schooner about 130 tons, same as the schooner my old man had.

He continued:

My old man also had the boomie *Yulan*. It took him three months to take a load of chalk to Scotland and come back. He was skipper at one time of the *Mystery* and of the *Justice*, and also of the schooner *Alarm*. She belonged to Ipswich, she did. Butcher had the *Laura* before my old man did. She was a big boomie and carried 200 tons of coal. I was mate of her for four years with my father. I left her at Whitstable and walked home to Woodbridge, 200 miles. She was too wet for me. I got a lift from Ingatestone to Ipswich on a furniture van. I had walked so far from Whitstable. By the time I got to Ingatestone I

had walked about a hundred miles and I hadn't any money. A chap gave me a couple of bob in a pub at Ingatestone. When I left the *Laura* my father gave me ten bob to go home.

Among the craft recalled by skipper Lewis, the *Yulan* met a particularly poignant end. She was bound from Belgium to London with paper pulp when she drove ashore on the Goodwins in a south-easterly gale at the end of January 1911. Her skipper, John Russell, had his two sons for crew. That night one of them was washed overboard. The skipper and the other son, Arthur, took to the rigging as the Walmer lifeboat searched for them in tow of the tug *Java.* Next day they sighted the wreck, but as they came alongside the *Yulan*'s mast fell, carrying away the skipper's second son with it.

Captain Harry Porter was another who went to sea with his father:

The *Eustace* belonged to Walker and Howard of Mark Lane, London. I joined her as a boy when my father was skipper and kept with her till my father retired. I then became her skipper, so I was cook, which is what the boy always was, then ordinary seaman, able seaman and then mate in her. I came home and found my father dying. I said "Father, I am leaving the *Eustace.*" He replied "My boy, you'll never do any good if you leave her." He was right. I took the *Davenport.* She belonged to Benstead, a shipwright in Vaux's yard. I couldn't do anything right for him so I left and was out of a berth for two or three months. I had been out of the *Eustace* for a year or so when she was lost on the West Rocks loaded with pitch.

My next vessel after leaving the *Davenport* was the *Mystery.* Dudley Ward, her former skipper, had died and his body was brought to Pin Mill in the *Mystery* where I took over. She previously had a tiller but Dudley Ward had fitted a wheel and also davits to her. When I took her a long tiller was aboard but I got rid of it as it was in the way. The *Mystery*'s wheel was very small and I didn't seem to have much power over her. One day I went in to Whitmore's and saw a fine wheel. I said "That is a fine wheel" and Whitmore said "Yes, do you want one?" I went up to the wheel and caught hold of it and I immediately knew it was the wheel of

the *Eustace.* I told Whitmore so and he informed me that the wheel had been salvaged from her. I could tell by a score on the wheel caused one day when raising the mast. By buying the *Eustace*'s wheel I was twenty-one years holding the same wheel.

So much for the skipper's view. The voice of the foredeck is not so often heard.

H. E. Taylor of Colchester sailed both with James Meachen senior in the *Alice Watts* and with James Meachen junior in the *Startled Fawn.*

I can tell you the *Startled Fawn* was a flyer, [he recalled]. But there was one characteristic about boomies that I never met up with in spritties and that was what we used to call "stamping her foot". Sailing light, as we often used to, she would lift her bow clear of the water and come down again with a resounding smack, making a terrific bang, and us inhabitants of the foc'sle didn't get much sleep. This of course could only happen in flat-bottom craft.

I suppose it was part of the discipline, but these skippers had to be called "Sir" by the crew, and the cook was invariably addressed as Toby. Why, I don't know but there was certainly no need to call him chef. Salt horse, jacky potatoes, rancid butter and old Mister Last's concrete biscuits were our main diet, very frugally served out by the mate from a well-locked cupboard.

Mr F. L. Last of Woodbridge recalled a typical bargeman's life, working his way up through the local spritties and finishing in a boomie. He started in the Maldon *Mermaid*, working hay and straw from Minter's Dock in Boyton Creek to Vauxhall, and lightering grain from Butterman's Bay to Colchester and Ipswich.

Then he went mate to Bill Eves in the little *Audacious* of Colchester, working brick rubbish from Wakering to Harwich for the roads. Next he moved with Eves into the *Falconet,* in living memory the baby of the Colchester fleet, but in those days considered quite a big barge, justifying a third hand. After that he had a spell in another small Colchester barge, the *Peace*, working brick rubbish and bricks from the London Brick Company's yard at St Osyth with some freights of coal from Colchester to West Mersea.

His last sprittie was another stack barge, the *Beaumont Belle*, and then he joined the boomie

*Laura* as third hand with James Lewis of Wood-bridge. The *Laura* was four-handed, and usually working shingle from Orford Haven to Hull, with coal back to Orford Quay. He recalled, 'We took on average a week from Orford to Hull. We have brought up in the Yarmouth Roads but it weren't very often as we used to get away down. I don't think she had a figurehead then.

Another Woodbridge man, David Farrow, went straight into boomies:

My first vessel was the *Emily Lloyd,* a boomie belonging to Burnham. She belonged to a man name of Smith. He had a big coal business, and had these barges on a purpose. I joined at Woodbridge. We went to Hartlepool for coal and took it to Burnham. It was the first sovereign I earned in my life. The skipper's wife gave me a shilling, the mate gave me a shilling and one of the crew gave me a bob. My fare was paid to Woodbridge. There was no railway between Burnham and Maldon then, so I went by carrier to Maldon and on to Woodbridge by train. The platform wasn't big enough for me. I had to take the sovereign to my father, but I said nothing about the rest.

The *Emily Lloyd* and the *Harold* both had flat sterns, like a sprittie — no counter. Ruffles and Garnham bought the *Harold* off Stoney, as Stone of Mistley was known. She was a proper bloody diving bell. She was a proper dirty bugger. The *Sussex Belle,* you could live on her as long as you like, but the other would proper drown you. She was a proper bloody submarine when away came the wind.

After leaving the *Emily Lloyd* I went to the *Empress of India.* It was in her I had six teeth knocked out when the handle of the leeboard winch kicked back. One tooth went between the mizzen mast and its tabernacle. I got nothing for this accident. There was no insurance then or employers' liability act. All the skipper did was ask me next morning if I was dead. The bloody old sod. My parents wouldn't let me go back in her. After recovering from the accident I went along with Jimmy Lewis in the old *English Rose.* When the *Emily Lloyd* was at Woodbridge the coal was whipped out, but I wasn't man enough for that.

## CHAPTER 18

# A Family of Skippers

Among boomie-barge skippers in Essex, the Meachen family were especially prominent.

Rudrum ('Rud') Meachen of Harwich started in the cod smacks, and was skipper of Groom's *Swift.* This was in itself unusual, for the smacksmen and bargemen generally lived in their own worlds. In fact, the only other smacksman I have heard of making this change was Bob Newman, who used to enjoy the long voyage to Iceland, and later tried working-day trips fishing out of Harwich in the *Curlew.* This restless life he found so little to his taste that he decided to go to sea again, and took the *Startled Fawn.* He did not make a success of it, due, according to one memory, to trying to sail a barge as if she were a smack — a significant reminder of the specialist knowledge and experience demanded by flat-bottomed craft.

Rud Meachen, on the other hand, found his *métier* in the ketch barges. After a spell in the old *Pearl*[1] he took an old Dutch curiosity called the *Advance,* to which he fitted leeboards to make her sail better, and then several dandies, including the *Brightlingsea,* which he passed on to his son, William.

His half-brother, James Meachen senior, after being skipper of the *May Queen, Enterprise* and *Flower of Essex,* took the *Alice Watts* from the time of her launch till he retired, spending most of forty years trading to Colchester gasworks, and ultimately owning the barge.

James's son, James Arthur Meachen, had the *Startled Fawn,* and another son, Herbert, took the *Gloriana,* but lost her in 1909 off Spurn Head

[1]Presumably the *Pearl* of Portsmouth, as the *Pearl* of Ipswich was not built till 1889.

George (Joe) Mynheer

on his first voyage, after which he reverted to mate with his father. A third son, Joseph, had the first barge built in Harwich, the sprittie *John Watts.*

A daughter of James senior married Mynheer, a shipwright at Vaux's yard, who fell out with the

Herbert Meachen

foreman while the *Llama* was being built and left to go to Curtis at Ipswich. Their son, George Mynheer (always known as Joe), went to sea in 1873 in a London barge called the *Emerald*, was in the *Tertius* in 1875, then in the *Flower of Essex* and *May Queen*, the schooner *Alma*, the *Active* as mate to his Uncle Rud, and the *James Garfield*. He then went into the railway boats as AB, but returned to boomies as skipper of the *Eliza Patience* and then of the *Pearl* of Ipswich, of which he became part-owner in 1898 and sole owner in 1931.

In his old age he visited the *Pearl* in Ipswich dock every day, lighting a fire in the cabin and tending the pumps. Finally in 1939 he announced that anyone who would take her away where he would not see her again could have her on payment of the debt for dock dues. The quick-witted skipper of the sprittie *Shamrock* discovered the amount was £28 10*s.* for which sum he acquired her. He then performed the remarkable feat of towing her to Gravesend with the *Shamrock* — for which he was sacked by his owners! There she was hulked, ending her days at Hoo under the name *Pearl Wood*.

Because of the length of his memory and the extent of his experience, Joe Mynheer was much consulted about the history of boomies, and is responsible for much of the information in this book. He recalled one occasion when three vessels were towed into Yarmouth, which had all once been skippered by Rud Meachen:

When I was mate of the *Active* my uncle Rud was skipper. We anchored in the Wold off Yarmouth with a heavy breeze from the south. Our chain broke before we fetched her up. Me and my uncle got the other anchor down, which brought her up, but she went across the *Sarah Lizzie*. His bowsprit swept our mizzen mast over and his stem cut through our gunwale. The *Sarah Lizzie* was a round-bottomed vessel with a billyboy stern. She had yards on her foremast and was ketch-rigged. We were towed into Yarmouth and the *Brightlingsea* was towed in by the same tug as us. The tug got £80 for the two of us, due to the salvage claimed on vessels and cargoes.

The skippers of the two barges were father and son, as W. B. Meachen had the *Brightlingsea*. At the same time a tug towed in the *Advance*, leaky. Fortunately coal is not a very valuable cargo, or the salvage claim would have been much greater. We were towed to Woodbridge with our coal and without our mizzen, and the shipwright at Woodbridge put a new mast in.

James Meachen's memories went back to the trade to Lisbon. He once had to complete a voyage there after it started with a particularly gruesome incident. Joe Mynheer recalled:

The *Alice Watts* was built for James Meachen; that is, he was to take her. John Watts was the owner. While the *Alice Watts* was building, the *May Queen* was on passage from London to some small port in Spain close to Lisbon with machinery abridge.[2] When Captain Webber got away from London clear of drink he found that although the *May Queen* had a very light draft, eight feet, there wasn't enough water at this little place for his ship. He cut his throat down the cabin in Plymouth Sound. The owner, John Watts,

---

[2]This term is not explained. I presume it refers to loading through the hatch and onto the deck, as was done with the *Problem*.

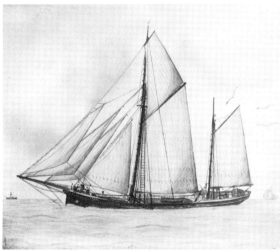

**Pearl.** *(Top)* The last of the Ipswich boomies portrayed by Reuben Chappell, and *(bottom)* George Doughty. *(Roger Finch)*

got my uncle, James Meachen, to go as sailing master and employed a ticketed man to take her across. They laid there and found there wasn't enough water and went to Lisbon to discharge.

Another little tale about Jimmy Meachen illustrates by contrast the intimately domestic scale of most of the boomie voyages, and the extent to which the skipper was indeed the master of his proud little craft.

Once, when the *Alice Watts* was lying in Harwich, James Meachen took his watch to Parsons the jeweller for attention. The voyage was then resumed, but as he sailed out of the harbour Jimmy puzzled as to whether he had suddenly grown stouter. At any rate the watch, rigged with the usual guard chain, felt unaccountable tight across his stomach. Finally the awful truth dawned on him. The *Alice Watts* was put about and sailed back into the harbour for her irate skipper to seek an explanation as to how his gold chain had lost four links!

Another Mynheer yarn from home waters shows the advantage of being a local man in the Deben, and contrasts with the troubles of the skipper of Harvey's *Susie*, ignored by the pilots in the same river, as mentioned in Chapter 12.

When I was in the *Active* we and two other barges, the *Mystery* of Harwich and the *Empress of India*, got into Woodbridge

**Pearl.** *(Top)* As the camera saw her, under way and *(bottom)* in retirement in 1937, when she lay in Ipswich Dock, tended by her skipper-owner Joe Mynheer

Haven and found the river was frozen. The other two barges were bound for the Woodbridge gas company. They had to send for the tug *Robert Owen* to tow them up. She was an old-fashioned paddle tug that belonged to Vaux. Si Keeble was skipper. He had no right to take us in tow but he did and broke the way for the three ice-bound barges, towing all three.

The last on the line got ashore in Troublesome[3] and the tug had to slip him. The second got ashore at Kyson; then he had only us and he had no right to tow us. We were bound for Melton. To make way for the other two barges Keeble towed us above the gas works quay and we managed to scramble into Hart's Dock.

The tug then went back to collect the other two barges. As we could not get up to Melton and customers had to be supplied, coal was taken out as customers wanted it. Keeble made no charge.

[3]Many rivers have an awkward reach called Troublesome. For the location of this in the Deben, and also of Kyson, see Arnott: *Suffolk Estuary.* Hart's Dock was also called Lime Kiln Quay.

On 17 November 1880, after a gale of wind, the *Lothair* was found ashore at Winterton with her bow damaged. There was no sign of life aboard, save a black retriever dog. The crew of five were all lost. It was assumed she had been in collision, and the crew took to the boat. The men came from Pin Mill, and the news caused much gloom there. The *Lothair* was got off and towed into Lynn. Thirty years later, soon after the War, she was wrecked entering Harwich. The skipper had not been in for many years and mistook the Beach End and the Rolling Ground buoys. When he discovered he was on a lee shore he let go his anchor but it was too late. She was loaded with stone and knocked her bottom out on the Andrews.

Captain Herbert Meachen recalled:

My father was in the same breeze of wind in the *Alice Watts*, as when the *Jabez* was lost and the *Lothair* had her crew washed out of her. I was a boy at school at the time. The *Ornate* was the first barge out of the Humber. There were about 200 sailing vessels with her. It came a dead calm and an awful swell made them all bump into each other. They were all on top of one another and couldn't get their heads the right way. Then the gale came up. The *Ornate* got clear and so did the *Alice Watts*. My father said he could hear people crying for help all that night, but couldn't do anything. He nearly capsized himself. He dursn't lower anything; if he had tried his sails would have been blown to ribbons. It depended which tack the vessel was on when the wind struck her. A barge light won't came round in a heavy sea.

Those vessels which had their heads the right way were all right, the others went ashore. Some tried to run into the Humber. *Jabez* run into Withernsea Pier and all her crew got drowned. The inhabitants of St Leonard's cottages near Hythe Quay at Colchester were nearly all widows. Aboard *Lothair* nothing was ever found more than a dog and a man's hat. The skipper was Captain Taylor of Trimley. They don't know what become of the crew or whether they took to the boat or not.

Joe Mynheer recalled another occasion when the prudent skipper got an offing and the unlucky one paid for lack of sea room:

I forget who had the *Warwick Castle,* built for Walker and Howard and Co. She had teak planks for the Tyne. I was in the *Pearl*, light. We were anchored in Bridlington Bay, summertime. The wind came in from the sea south-easterly. We got our anchor and went on our way. When we opened Flamborough Head we had a wonderful sea coming in east-north-east. I didn't like that so kept off the land as far as the wind would take me. He kept down along the land. The wind died away to a dead calm and the sea knocked him in under Speeding Cliff and she became a total wreck. I had a long way to go to knock me in. A gale came in at ten o'clock. We run back to Bridlington Bay. I sailed past Flamborough Head at daylight and sailed through his timber. I saw the sails of the *Warwick Castle* white against the cliff. The skipper rowed his boat to Filey before the gale came.

131

CHAPTER 19

# The Coal Trade

Nothing emphasizes more clearly the importance of the coal trade to the profitability of the big barges than turning the faded pages of an owner's account book. Scanning the surviving cargo-books, laboriously completed at the end of each voyage by the skipper (as ordained by the Board of Trade), confirms the fact. Coal from Tees and Wear, from the Tyne, from Keadby, Goole and farther down the Humber at Grimsby, from Saundersfoot and Cardiff to the west, all regularly figure in the records. Coal was carried all round the coast and across the Channel by boomies from their first emergence as a type. As early as 1866 the Ipswich *Quintus* foundered off Sandgate, loaded with Tyne coal, and the trade continued to drown bargemen and wreck barges until the end. The *John Ward, Earnest, Reindeer* (of Ipswich), *Brightlingsea, Gloriana, Trim, Pioneer* (of Maldon) were all lost on the coal coast, and the *Friendship*, under 'Britisher' Lambert, was run down, coal-loaded, off Spurn Head.

A cargo of coal from the Tyne delivered to Cromarty by the *Alice Watts* in 1878 probably represents the northern limit of the coal trade for cargoes from the North-East coal ports. Par in Cornwall was the most westerly port of delivery. But Sunderland, Hartlepool and the Tyne were not the only source of black diamonds. Rounding Start Point, on the South Devon coast, a boomie, decks awash with Wallsend house-coals, might well hail a ketch barge loaded down with Welsh anthracite, bound up-Channel towards an Essex maltings on the Stour. The trade provided cargoes until the end of the era of the boomie barge. The last voyages made by the boomies were with coal from the Humber; the *Sussex Belle* was lost in 1927, bound from Keadby with coal for Orford,

the *Harold* the next year, and as late as 1939 Everard's *Martinet* was still delivering gas-coal to Margate.

The great majority of the portraits of the boomies which decorate these pages were painted while their skippers waited for their turn to load beneath the wooden coal drops. J. Fannen worked at Newcastle, and Reuben Chappell first at the inland coal-port of Goole on the Humber and later at Par. One must feel that even allowing for the great change in values the five shillings or so they charged for their work was well spent.

Even if the five shillings paid for a painting represented a great deal of heavy work on deck and aloft, it could be spent with the knowledge that coal work, if not particularly well paid, was at least regular, and a skipper could find profit in freighting his own ketch and selling the cargo for himself. As a single commodity coal outnumbers all other cargoes, even such stand-bys as timber, cement and stone. It would not be inaccurate to state that taken together at least one-third of all the paying voyages made by the big barges were in the coal trade.

A coal cargo — earning between five shillings and eight and sixpence a ton, a sum carefully calculated on how far down-Channel it was to be delivered, the difficulty of entering the port, and the amount of unavoidable expenses involved — underpinned the profitability of a ketch barge. It enabled her owners to secure a steady 10 to 12 per cent return upon their investment until the beginning of the First World War. The rate for coal cargoes dipped during the 1880s and then recovered to maintain a steady level, only slightly eroded by inflation. The long-delayed enforcement of load-line regulations in 1887 had the

Colchester gasworks colliers on the Tyne, believed to
be **Gloriana, Startled Fawn, Alice Watts, Antelope** and
**Hesper**

effect of reducing the paying capacity of some
sailing coasters, and affected profits to a small
degree. Then for a short time, after 1917, the
intensifying war at sea produced astronomically
inflated freight rates. But when peace returned in
1918 a new world arrived which soon proved it no
longer held a place for the sailing coaster.

By the time the bigger boomies began to prolifer-
ate, steam had proved triumphant in capturing
the vast coal trade to the metropolis. Although as
late as 1863 only a quarter of the sea-borne coal
delivered to London arrived by screw collier, ten
years later the position was reversed, and
shipping-owners of the North East coal-ports and
elsewhere were disposing of sail tonnage as fast as
they could. The *Gloriana* took coals from Hartlepool to London in 1876, but it was one of the last
freights delivered there by a boomie. Nevertheless, at the smaller ports all down the east and
south coasts, for half a century or more after the
arrival of the steam collier, sail still could survive.
With a smaller crew, if only by one seaman less

than the brigs and brigantines, and with a simpler
sail plan to provide and maintain, a balance
between economy and seaworthiness could be
struck which enabled a trading profit to be made
in the traditional way.

A merchant with a quayside business, such as
Beaumont at Ipswich or Middleton of Harwich,
could still profitably hold shares, together with
the skipper, the ships' chandler and the ships'
biscuit-baker, in a small sailing vessel spending
much of her time in the coal trade. In contrast to
the older schooners and brigs, there was no
ballast to buy and load before she even left the
river, and then discharge, while the building price
was about two-thirds the cost of a round-
bottomed craft. The merchant at a small port was
traditionally used to financing the two hundred
tons or so that the older brigs and schooners
brought to his quay, and he was disinclined to
extend his financial commitment beyond this
point. The high running and overhead expenses
of a steamer demanded that the merchant must
accept some three times that amount of cargo,
pay for it and then store it on his relatively small
quay.

In addition to this the steamer was anxious to

be gone, to be at sea for another paying cargo long before the primitive discharging arrangements available at the time could cope with such an influx. A charter survives for the *Emily Lloyd*, dated November 1899, for a coal voyage from Sunderland to Rye for which the ship was fixed at 8s. 6d. per ton. Without engineers to pay or expensive machinery to keep in employment, she could afford to stipulate that a minimum of only thirty-four tons were required to be discharged each working day, permitting a leisurely weighing and bagging of each hundredweight as it emerged, in the traditional bushel basket, from the grimy hold. Even the collier brigs of the early nineteenth century were expected to whip out their cargoes at the daily rate of eighty tons.

The owners of the gasworks were not so limited in their financial arrangements, but in many towns along the east and south coast the industry had been established several decades before the arrival of the railway, and was naturally sited on a tidal quay. The wrench required to realign them with the iron road was never made, and they continued to use sea-borne coals. The same applied to the older breweries and maltings — both consumers of coal and producing products that could be water-borne, sometimes in the same bottom that delivered their fuel.

Even if rail-borne coal from the nearer Midland pits could be purchased at a marginally cheaper price, its trans-shipment meant that delivery by water was more convenient. King's Lynn had its own coal hoists where Midland coal was tipped into colliers, sail and steam, for coastal delivery. Even after the heyday of the boomies several Thames estuary ports took coal from spritsail barges, cargoes which were loaded at Limehouse from a hoist supplied by rail.

Not only was there a reluctance among coal factors along the English coast to change long-established patterns of trade; on the north Normandy coast half a dozen small ports continued to import Tyne and Wear coal as they had done since medieval times. Fécamp, Saint-Valéry, and, after a long tow up the Seine, Rouen, all saw boomies discharging coal. The *Eliza H* was lost bound towards Saint-Valéry and the *Garibaldi* off Saint-Malo.

Another coal voyage was the one to the westward. Saundersfoot today is a small, forsaken Pembrokeshire harbour on the western shore of Carmarthen Bay. Although by 1830 the port had achieved a substantial stone pier, it remained a drying harbour, serving an agricultural area, ill suited to large vessels. A decade later the exploitation of rich anthracite seams near by

crammed the bay with little brigs and sloops from as far afield as the East Coast waiting their turn to load at the wharves, while a shipyard had been established to repair craft and build ketches and schooners. The cargoes were delivered along tramways which linked the mines to the harbour and the wooden funnels down which the anthracite was shot, built on to the specially constructed timber wharves.

Anthracite was always in demand by maltsters on East Anglian estuaries and along the Thames to fuel their drying kilns, and they found Saundersfoot a convenient source. As congestion grew, the mushrooming South Wales coal-ports became increasingly contemptuous of the demands of small wooden coasters, which were forced to look elsewhere for cargoes. The less favoured harbour of Saundersfoot remained available to them. Small, and with relatively primitive loading facilities beside mud berths which dried out at low water, it was shunned by steamers anxious for a rapid turn-round. Nevertheless, it was acceptable to the survivors from the slower-moving economy, and especially favourable for the boomies.

*Justice*, *Goldfinch*, *Thalatta*, *Record Reign* and *Eliza H*, among many others, loaded fuel at Saundersfoot for the maltings at Snape, Faversham and Mistley, facing the dangers of 'rounding the land' and then the long slog up-Channel. Fortunately, the malting season commenced in early autumn, and maltsters and brewers accumulated stocks before the equinoctial gales set in. On one occasion the *Active* and *Alice Watts* both completed loading at Saundersfoot on the same day. The *Active* was not long new off Vaux's Harwich shipyard, and had carried a valuable cargo of artificial fertilizer from Ipswich to Drogheda, and then fixed a freight of Welsh anthracite. Confident of his new command, her skipper offered Jimmy Meachen of the *Alice Watts* a wager on the result of a race back, for both were bound for Harwich. Unfortunately, the duration of the voyage is not recorded, but the *Active* reached the Sunk light-vessel ahead of her rival, only to be becalmed, with the *Alice Watts* five miles astern. Determined to make port first, the *Active* took the paddle tug *Harwich* into the harbour, where the crew learnt that under cover of darkness the *Alice Watts* had slipped in and had already delivered her cargo at Mistley maltings.

Others making the long haul to the Severn Sea were less lucky. Of the generation before the boomies the little 48-foot round-bottomed ketch *Halcyon* of Ipswich was lost off Saundersfoot in 1862.

An outlet for the mines of the Great Northern Coalfield on the North-East coast, Seaham Harbour may be compared to Saundersfoot, for it provided a haven for the boomies and other small sailing vessels as they were gradually elbowed out of the coal-ports on the Tyne and the Tees by steamers. There was hardly one which did not inscribe 'Coals, Seaham Harbour' in its cargo book at some time. Although Saundersfoot shipped out its last cargo in 1930 Seaham Harbour is still available for coasters, while its antique coal drop (beneath which scores of ketch barges had loaded) became literally a museum-piece at Beamish, County Durham.

The coal-ports were not only the providers of a staple cargo; they conveniently imported scrap-iron and teak for shipbuilding while sometimes a cargo of grain could be fixed for the millers of Newcastle. Explosives for the mines were occasionally sent from Gravesend and Oare in North Kent by ketch barges, for the PLA did not permit powered vessels to load such a potentially dangerous cargo. With explosives aboard, no fires were allowed below, and a boomie without a galley on deck rigged an iron stove against the forward rail. Despite the legendary Geordie thirst, malt for brewing was rarely dispatched there. Three or four successive coal cargoes in the hold were a deterrent to a merchant entrusting a valuable commodity such as malt that was easily contaminated. Newly launched tonnage, unless expressly built for the coal trade, avoided it for as long as possible, but eventually all succumbed.

CHAPTER 20

# The Collier's Life

While the skippers and mates of boomies in the coal trade were men who by long and hard-won experience, often motivated by a financial involvement in their command, could cope successfully with all but the most overwhelming emergency at sea, the same could not always be said of the crews. They, poor fellows, 'went to sea for the grub and earned their money working the cargo'. Most were drawn from a group who, lacking any skill with which to bargain for any better employment, knew that a berth in a boomie barge in the coal trade would at least provide a stove around which to warm themselves when off watch, a cot in which to lay their 'donkey's breakfasts' (as their straw mattress was called) and food which, even if meagre, was better than workhouse skilly. They provided the muscle power to wind out the cargo on the donkey winch, bring up the anchor and set the sails. In return they received a livelihood scarcely above subsistence level.

When Captain George Mynheer temporarily left the coasting trade in the *Eliza Patience* and *Pearl* to go into steam he could do nothing better than secure a position as an able seaman on the railway steam boats. What chance was there then for the deck-hand of improving his lot, unless, of course, he was the son or nephew of a skipper showing his worth at sea? This meant that in a crisis, especially in the dark days of winter — and working the coast under sail in a vessel built and maintained on the edge of economic survival, life was a series of crises — the whole crew could not always bring to bear the instinctive skill that the situation required. Indeed, if contemporary accounts are to be believed, they hindered those who could.

But if the fo'c'sle hands sometimes lacked professionalism they were only one of the many factors that made the skipper's life a demanding one. To the casual viewer, a blue back chart labelled 'North East Coal Trade' seems to offer numerous places of refuge from contrary winds and sudden gales. This is far from the truth. Going north, once Harwich harbour was left astern (where a knowing skipper could anchor between the Guard buoy and the end of the pier, and so avoid harbour dues) there was nowhere to provide real shelter before the Humber was reached. Yarmouth Roads provided some shelter

At Bridport, considered one of the worst harbours to 'take' down-Channel. An unidentified ketch barge is discharging with cargo derrick. Note unusually long quarterboard *(From a postcard dated 1912.)*

inside the Scroby Sands, but this was only limited protection, as the *Sussex Belle* and the *Britannia* among others found to their cost. The Wash, with its sands, could prove a death-trap, and even the Humber, with the protection of Spurn Head from northerly gales, had prodigious tides and fleets of blundering steam trawlers entering and leaving. Farther north of the Spurn, Bridlington Bay was known as the 'Bay of Safety'. The bay and the off-lying Smithic Sands give shelter, except from gales from the south-east, when it becomes a dangerous lee shore. The harbour of Whitby which saw the dramatic end of the *Star* of Colchester (described in Chapter 10) was scarcely a satisfactory bolt-hole, and the Tyne bar held its own terrors. Small wonder that, particularly in winter, a boomie skipper's coal voyage was a series of undignified scurries from one precarious refuge to another.

Once a place in the tiers of waiting sailing-ships was secured, a further struggle, but of a different kind, awaited the skipper of a small coaster. To get a berth beneath the coal-drops required diplomacy, sometimes assisted by outright bribery, combined with opportunism. Steamers had priority, and forced sailormen to the end of the queue. Membership by some skippers and owners of the Masonic brotherhood, indicated by ketches named *Corinthian*, *Boaz*, *Mystery* and *Masonic*, was no guarantee of a barge securing its proper place when its time came.

Captain Porter also recalled how in the *Mystery* he was waiting for coal at a staithe in Sunderland about 1910 when his mate suddenly said, 'Here comes your coal.'

I saw three trucks had broken away from the train and were running down the incline [he recalled]. I knew they were not for me as the trucks were too big. The first truck ran over the staithe and fell from a height of twenty or thirty feet over the main boom and deck and into the hold with thirteen tons of coal. The second turned on its side and was caught up on the staithe and this held up the third truck. Fortunately no one was injured, though the bowsprit was broken and the deck was damaged. I wired to Harwich, telling of the damage, and received a wire back saying "Wait for tug." The Board of Trade official inspected me and said I wasn't fit to go to sea. I said a tug was coming to fetch me. So he gave me permission provided no one was aboard and the *Mystery* was towed like a log. So I lashed the helm amidships.

When the tug arrived I was having my dinner. I said, "We had better be off before the inspector arrives again." The tug's skipper said, "Well, a few minutes while you finish your dinner won't matter." However, suddenly the official arrived. He objected that the tug wasn't a seagoing tug. I told him the tug had been going to sea for years. Then' he said, "She hasn't any lifebuoys or a boat." I said, "Well, we can supply her with those from the *Mystery*." At last the official gave his permission to proceed to sea and he left.

We found that the boat took up too much room on the tug so in case the official should see us leave we hid the boat by putting it in the *Mystery's* hold and left hurriedly in case he came back. The *Mystery* swam perfectly behind the tug the whole way to Harwich.

Spectacular accidents such as the one that occurred to the *Mystery* were rare. Usually it was the long wait, tied up in an industrial wasteland, begrimed with coal-dust and constantly on vigil to ensure that their turn to load was not missed, that made nagging difficulties. But eventually — and a wait of weeks was not uncommon — a cargo was shot into the hold, and it was trimmed.

Trimming was part of the crew's work, assisted by a shore-based gang. Here the big hatches of the boomies helped; by working her fore and aft by adjusting the warps some of the drudgery could be avoided. The 'pulled-out' look of the ketch barge's sail-plan, compared with its West Country counterpart, originates from this long main hatch which became progressively longer as the type developed. Nevertheless, shovelling the cascade of coal — ten tons at a time — from the drop's spout into the wings (as the space beneath the sidedecks was called) and the cupboards (as the hold immediately forward of the after bulkhead was known) provided enough exercise to engender a healthy thirst. A good cargo was largely composed of large coals which defied shovelling and had to be manhandled into position. It is interesting to note that in the oldest account books that survive of boomies that worked in the trade their cargo is still measured in 'keels', rather than tons, although loading coals from these barges, traditional to the Tyne, had ceased decades before.

The long voyage to the north or down from the Tyne sometimes gave the opportunity of a run before a fair wind, a time when the older boomies' squaresails came into their own. Later squaresails were bent on to a yard on deck and then hoisted on the foresail halyards with the foot boomed out to windward. When running before a breeze it might be thought that a barge could stow her mainsail, save the risk of a gybe in a seaway and run comfortably for ever in this fashion. However, it was seldom done. When the time came for it to be prudent to stow the mainsail under these conditions it would be almost impossible to set it again in the event of a change in the direction of the wind, an all too likely event in the North Sea. With a closely reefed mainsail set it might be thoroughly uncomfortable running, but the sails were prepared for heaving to, or for the sheets to be hardened in for working to windward and avoiding a lee shore.

When a boomie crossed Tyne Bar in winter the skipper well knew that the question was not 'Shall we meet a gale?' but 'When will we meet one?' However, the most treacherous time was autumn, when a succession of fine October days, calm with a north-east breeze and a slight swell swirling the coal-dust in the scuppers, would tempt out a fleet of laden sailing-craft. A rapid and unheralded deterioration with a change of wind-direction could find the motley fleet pinned against a lee shore, and no refuge to run to. The cautious skipper of a traditional collier brig would have worked out well to windward. Risking the heavy seas in open water, well reefed down — for his numerous sails could individually each be tackled with comparative ease — he could plug on or heave to under trysail and reefed jib. Rising and falling in the same heavy sea, the flat bottom of a light barge would strike the water and send a ghastly shudder through the whole fabric, and this could even occur in a loaded vessel. Reefing was also less simple. Before reefing the big mainsail a boomie had her topsail, hooped to the topmast, to deal with. Stowing it in a gale must have required all the strength a seaman aloft could muster, for it did not have the heavy dressing of a spritsail barge's topsail to deaden it. It is strange that the Westcountryman's deep-sea method of setting a topsail on a wire jackstay, set up on the deck, was never widely adopted, except in a few cases of barges setting square topsails. Instead skippers adhered to the spritsail barges' traditional method — more suited, one would have thought, to estuary work.

The huge mainsail of the 200-tonners must also have been a handful, particularly before the days of roller reefing (see Chapter 2). There was a tendency for the mizzen to be increased in size, and the mizzen topmast carried by such as the *Europa*, *Stour* and *James Ward* was probably an

attempt to give more canvas to the smaller mast, at the expense of the mainsail, and to even up the size of their respective areas.

From the outbreak of war in 1914 all these difficulties were multiplied by the hazards of unlit

The evolution of the boomie barge in general, and of most individual boomies, usually showed a trend away from traditional elaboration towards simplicity, and the saving of gear and manpower.

**Empress of India** was an exception. The portrait *(top)* shows her as she was originally rigged in 1876, setting only one jib on a sliding bowsprit, and jackyard topsails which probably did not set too well close-hauled. (She also has a chain peak halyard.)

In the later portrait *(bottom)*, probably dating from soon after 1900, she has been given a long standing bowsprit, with a stem knee. Two jibs are set, in addition to a jib-topsail, all diagonal-cut. The topsails are better suited for windward work, and the mainsail has roller reefing. But, surprisingly, she is still tiller steered.

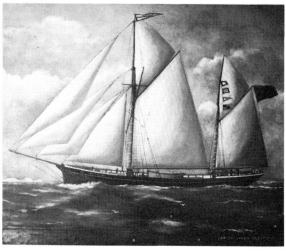

channels and enemy action. Unrestricted submarine warfare against Allied shipping commenced in 1917. Prior to this, while freight rates had risen, many barges had been taken up by the Government, for months at a time, to be used as floating warehouses at Hull and London. Unsuited to this work, the last of the square-rigged colliers — among them the grimy collection of the Whitstable Shipping Company — were laid up, few ever to sail again. However, with an acute shortage of tonnage the smaller and handier ketch barges were found a part to play in the war effort. Not only would their shallow draught assist them in clearing minefields but, it was argued, a U-boat would hardly be prepared to expend a torpedo against such an insignificant target, while it would be disinclined to surface and sink it by gunfire in the closely patrolled waters of the Channel.

Freight rates rose to unprecedented heights. Coal from Hull to the French Channel ports was the most profitable, and for the first time it paid to fit engines as the Dutch had done to their *tjalks* and the Scandinavians to the *jachts* years before. Revived with an engine, the *Laura* was lost on her first voyage, mined off Boulogne with coal, but the *Thalatta*, now an auxiliary, was luckier. Both *Boaz* and *Cock o' the Walk* were casualties, the former being sunk by a submarine off Cap Barfleur. The *Olympia* was also lost in this work.

Details of a round voyage by the *Dannebrog* give some idea of the profits that could be made. She fixed coal from Hull at £8 10s. a ton, with a gratuity of an extra 8s. if delivery could be made by a certain date. The deadline was met, and a cargo of pit props was secured for a return cargo at the rate of £3 10s. per ton on the barge's deadweight tonnage. Captain Wife cleared something like £1300 after settling expenses and paying the crew.

Crews were difficult to find, and for the first time could command an adequate wage. Owners partially met this problem by fitting motor-winches which were used for discharging cargo and anchor-work on an undermanned barge.

The bubble of inflated freight rates burst with the armistice of 1918, although a minor boom continued in cargoes of pitch, desperately needed for the repair of the war-torn roads of the battle area. Now, however, the resources that had been devoted to the development of the diesel engine during wartime inevitably led to its adoption in low-tonnage commercial vessels. A diesel engine required little space and did not need big bunkers for its fuel, neither did it require an engineer or a stoker, yet it could provide a reliable service to merchants, and pushed towing charges from the expense sheet. The motor-coaster had arrived, usually flying the Dutch flag, and such cargoes of coal as it did not deliver the motor-lorry eagerly carried from the nearest station coal-yard.

Unidentified ketch, probably at Tilbury before the First World War. She has old-fashioned point reefing, and a jib-headed topsail hooped to the mast. The sprittie on the left is a reminder that long quarter-boards were not confined to boomies, before continual loading in the London docks made them too vulnerable to damage from swim-headed lighters.

CHAPTER 21

# One Night in the North Sea

Let this record end, not with a tale of heroism or dramatic shipwreck, or a yarn by one of the celebrities of the coasting trade, but with a bleak little picture of an incident such as must have been all too commonplace on the desolate Yorkshire coast in the distant days of ill-found ships and inexpert sailors.

No account of a little scene of confusion and tragedy in the North Sea a century ago can be more vividly authentic than the skipper's own detailed memory, written down immediately afterwards. Such a record remains of the fatal collision between the schooner *Fanny* of Colchester and the Maldon ketch barge *Triumph*[1] off Scarborough in February 1873.

The two craft were both bound for the North. The *Fanny* had sailed with a crew of six, three-quarters loaded with 120 tons of chalk from Greenhithe, for Newcastle, while the *Triumph* was light from Burnham to Sunderland with four hands. Both had been over a week on the passage when they found themselves in close company off the Yorkshire coast.

It was a February night, with a strong wind from the north-west, and a heavy sea. The *Fanny* had her topsail, single-reefed mainsail, jib, square foresail and forestaysail.[2] She was on the starboard tack, six or seven miles off Scarborough, when she saw the *Triumph's* green light away to port. The mate called to Captain Martin Mann, 'Come and look up here.' In the moonlight they picked out the ketch and saw her lower her mizzen peak. 'She's going to bear away,' said the skipper.

Then the main peak slacked down and the mainsheet was eased off. When she was 400 yards away they glimpsed her red light — sign that she should go clear. But she would not bear away. Her helm hard up, she sheered along the *Fanny's* port side, striking her bow and knocking off her jibboom. The *Triumph's* bowsprit and crosstrees were also broken.

Aboard the *Fanny* they could do nothing but put the helm down in an attempt to ease the blow. Water began pouring in through the battered bow.

'We'd better make a jump,' said Mann, but as

[1]The *Triumph* was built at Stow Creek, Burnham, Essex, in 1842, an early date for a ketch barge. Her small size (68 feet long) and square stern make it possible she was originally a sloop or a sprittie. She was owned for the first thirty years of her life by Benjamin Cackett of Hullbridge, who seems to have been her owner at the time of the collision. Three months after the inquiry, on 9 June 1874, she was sold by order of the High Court of Admiralty (suggesting the likelihood of civil proceedings) to William Mills of Colchester, who died the same year. She then reverted to the port of Maldon, having several owners, including William Green of Stow Maries, skipper and part-owner of the *Trim* and part-owner and occasional skipper of Smith's *Dauntless*. In 1886 she was sold to Augustus Hughes of Mark Lane, and though her registry states she was broken up she was in fact rebuilt at Greenwich in 1887 as the sprittie *Coombdale*, No 101906, owned by Edmund Hughes of the London and Tilbury Lighterage Company.

In 1906 *Coombdale* sank off Woolwich dockyard after a collision with *ss Player*, but was raised and later passed into Theobald's ownership. In 1919 she was surprisingly owned in Dundee, where she was managed by Alexander Reid, though her port of registry remained in London, but by the 1930s she was back in home waters, owned by the Brice family. She finally ended her days on Cliffe Marshes — so what remained of the original *Triumph* was then over a century old.

Captain Martin Mann, skipper of the *Fanny*, was doubtless a relative of John Mann, the Colchester shipbuilder, but I have found no records of this interesting family.

[2]The contemporary report in the *Essex Standard*, 13 March 1874 says Foretrysail, which I take for an error.

Winter's toll: the end of many an East Coast voyage
An unidentified wreck, believed to be at Shingle Street,
Suffolk. The stowed sails and raised leeboard suggest
the barge drove ashore lying at anchor, caught in a
bitter easterly. *(Suffolk Photo Survey)*.

the four hands on deck scrambled aboard the
*Triumph* he remembered that the boy, his cousin,
was asleep below in the cabin. He leapt back for
him and at that moment the two ships broke away
from each other. 'We shall have to get your boat
out', the *Fanny's* mate told the *Triumph's* skipper, but his reply was, 'It's no use. It's too
shallow.' The *Fanny's* boat was equally useless.
'She had had a nip,' said the mate, 'which made a
hole in her side. Also she had a hole in her
bottom, patched with zinc.'

So the *Triumph* set off into Bridlington Bay
with the *Fanny* following, or so they hoped and
thought. Her lights at least were good, burning
bright with the best colza oil. But presently they
were no more to be seen.

This story was told to an inquiry held in
Colchester Town Hall, with the mayor and
deputy mayor acting as Justices appointed by the
Board of Trade, assisted by Captains White, RN,
and Sceales, as nautical assessors. What their

worships made of it one wonders, and more
importantly how much understanding had those
four-ring captains for conditions aboard a little ill-
found coaster on such a night?

Captain White was insistent, despite the evidence, that the *Triumph* must have been sailing
fast to have sunk the *Fanny,* but the whole picture
is of a craft so checked by a lumpy sea that she
had not sufficient steerage way to answer her
helm. If he had asked why they did not give her a
bit of leeboard to make her pay away we would
have more respect for his authority!

When the skipper of the *Triumph,* James Bryant,
came to be examined, he first told his story by
word of mouth, mentioning that the *Triumph* was
always unhandy light, and that they had the port
leeboard up, and had also picked up the other
before they saw the schooner's light. Then he
handed in his written evidence. Here it is, only a
little condensed:

At 30 past 3 a.m. heard the mate say lower
the mizzen peak; captain looked up to see
the cause; saw a red light on our starboard
bow about four hundred yards distant; Cap-

141

tain immediately jumped on deck; let go the main sheet and help the mate shove the helm up to port; mate let go the helm to let go the mizzen sheet; by that time we came into collision with the *Fanny* of Colchester, striking her with our stem and starboard bow on the port bow; knocking the *Fanny* onto port tack; blowing very stiff; *Fanny* fell alongside; by that time four of the crew of the *Fanny* jumped on board the *Triumph*; the *Fanny* struck very heavy but only once; she then came under our stern and squared before the wind for a time; the bowsprit carried away; halyard hook broke aloft, could not get the jib down, had to strap it into the rigging; square-sail yard broke, the gear flying about in all directions; helm hard aport, would not go off no further than SE; the *Fanny,* as far as I could see, away from our lee rigging; running tackle broke; the mate then came aft and said he had cleared away for'd, all but the bowsprit; he said he could not get it in; I said "You must"; the mate said "Somebody else must come"; I said "There is seven of you"; then went and got it in; we then lowered the mainsail partly down; got the *Triumph* before the wind; gave orders to truss the mainsail up; truss pendant broke by misfortune; we gybed onto starboard tack; had the *Fanny* on our port bow; heavy sea running; we then gybed again onto port tack; knocked the compass binnacle out; put the light out; called the boy to see after it; sky overcast; captain could not see where he was going as the mainsail was so low; broached to a bit; saw the *Fanny* abaft the leach of the mainsail; hard aport again; I then turned my head — saw the *Fanny's* green light; I then said "The *Fanny* is hove-to"; we then lowered the stay foresail; pulled the mainsail up; pinned in the mainsheet; we then headed east; *Fanny* bore WNW about one-third of a mile; there then came on a hailstorm; we lost sight of Scarborough light; lost sight of

*Fanny's* lights about ten minutes; afterwards saw Scarborough lights; no more see *Fanny's* lights; we then judged to be about 5 a.m.; we then kept hove-to; about 6 a.m. lower masthead cap gave way, expecting to see the mast come down; we laid till 30 past 6; then bore up for bay as one and all said "If the *Fanny* is survived she must be gone into the bay", but sad to relate no *Fanny* was to be seen; landed the crew, four in number, at Bridlington quay by the *Triumph's* boat.

It is a graphic picture of a scene from which nobody except poor Captain Mann emerges with much credit, and inevitably the inquiry ruled:

> The *Triumph* was wholly in default and the mate, who appears to be an inefficient seaman, is to blame for it, not having kept a proper lookout. There was not sufficient effort to save the lives of the captain and boy left aboard the *Fanny;* that James Bryant's certificate be suspended for six months; that the owners of the *Fanny* knew the unserviceable state of the ship's boat and that the boat of the *Triumph* appears to have been fit only for river purposes.

Apart from reflecting that the owners got off remarkably lightly — which was perhaps according to the custom of the age — and that the high-ranking officers showed scant courtesy and consideration towards mariners in humbler callings — which has always been the custom up to and including the present time — one is left to wonder what a certificated master was doing in charge of a ketch barge. Presumably times were hard and he could not find any grander command. But in that case what difference did the suspension make to him? Poor old boy, I hope it made none at all, and that he was never again caught on the port tack, for he sounds an honest man; indeed, the honesty of his testimony may well have been his undoing.

# APPENDIX 1
# The Big-barge Fleet

This summary lists the boomies, from sloops to square-riggers, of which we are aware, and includes a number of entries and details contributed by Peter Ferguson. It does not aim to include all the material in the preceding chapters, but rather to summarize salient points and add some factual details omitted from the main text. More detail concerning the builders mentioned will be found in Appendix 2.

The 'near relations' of the boomie — notably billyboys, some round-bilged ketches, and Dutch-built 'klippers' — have been excluded, even when they were fitted with leeboards. References to them are noted in the index of ships' names.

Tonnages are as far as possible registered, but references are sometimes loose, and in some cases nett tonnages have probably been quoted. Moreover, many boomies were registered on several occasions and given different tonnages, sometimes (thought not always) with a view to obtaining a reduction. This figure should therefore be treated as a rough guide to size.

The dimensions quoted are length in feet (between perpendiculars; that is, between the points where the outer edges of stem- and stern-posts meet the water); and depth (from a point under the deck amidships to a point directly beneath, alongside the keelson). These dimensions also vary surprisingly as measured for different registrations, and there are discrepancies, particularly as to rig and ownership, between the *Mercantile Navy List* (the prime source), *Lloyd's Registers* and the shipping registers at the Custom Houses. It seems that boomies converted, for example, from schooner or dandy to ketch did not always have the alteration recorded for the *Mercantile Navy List*.

Ownerships are quoted from *Mercantile Navy Lists* which happen to be in our and Peter Ferguson's possession (chiefly 1881, 1890, 1893, 1919 and 1934); *Lloyd's Registers* have also been consulted where possible, though only a minority of boomies were built to Lloyd's classification. 'M.o.' indicates managing owner. Official registry numbers are quoted where available. Where rig is not specified assume ketch.

Descriptions in quotation marks are mostly the comments noted and taken down by the late Dr J. Groom of Harwich, or sometimes details from *Lloyd's Registers*. In a few cases where contradictory records exist the alternative versions are included.

**ACTIVE of Harwich    744380**
Built by Vaux at Harwich, 1877. 97 tons. Owned by R. Lewis, skippered by 'Rud' Meachen. Sister to same owner's *Sylph*. Run down and sunk off Beachy Head, June 1888 (Deptford to Plymouth, Government stores). Crew landed at Brixham.

**ADA of London    657190**
Built at Ipswich, 1872. Owned (1881 and 1890) by W. B. Fisher, Greenwich, and (1894) by J. Scovell, Hampshire.

**ADA of Portsmouth    68565**
Built by J. T. Crampton at Landport, 1873. 77 x 19 x 7, 68 tons. Four years A1 at Lloyd's. Owned (1873 and 1890) by builder.

**ADA of Rochester    67032**
Built by E. Gill at Rochester, 1872. 68 tons. Owned (1890) by builder.

**ADA GANE of Harwich    84033**
Built by Vaux at Harwich, 1882. 96 x 22.4 x 8.4, 110 tons. Built for W. S. Gane, and named after his grand-daughter. For many years commanded by Captain Day, formerly of the *Stour,* with his son as mate, working coal to the Channel ports. On his retirement at the age of seventy-five after the First World War, sold to Fred Crundall of Dover, and renamed *Askoy*. After being used as a towed lighter, sold to Faversham and re-rigged as a yacht under the name *Leigh Hall*.

**ADSEY of Faversham    47864**
Built by Taylor at Sittingbourne, 1863. 64 tons. Owned by Charles Wood of Milton and (1881 and 1890) by W. J. Mitchell, London.

**ADVANCE of London**
Built at Limehouse, 1854. 101 tons. Nine years A1 at Lloyd's. Owned by Fox and Sons, London. The first recorded flat-bottomed schooner. Owned (1872) by J. Fox, Limehouse. Out of register by 1881.

**AGNES**
Built by Shrubsall at Sittingbourne, 1874. 109 tons, loading 200 tons.

Schooner. Run down, January 1878.

**AGNES AND CONSTANCE of Rochester    97711**
Built by Curel at Frindsbury, 1889. 66 tons. Owned by James Little, Strood, Kent, and (1919) by J. T. Rayfield, Gravesend, and (1934, as sprittie) by J. Francis, Colchester.

**ALCYONE of Harwich    84038**
Built by Vaux at Harwich, 1884. 95 x 22.5 x 8.2, 108 tons. Owned by Hempson and Dale of Shotley. Sold to London 1905. Out of register by 1919. Broken up 1928. Usually known as the *Elsie Owen*.

**ALERT of Ipswich    95305**
Built at Ipswich, 1888. 95.8 x 20.4 x 7, 85 tons. Owned (1890) by W. Bayley, jun., Ipswich and (1894) by Alfred Bayley (managing owner, A. S. More, Leadenhall Street). Out of register 1923.

**ALEXANDRA of Poole    95655**
Built by J. Allen & Co at Poole, 1891. 85 x 20.2 x 8.3, 86 tons. Owned by F. Griffin, Salisbury, and later by F. Nicholls, Whitstable. The last boomie at Whitstable after the loss of *Malvoisin* in 1929.

**ALICE of London (later of Manchester)    73695**
Built by Holman at Topsham, 1876. 61 tons. Built as sprittie. Converted to ketch and owned (1881 and 1893) by W. Bushell, Dover. By 1919 registered at Manchester, owned by Alfred Bowen. Out of register by 1934.

**ALICE MAY of Ipswich    109205**
Built by McLearon at Harwich, 1899. Named after wife and daughter of R. J. Smith of Felixstowe, first owner. Owned (1934), as mulie by R. & W. Paul, Ipswich. Still afloat.

**ALICE WATTS of Harwich    672640**
Built by Robertson at Ipswich, 1875. 100 x 24 x 8, 119 tons. Schooner with figurehead, and the first boomie to be built with a

wheel. Owned (1881) by J. Watts, Harwich. A regular collier to Colchester gasworks, owned by her skipper James Meachen. Managing owner (1919) F. Crundall, Dover. In 1920s owned by Anderson of Whitstable, and finally by Whitstable Shipping Co. After being laid up at Whitstable for some years, towed to Deptford for breaking up.

**ALPHA of Faversham    528910**
Built by R. M. Shrubsall at Milton, 1865. 137 tons, loading 280 tons. Three-masted schooner for S. Court at Milton. Owned (1893) by E. Goldfinch, Whitstable. Lost February 1897, H. Sandy master.

**ALPHA of Ipswich    22184**
Built by W. Bayley at Ipswich, 1858. 80.5 x 19.1 x 6. Tuck stern barge. Stranded and lost 1878.

**AMAZON of Harwich**
Built at Brightlingsea, 1856. 67 tons. Boomsail. Owned by Luke Richmond, Harwich. Out of register by 1881.

**AMY of Harwich    67258**
Built at Harwich by Parsons & Cann, 1873. 98 tons. The first boomie by these builders. Round stern. Owned (1881) by G. Cann, Harwich, and (1890) by J. Godfrey, Plashet, Essex. Sunk near Spurn Head 1897. Crew saved by lifeboat.

**ANN GOODHUGH of Faversham    60243**
Built by Goldfinch at Faversham, 1872. 82.5 x 21 x 6. Built partly of old timber for W. G. Dawson & Co, Faversham. Last in register, 1879.

**ANNIE of Littlehampton    75232**
Built by Harvey at Littlehampton, 1877. 64 tons. Owned by builders. Run down off Dover by French mail steamer *Pas de Calais*, 1901.

**ANNIE FLORENCE of Portsmouth (later of Faversham)    76908**
Built at Emsworth, 1878. 96.5 x 23.1 x 8.7, 130 tons. Brigantine, ketch-rigged in 1881. Owned (1881) by J. T. Crampton,

Portsmouth and (1893) by S. Payn, Faversham. Out of register by 1919.

**ANTELOPE of Harwich    56435**
Built by Aldous, Brightlingsea, 1869. 100 x 23.2 x 8, 116 tons. Colchester gasworks collier noted for speed. Owned (1881) by W. T. Griffiths, Ipswich, and (1890) by L. Richmond, Dovercourt. Sold to C. V. Hardy at Hull after being ashore on Yorkshire coast. Then (about 1909) sold to Denaby and Cadeby Collieries. Managing owner (1919) A. Westcott, Plymouth. Register closed November 1929.

**ARUNDEL CASTLE of London    95491**
Built at Clymping, 1888. 100.5 x 23.5 x 8.5, 135 tons. Oak frames, pitch pine and elm planking. Owned (1891) by T. Howard, London. Under Walter Ward loaded stack of timber from Christiania and was hove-to with it for three days off the Dogger. Between 1890 and 1893 foundered off the Casquets in fine weather, having laid in a bad berth. Sank in ten minutes. Crew got in boat, cut gripes and floated off hatch.

**ATHOLE of Shoreham    97783**
Built by Harvey at Littlehampton, 1892, 128 tons. Square topsails. Owned (1893) by Gates of Shoreham, and (1910) by F. Lennard. Out of register by 1919.

**AZARIAH of Ipswich    79054**
Built by W. Bayley at Ipswich, 1878. 79.7 x 17.9 x 6.3, 64 tons. Owned by Robert Peck and (1918 and 1938) by C. J. Butler, Ipswich. Converted to sprittie.

**BELMONT of Faversham    104933**
Built by Whitstable Shipping Company at Whitstable, 1895. 104 x 24.1 x 9.6, 149 tons. No leeboards. Modification of *Zebrina*, but found too heavy to work with this rig. Sold and converted to three-masted lighter. Owned (1919) by Herbert Payne, London. By 1934 registered at Portsmouth as *Camber*, owned by Fraser and White. Hulked at

Velder Creek, Portsmouth.

**BESSIE HILLER of Faversham    80519**
Built by Goldfinch at Faversham, 1881. 80 tons. Named after Bessie Hiller Thomas, daughter of her owner, William Goodhugh Dawson. Lost November 1893. Had not complied with surveyor's requirements, so Harwich Barge Alliance refused claim, and rejected private subscription.

**BIRTHDAY of London    81547**
Built at Charlton, 1879. 65 tons. Owned (1881) by G. A. Rooke, Bermondsey, and (1890 to 1910) by J. L. Strood. Out of register by 1919.

**BLANCHE of Ipswich    86622**
Built by Bayley at Ipswich, 1884. 82.6 x 19.4 x 6.6, 68 tons. Owned (1890) by Edward Garnham, Chelmondiston. Converted to sprittie, and owned (1910) by F. Smith and (1921) by Nimrod Ltd, London, and (1919) by J. Carter, Surbiton, and (1933) by Peters, Southend. Out of register by 1934.

**BOAZ of Ipswich**
Built by Harvey at Littlehampton in 1908. 92 x 22 x 8, 93 tons. Owned (1910) by J. Harvey. Name of Masonic significance. Bought by Wynnfield Shipping Co., Grimsby, 1916. Sunk by German submarine off Cap Barfleur, 31 March 1917.

**BOLHAM of Poole (later of Chester)**
See *Sarah Colebrooke*.

**BONA of Ipswich    10923**
Built by Harvey at Littlehampton, 1898. 79 tons. Owned by F. B. Garnham of Chelmondiston. Lost on Prawle Point, August 1908. Crew reached Dartmouth in own boat.

**BRIGHTLINGSEA of Harwich    56434**
Built by Aldous at Brightlingsea, 1869. 99 tons. Round-sterned dandy setting square topsail. Owned by John Watts of Harwich, and later by Rudrum Meachen, Harwich, who was succeeded as

skipper by his nephew, H. Meachen. He lost her on the Leman and Owers Sand off Cromer, bound from the North with coal, 30 October 1891. Crew saved by Caister lifeboat.

**BRILLIANT of Portsmouth    81020**
Built by J. T. Crampton at Landport, Hants, and owned by him. 49 tons. Sister to *Sapphire*. Out of register by 1890.

**BRITANNIA of Harwich    99451**
Built by Vaux at Harwich, 1893. 86.3 x 20.3 x 6.5, 70 tons. Owned by Robert Lewis, and (1910) by R. L. Gooch and by J. Sparrow, Bristol Arms, Shotley, and later by Ned Goodman (skipper) and his son (mate). Rebuilt at Ipswich after First World War. Last boomie built by Vaux. Lost at Gorleston about 1930.

**BRITANNIC of London    98198**
Built at Southtown, Suffolk, 1891, 79 tons. Owned in Brightlingsea by (1897 to 1910) William Pannell and (1902) by Angier. Out of register by 1919.

**BYCULLA of Ipswich    95301**
Built by W. Bayley at Ipswich, 1887. 85 x 20 x 6, 77 tons. Transom stern. Owned by Garnham, Chelmondiston. Lost with all hands 10 September 1903.

**CAMBER of Portsmouth**
See *Belmont*.

**CARISBROOKE CASTLE of London    98104**
Built by Cann at Harwich, 1890. 97.8 x 24.4 x 8.9, 76 tons. Owned by Walker and Howard and (1919) by T. Scholey, Greenwich, and (1927 and 1938) by S. W. Burley, Sittingbourne.

**CARLBURY of Harwich    81161**
Built by Vaux at Harwich, 1879. 97 tons. Owned by J. Brackenbury, Kirby, Essex. Lost 18 October, 1882.

**CARRIE LOUISE of Shoreham    97732**
Built of pitchpine by Stow at

Shoreham, 1890. 86.5 x 21 x 7, 77 tons. Owned by E. J. Reeves of Brighton and by Watson and Gill. Disappeared with crew of six on passage Cherbourg to Rochester, 8 September, 1903. Boat found off Dunkirk.

**CECILIA of London        18295**
Built at Sittingbourne, 1903. 80 tons. Owned (1919) by E. J. and W. Goldsmith, London. Became powder hulk for Woods of Gravesend, renamed *Cecil Wood*. A sprittie by 1919, but had fiddle head and code flags, suggesting boomie origin.

**CLYMPING of Littlehampton        105598**
Built by Harvey at Littlehampton, 1909. 93 x 23.4 x 8.3, 121 tons. Owned (1910) by J. Harvey and (1919) by Wynnfield Shipping Co. and (1927) by C. J. Perkins. Sailed out to British Guiana, 1930, and owned there (1938) by Booker Brothers, London.

**COCK OF THE WALK**
Built by Goldfinch at Faversham, 1882. Apparently lost before registration.

**COCK O' THE WALK of Weymouth        63913**
Built by Hartnell and Surridge at Millwall, 1876. 96.8 x 23 x 8, 100 tons. Owned by Richard Cox of Weymouth, and (1910) by H. Strange. Captain Bloomfield left the *Tertius* to take her new, but she was not a success till Captain Strange moved her mainmast aft and her mizzen forward. Sunk by German action in First World War.

**CORINTHIAN of London        101949**
Built by Beeching at Yarmouth, 1892. 97.5 x 21.3 x 7.9, 94 tons. Owned (1893) by Walker and Howard, also by Garnham of Chelmondiston and (1919) by H. Covington, Battersea. Lost October 1919, on Goodwins. Crew saved by lifeboat.

**CROWPILL of Bridgwater        67254**
Ex-*John Wesley* (qv). Owned (by

1890) by John Sully, Bridgwater, and (1919) by J. Samuel White & Co., Ltd, East Cowes.

**CYLLENE of Harwich        67255**
Built by Parsons and Cann at Harwich, 1873. 98 tons. Owned (1880) by R. S. Barnes, Harwich. Lost with her master, Jacob Fance of Brightlingsea, off Beachy Head, 23 January 1883.

**CYMRIC**
See *Success*

**DANNEBROG of Harwich        109881**
Built by McLearon at Harwich, 1901. 71 tons. First owned by S. R. Groom and (1919) by Archie Wife, Ipswich, and (1934) by Cranfield Bros, Ipswich. Built as ketch. Converted by 1919 to mulie, then to sprittie. Traded as auxiliary, then motor barge. Restored by Taylor Woodrow, 1970s. Still afloat.

**DARNET, THE, of Rochester        67048**
Built at Rochester, 1873. 78 tons. Owned by R. Lewis, Harwich, and (after 1890) by William Frost, Tollesbury. Took cement from Medway to Holland for building of North Sea canal. Both masts lowered. Driven ashore on Wainfleet Sands 11 July 1909, but got off. Broken up by 1918.

**DAUNTLESS of Maldon        68311**
Built by Spencelaugh at Sittingbourne, 1873. 96.8 x 23.2 x 8.1, 143 tons. Built to Lloyd's class but not surveyed after 1874. Tuck-stern schooner, converted to ketch. Owned by John Smith, Burnham.

**DAVENPORT of Ipswich        65379**
Built by W. Colchester at Ipswich, 1877. 86 x 19 x 6, 82 tons. Registered as dandy, altered to ketch with brailing mizzen, then to half-sprit. Owned (1881-90) by J. Hooker, Ipswich, and (1919) by Robert Rutherford, London, and (1934) by Roy Rands, Ipswich. Foundered at anchor off Eastbourne, February 1936, bound

Plymouth to Ridham Dock with bricks and fireclay. Sank near pier when pumps choked.

**DIAMOND of Portsmouth        81011**
Built by J. T. Crampton at Portsmouth, 1879. 49 tons. Owned by builder and (by 1919) by Henry Crampton, Portsmouth, and (by 1934) by Henry Raynard, Portsmouth.

**DIANA of Rye        80258**
Built by Smith at Rye, 1891. 100 x 23.5 x 8.4, 144 tons. Owned (1906) by J. S. Vidler, Rye, and (1919) by Haig Hall Steam Ship Co. Ltd, Cardiff (m.o. Sven Hansen). Out of register by 1934.

**DOLGWANDLE of Littlehampton        88824**
Built by Harvey at Littlehampton, 1891. 70 tons. Owned (1891-1910) by C. Parry, London, J. Harvey managing owner. Sold to French owners and renamed *Gravelines III*. Owned (1910) by Mrs A. M. Boatwright and (1917) by Mrs F. Bayley, Greenhithe (m.o. Frederick Bayley), when registered as 'formerly *Wandle* and *Dolgwandle*'. But registered as *Dolgwandle*, 1892. Out of register by 1934.

**DORIC of London        99096**
Built by Vaux at Harwich, 1892. 142 tons. Owned by H. Shrubsall, London. Described at launch as schooner, but registered as ketch.

**DOVERCOURT of Harwich (later of London)        54523**
Built by Aldous at Brightlingsea, 1865. 82 tons. Round-stern dandy setting square topsail, owned first by J. Watts, Harwich, sold to London 1889 to Tank Storage and Carriage Co. Ltd (m.o. David Caird), and in 1893 owned by the Kerosine Company Limited, London (m.o. Thomas Howard). Out of register by 1919.

**EARNEST of Ipswich        29856**
Built by Bayley at Ipswich, 1861. 87.5 x 21 x 7, 85 tons. Eight years A1 at Lloyd's. Described as 'sloop

similar to *Tertius',* but registered as ketch. Also described in Lloyd's Register, 1873-4, as a barque, presumably a misprint for barge. Sold by Bayley & Co. 1872-3. Owned (1881) by Ezra Dale, Shotley, Suffolk. Lost with all hands 25 January 1883, with timber, Ipswich to the Tyne.

**EASTERN BELLE of London   89496**
Built by Colchester at Ipswich, 1883. 86 x 21.6 x 7.4, 89 tons. Owned by Herbert Hawkins, London, and English and Continental Shipping Co. 'A hard-headed old cow.' Traded to Lisbon. Out of register by 1919.

**EDITH of Ipswich   58533**
Built by Lambert at Ipswich, 1867. 92.1 x 21.6 x 7.1, 97 tons. 'Flat-bottomed schooner'. Six years A1 at Lloyd's. 'Ipswich coaster.' Owned by W. Lee. In register 1873, but out by 1881.

**EDITH WOOD of Faversham   52896**
Built by Taylor at Sittingbourne, 1865. 96 tons. 'Clipper schooner barge.' Maiden voyage to Middlesbrough in December with owner (Charles Wood of Milton, Kent) and party aboard. Wood still owner, 1890. Converted to sprittie by 1893. Out of register by 1919.

**ELIZA H of Harwich   84029**
Built by Vaux at Harwich, 1881. 110 tons. Owned by John Holmes of Harwich. Named after Eliza Holmes, his daughter. Had figurehead, but did not set square topsail. Lost on Longsand, December 1902, with coal, Goole to Saint-Valéry. Captain Jim Stone and crew of three rowed to Sunk light-vessel. Barge later came off the sand but sank in deep water, and was blown up.

**ELIZA PATIENCE of Ipswich   86619**
Built by Orvis and Fuller at Ipswich, 1883. 76 tons. George Mynheer's first command. Owned (1890) at Dungarvan, Co. Wexford, Ireland (m.o. W. H. Orvis, Ipswich). Lost 10 September

1903, on Holkham Beach, Norfolk (oil-cake, Hull to Lowestoft). Crew saved by Wells lifeboat.

**ELIZA SMEED of Rochester (later of Swansea)   49842**
Built by Smeed at Sittingbourne, 1865. 140 x 27.8 x 13.2, 345 tons. Barquentine described as 'three-masted clipper schooner'. Named after George Smeed's daughter. Loaded 500 tons. Owned (1880) by E. Sellin, Rochester, and (1882) by J. Bevan, Swansea, where registered. Sold to USA, and lost off New Jersey.

**ELIZABETH of Maldon   2644**
Built at Maidstone, 1840. 64 tons. Owned (1881 and 1893) by J. Float, Heybridge. Out of register by 1919.

**ELIZABETH LITTLE of Rochester   11018**
Built at Frindsbury, 1847. 64 tons. Sloop 'similar to *Tertius*'. Took deals from London to Southampton and returned with Portland stone to Pimlico. Also in beach trade. Converted to sprittie after 1890. Owned (1881) by W. B. Little, Upnor, Kent, and (1890) by J. Westwood, Napier Yard, Millwall. Out of register by 1919.

**ELLEN SMEED of Rochester   67044**
134 tons. Rebuild of *Henry Everist* by Smeed of Sittingbourne, 1872. 107.8 x 22.6 x 8.8. Three-masted schooner with jibboom and figurehead. Owned (1881) by G. Willson, Sittingbourne, and (by 1890) by C. W. Marshall of Faversham. Stranded at Palling 1908, but got off. Last owned by Bull Line of Newhaven. Sailing till 1912.

**EMERALD of London   73662**
Built at Harwich, 1876. 83 tons. Owned by Walter Watts, Harwich. Converted to sprittie by 1881, but reconverted to ketch by 1890, owned by E. J. Goldsmith of Grays.

**EMERALD of Portsmouth   76903**
Built by J. T. Crampton at Landport, 1877. 34 tons. Owned

(1881 and 1890) by builder, and (1919) by Harry Crampton, Portsmouth. Out of register by 1934.

**EMILY of Maldon (later of Ipswich)   63550**
Built by Lambert at Ipswich, 1869. 88 x 20 x 7, 85 tons. Owned by J. Rogers, Maldon, and (1873-4) by M. Capon as Ipswich coaster, G. Jennings master. Lost October 1881.

**EMILY LLOYD of Maldon   68366**
Schooner built by Taylor at Sittingbourne, 1872. 95 x 24 x 9, 126 tons. Thirteen years A1 at Lloyd's. First named *William Levitt* after manager of Elmley Cement Works. Sold (1876) to John Smith of Burnham and E. Lloyd. By 1880 Smith sole owner. Lost at sea November 1899.

**EMILY SMEED of Newhaven (later of Aberdeen, 1919, and Peterhead, 1934)   67034**
Built by Smeed at Sittingbourne, 1872. 133.3 x 25.8 x 13.3, 272 tons. Big barquentine particularly notable for depth. Converted to three-masted schooner by 1890. Loaded 750 tons. Owned (1890) by Neil Bull, Bull Line, Newhaven. Sold to Aberdeen (1903), and hulked there until 1919. Owned (1919) by Craske Ltd, Lowestoft, and (1934) by F. O. Mullender, Lowestoft. Jury-rigged as lighter, 1930.

**EMMA of London   50141**
Built by Hartnell and Surridge, Limehouse, 1864. 86 tons. Dandy with boom 48 feet long, skippered by Rudrum Meachen. Converted to ketch by 1881. Owned (1893) by Mrs Sarah Forster, Harwich. Lost 1895.

**EMPRESS of Harwich   74435**
Built by Vaux at Harwich, 1876. 64 tons. Owned (1881, as sprittie) by John Watts, Harwich, and (1893, as ketch) by G. Hayward, Chelmondiston, and (1920) by G. Hardie, Southampton.

**EMPRESS OF INDIA of Ipswich    65376**
Built by Curtis of Ipswich, 1876. 85 x 20 x 7. 71 tons. Owned (1881-90) by John Baker, Ipswich. Collier to Woodbridge under Captain Thomas Douse. Lost at Caister, 4 September, 1910, loaded with glass bottles. Crew saved by lifeboat. Wreck sold for £11 and broken up.

**ENDEAVOUR of Ipswich**
Built at Ipswich, 1865. 87.9 x 20.4 x 7.1, 77.5 tons. Transom stern. Converted from dandy to ketch. Lost October 1869 at Brancaster.

**ENTERPRISE of Harwich    67260**
Built by Vaux at Harwich, 1874. 71 tons. Transom stern. Set jib flying on traveller. Owned (1881-93) by G. Walker, London, and (1910) by W. T. Howard and (1919, still as ketch) by London and Rochester Barge Co. Ltd, Rochester. Out of register by 1934.

**ENTERPRISE of Portsmouth    81001**
Built by J. T. Crampton at Portsmouth, 1879. 275 tons. Barquentine-rigged collier for owner's use. Out of register by 1893.

**ENTERPRISE of Rye    80254**
Built by Smith at Rye, 1888. 116 tons. Owned by E. Bayley of Rye. Lost November 1893.

**ENTERPRISE of Yarmouth    92983**
Built by Bessey and Palmer at Yarmouth, 1891. 109.5 x 24.8 x 10.3, 168 tons. Three-masted schooner with leeboards. Owned by Bessey and Palmer, coal merchants, but not considered a success. Later traded as motor-barge. Out of register by 1919.

**ERA of Harwich    56422**
Built by Aldous at Brightlingsea, 1867. 79 tons. Owned by W. T. Middleton, Harwich, and (1877) J. Whitmore, Harwich, and (1881) J. Pengelly, Ipswich. In October 1891 ashore at Gorleston with coal, Sunderland to Mistley. Crew saved by rocket line. Barge got off and

lost by fire at Pattrick's Wharf, Dovercourt, January 1893.

**ERIC of London    99050**
Built by Harvey at Littlehampton, 1892. 75 tons. Owned (1901) by T. W. Howard. Out of register by 1919.

**ESTHER SMEED    58479**
Built by Fred Sollitt at Smeed's yard, Sittingbourne, 1868. 494 tons, loading 800 tons. The biggest barge ever built. Named after owner's daughter. First rigged as barque, but traded to Ireland as three-masted schooner. Stranded in Baltic 1878, got off, but out of register after this date.

**ETHEL EDITH of Ipswich (later of Faversham)    97684**
Built by Robert Peck at Ipswich, 1892. 88.5 x 23 x 7.9, 97 tons. Mast in keelson. Owned by builder, and (by 1919) registered at Faversham and owned by Arthur Wenban, Milton Regis. Owned (1920s) by John Sawyer of Brightlingsea, and (from 1928) F. Mumford, Stanford-le-Hope. When she blew ashore at Yarmouth Captain Angier of Brightlingsea saved her by paying out a kedge on a wire over her stern, and so getting her ashore broadside. Houseboat at Pin Mill till 1960s; now derelict there. Master from 1934 till after War, S. H. Sharman.

**EUROPA of Rochester    58530**
Built by Taylor at Sittingbourne, 1871. 100 x 22 x 9, 98 tons. Built as schooner for A. D. Robinson's cement trade. Converted to ketch after 1881. Owned (by 1890) by Doughty of Margate.

**EUSTACE of Rochester    90982**
Built by J. Bird at Teynham, Kent, 1886. 62 tons. Built for J. Westwood, Napier Yard, Millwall, and later owned by Walker and Howard. Converted to sprittie. Lost on West Rocks, Harwich, 1908.

**EVELYN of Rye    105103**
Built by Smith at Rye, 1900. 85 tons. Owned (1910) by G. Coote, Rye, and (1919) by F. T. Everard,

Greenhithe. Out of register by 1934.

**FAITH of Colchester    26856**
Built at Brightlingsea, 1858. 74.9 x 17.2 x 5.7, 58 tons. Transom stern. Boomsail converted to sprittie after 1890. Owned (1881-90) by Robert Shead, Colchester. Out of register by 1919.

**FANNY RAPSON of Rochester    55160**
Built by Taylor at Sittingbourne, 1866. 101 x 21 x 8, 122 tons. Brigantine (1881), but converted to ketch by 1890. Owned by C. Burley, Sittingbourne. Out of register by 1919.

**FEARLESS of Ipswich (later of London)    65377**
Built by Colchester at Ipswich, 1876. 90 x 21 x 8.2, 108 tons. Owned by Frank Christie of Ipswich (coal merchant and brother of William Christie, foreman to Vaux, Harwich) and (1910) by Whitmore of Harwich. By 1919 registered in London, owned by Walter Waugh. Out of register by 1934.

**FLEETWING of Harwich    56425**
Built at Ipswich, 1867. 89 tons. Owned by Luke Richmond, Harwich. Out of register 1880.

**FLOWER OF ESSEX of Harwich    18094**
Built by Hartnell and Surridge, Limehouse, 1857. 67 tons. Dandy converted to ketch (perhaps after being dismasted in collision with brig *Rebecca Jane*, 1864). Owned (1881) by John Watts, Harwich, and (1890) by Thomas Howard and George Walker and (1908) by T. Howard and (1919) by John Rayfield, Gravesend, and (1934) by Mrs E. Rayfield.

**FORERUNNER of Arundel**
Built by Harvey at Littlehampton, 1862. 55 tons. Four years A1 at Lloyd's. Owned by builders. Sold 1881 to Henry Burton, Newport, Mon., who still owned her in 1891. Out of register by 1893. Probably the pioneer Harvey ketch barge.

**FORTUNA of
Portsmouth    98456**
Built by Foster at Emsworth, 1892.
100 x 24.3 x 7.8, 113 tons.
Brigantine uniquely fitted with
centreboard instead of leeboards.
Owned by J. D. Foster, and used
by him for his own Emsworth coal
business. Out of register by 1919.

**FRANCIS of Harwich    78971**
Built by Parsons and Cann at
Harwich, 1877. 77 tons. Converted
to sprittie by 1881. Owned (1881
and 1890) by Martin Sanders,
Harwich. Out of register by 1919.

**FRANCIS, THE, of
London    52763**
Built at Lambeth, 1865. 55 tons.
Dandy converted to sprittie by
1881. Owned (1881 and 1890) by J.
Cann, Old Kent Road, London.
Foundered off Longsand, 22 July
1909.

**FRIENDSHIP of
Colchester    93979**
Built by Taylor at Sittingbourne,
1890. 117 x 25.5 x 10.6, 207 tons.
Three-masted schooner. Could
carry 490 tons. Owned by J. Smith,
Burnham. Run down and sunk off
Spurn Head, February 1912.

**GARFIELD of Rochester    84440**
Built at Sittingbourne, 1882. 74 x
14 x 5, 38 tons. Built as sprittie, and
owned (1890 and 1919) by Smeed
Dean. Rebuilt and converted to
ketch, but again sprit-rigged in
1934, owned by APCM. Became
mooring barge. Broken up at
Northfleet, 1952.

**GARIBALDI of
Faversham    28457**
Built by Goldfinch at Faversham,
1861. 44 tons. Converted to sprittie
by 1881. Owned (1881) by G.
Baker, Whitstable, and (1893) by
F. J. Doughty, Margate. Possibly
the first true Kentish ketch barge.

**GARIBALDI of
Rochester    45552**
Built by F. Sollitt at Smeed's yard,
Murston, 1862. 70 tons. Owned
(1881) by Henry Erb, Rochester
and (1893) by Walter Howard,
London. In 1908 converted to

sprittie by Parker of Bradwell.
According to her skipper, J. Culf,
was built with square stern, but had
round stern added when she was
sheathed. Worked up the Rhine.
Had pump windlass and short iron
tiller with chains to wheel. Lost off
Saint-Malo, June 1909.

**GARSON of Yarmouth (later of
Ipswich)**
Built by Mills and Baker at
Yarmouth, 1864. Registered as
cutter (perhaps meaning sloop or
dandy), but altered to ketch 1884.
Owned (1881) by J. W. Bennett,
Yarmouth. In 1893 ashore near
Winterton and sold at heavy loss by
her owner, John Finch of Mistley,
to A. B. Castle of Yarmouth, who
succeeded in unloading and
refloating her. Owned (1919) by
Albert Scholey, London, re-
registered at Yarmouth. Assisted
into Poole by Swanage lifeboat
1923. In 1926 converted to
clubhouse for Erith Yacht Club.
Bowsprit in centre, mast in
keelson, no bowboards of
quarterboards. Transom stern. No
square topsail. 'Not very fast.'

**GAZELLE of Ipswich    65378**
Built by Curtis at Ipswich, 1877.
91.8 x 22.6 x 8.3, 103 tons. Owned
by Alfred Beaumont, coal
merchant, Ipswich. Sunk in
Gravesend Reach by ss *Avoca*,
June 1898, but evidently raised.
Owned (1905 and 1918) by W. E.
Colebrooke of Rye. Out of register
1919.

**GEM OF THE OCEAN of
Faversham    75274**
Built at Faversham, 1877. 68 tons.
Owned (1881) by George Bassant,
Faversham, and (by 1890) by
Charles Forster of Harwich,
sailmaker. At one time skippered
by Henry Dobson of Maldon, who,
according to his disgruntled mate,
'put too much bleeding stone in
her'. Lost with all hands off
Dungeness, November 1892,
including Captain Walter Ward of
Pin Mill and his son Alfred.

**GENERAL CATHCART**
Built by Goldfinch at Faversham,
1857. 97 tons. Schooner. Nine

years A1 at Lloyd's. Wrecked on
Shipwash, October 1861. Crew
saved by salvage smacks.

**GENERAL GORDON of London**
Built by Harvey of Littlehampton,
1885. Run down by a steamer while
commanded by Captain Charles
Stone of Mistley before 1890.

**GENESTA of Faversham    89858**
Built by R. M. Shrubsall at
Sittingbourne, 1887. 69 tons. Built
for T. Bassett of Milton (owner,
1890). Owned (1893) by E.
Trussell, Burnham. Out of register
by 1919.

**GENESTA of Harwich    91327**
Built by Vaux at Harwich, 1886.
99.7 x 22.5 x 8.5, 113 tons. A1 at
Lloyd's. Owned by W. S. Gane
(m.o. Harry Stone) and (1910) by
Archie Wife of Foulness, Essex,
and (1926) by Handley of
Tollesbury and (1934) by R. G.
Jackson, Lambeth. Recorded as
wrecked near Exeter, but a photo
of her as a houseboat in north
Cornwall suggests that she was
salvaged without much damage,
and casts doubt on the location of
her final stranding.

**GEORGE SMEED of
Rochester    55181**
Built by F. Sollitt at Sittingbourne,
1866. 156 x 30.5 x 15. 477 tons.
Built as barquentine. One of
George Smeed's colliers, for his
NE coast trade. Could load over
700 tons. Owned jointly by Smeed
and William King (her skipper),
who became her sole owner and
sold her to Norway, 1879.

**GIPPESWIC of Ipswich**
Built by Harvey at Littlehampton,
1912. 92 x 23 x 7, 92 tons. Owned
(1912) by F. Garnham, Ipswich,
and (1917) by Wynnfield Shipping
Co., Grimsby. Sunk by German
submarine off Cap Barfleur, 31
March 1917.

**GLENAVON of
Rochester    113716**
Built at Borstal, 1903. 70 tons.
Owned (1919) by John Wilks,
Deal. Out of register by 1934.

**GLENMORE of Rochester    113710**
Built at Rochester, 1902. 61 tons. Converted to sprittie. Owned (1919 and 1938) by W. R. Cunis, London.

**GLENROSA of Harwich    84037**
Built by Parsons and Cann at Harwich, 1884. 87 x 20 x 6, 70 tons. Converted to sprittie by 1934. Fitted 72 h.p. engine, 1929. Owned (1890) by John Whitmore, Harwich, and (1919) by E. Cullum, Ipswich, and (1934) by Humphrey and Grey (Lighterage) Ltd, London.

**GLORIANA of Harwich    67246**
Built by Vaux of Harwich, 1871. 101.6 x 22.8 x 7.3, 116 tons. Named after American racing yacht. Owned by W. T. Middleton, Harwich. Originally carried 150 tons, but was built up 12-15 inches amidships to carry extra 50 tons. Kept jibboom till late date, and never had wheel or square topsail. Lost under Captain H. Meachen on the Inner Banks, Spurn Head, January 1909.

**GOLDFINCH of Faversham    89869**
Built by Goldfinch at Faversham, 1894. 98.5 x 22.7 x 9.2, 118 tons. Schooner. Owned (1910) by J. Hodge, Faversham, and (1919) by George Hodge, then by her skipper, J. H. Waters, Faversham. Double topsail sheeting to mizzen. Carried 250 tons. Sailed out to West Indies 1930. Owned there (1938) by Booker Brothers, London. Hulked 1947, when owned by J. Sibley of New Amsterdam.

**GRAVELINES III**
See *Dolgwandle*.

**GREENHITHE of London    68544**
Built by Keep at Greenhithe, 1874. 114 x 28 x 8, 162 tons. Three-masted schooner, coppered. Loaded 400 tons. Owned by A. Keep, sold to France and owned (1882) by J. P. Bryant, Saint-Brieve, Côte du Nord.

**HANNAH of Maldon    11080**
Built at Millwall, 1838. 69.5 x 17.1 x 6, 59 tons. Owned by James Strutt, Maldon.

**HANNAH AND SARAH of London**
Built in London, 1853. 78 tons. Ketch. Six years A1 at Lloyd's, oak and elm. Owned by Groves & Co. Voyage (1862, Siddall master) London – Antwerp. Out of register by 1881.

**HAROLD of London    112737**
Built by White at Milton-next-Sittingbourne, 1900. 90 tons. Named after builder's son. Owned (1910) by Stone of Mistley, then Ruffles of Ipswich and E. Garnham of Chelmondiston, and finally George Battershall of Grays. A frequent collier to Woodbridge, loading 180 tons. Lost on Lincolnshire coast, near Mablethorpe, March 1928.

**HARWICH of Harwich    56427**
Built by Aldous at Brightlingsea, 1867. 85 tons. Owned first by John Watts at Harwich, sold about 1881 to R. O. F. Steward of Nottington, Dorset, and by 1919 to J. W. Whitmore of Ipswich and her skipper Walter Rands. Owned (1930) by S. English, Yarmouth, and (1931) by A. Venton, Hull. Lost on North Scroby, December 1931.

**HENRY EVERIST**
See *Ellen Smeed*.

**HESPER of Harwich    81162**
Built by Vaux at Harwich, 1879. 101 x 22 x 8, 114 tons. Owned (1881) by Isaac Heighs, Brightlingsea, and (1890) by J. Whitmore, Harwich, and (1919) by William Jessop, Boston, Lincs. Colchester gasworks collier under Captain Dan Hatcher. Driven ashore and lost in Yarmouth Roads through anchor cable parting, 8 November 1921.

**HUDSON of Ipswich (later of Maldon)    79055**
Built by Robertson at Ipswich, 1878. 81 x 19 x 6, 64 tons. Transom stern. Owned (1881) by George Smith, Union Wharf, Kingsland, Middlesex, and (1890) by Henry D. Smith, London, and (1908 as sprittie registered at Maldon) by A. R. and S. Sales, London.

**HYDROGEN of London    123640**
Built by Gill at Rochester, 1906. 94.8 x 22 x 7.3, 98 tons. Built as tank barge for tar oil, and first owned by Burt Boulton and Hayward, voyaging to the Firth of Forth. Tanks removed and converted to mulie. Owned by Smeed Dean in 1920s. Sailed from Spurn Head to Milton Creek, Sittingbourne, in 24 hours in 1921. Owned (1934) by G. Andrews, Sittingbourne, and in final trading (1944) by A. Sully. Converted to auxiliary spritsail barge 1940. Still afloat.

**IDA of Ipswich    81989**
Built by W. Bayley at Ipswich, 1881. 94 x 23 x 9, 123 tons. Owned by R. & W. Paul, employed in coal and grain trade. In 1890 ashore on French coast, salvaged and sold to Whitstable. Out of register by 1919.

**INVICTA of Rochester    47863**
Built by F. Sollitt at Smeed's Yard, Sittingbourne, 1863. 86.2 x 20.4 x 8.4, 104 tons. Built as schooner, cut down to ketch, later converted to sprittie. Loaded 200 tons.

**ISABELLA of Rochester (later of Harwich)    20004**
Built at Maidstone, 1840. 93 tons. Three-masted schooner. Owned by W. Crockford, Chatham, and (1871) by George Smeed, Sittingbourne, and (1881) by James Clinch, Rochester, and (by 1890) by C. Doughty, Margate. In November 1894, wrongly described as 'of Faversham', towed into Harwich damaged and sold there to Middleton for £123. In 1897 registered at Harwich, wrecked at Winterton, parting from her anchor and striking half a mile from the shore. Lifeboat could not launch. Coastguards got a line aboard but it twisted and could not be used. Finally lifeboat was pulled off on coastguard's line, saving the

mate, S. Spalding, and the boy, William Turner, both of Ipswich, but the skipper, Captain J. Mann of Ipswich, and A. Murrell of Yarmouth were lost.

**IVY P of Ipswich (later of Dublin)      97690**
Built by Peck at Ipswich, 1893. 79 tons. Owned (1910) by R. Peck and (1919) by W. J. Ireland, Liverpool. Registered in Dublin in 1930, owned by William Morgan, Wicklow (m.o. K. Wetherall, Liverpool). According to one account, lost in Wicklow Bay soon after this date. According to another account, destroyed by an incendiary bomb in Liverpool Docks, 1941.

**JABEZ of Colchester      47808**
Built by Aldous at Brightlingsea, 1863. 71 tons. Dandy (or perhaps sprittie) altered to ketch. Owned (1878) by R. Shead, Colchester. Capsized, wood-loaded, at Withernsea, Yorkshire, November 1880, and lost with her crew of four, all from St Leonard's Cottages, Colchester, which were left inhabited by widows.

**JAMES BOWLES of Colchester      52977**
Built by Aldous at Brightlingsea, 1865. 71 tons. Owned (1881 and 1890) by J. Bowles, Tollesbury, and (1893) by Gill, Rochester. Collier to Tollesbury. Sold to Portsmouth 1897, and owned (1919) by P. W. Gilbert, Gosport. Out of sea-going register by 1934, but afloat as lighter in 1940s.

**JAMES GARFIELD of Ipswich      81992**
Built by Curtis at Ipswich, 1881. 81 x 21 x 7, 81 tons. Owned (1893) by T. Wellum of Brightlingsea, and (1910) by J. Hooker. In April 1883 was hove-to off Whitby bound from Ipswich to Scotland with broken tiller. Her master, Captain Wheeler of Colchester, was taken off by a German schooner, and the derelict barge was later picked up and taken into the Tyne. Register closed 1913.

**JOHN WARD of Rochester      67022**
Built by Smeed at Sittingbourne, 1871. 103.8 x 22.6 x 8.1, 123 tons. Schooner similar to *Alice Watts* with jibboom, fidded mizzen topmast, square topsail and topgallant rigged on parrel round topmast, and short double crosstrees. Ketch by 1881. Owned (1879) by Burham Brick Co. Between 1885 and 1890 sailed from Tyne and disappeared.

**JOHN WESLEY of Harwich      67254**
Built by Norman at Harwich, 1873. 90.7 x 24.2 x 8.5, 128 tons. Built of oak, and at that time the largest barge built at Harwich. Owned first by 'Porky' Norman, butcher, and Jonathan Brewster, baker, both devout Wesleyans, and (1881) by C. F. Williams, Plymouth. Sold to J. G. and R. Sully of Bridgwater, February 1888, and three months later burned out 'in the bay four miles from Burnham'. Rebuilt by Sully as lighter *Crowpill* (qv), 184 tons.

**JUBILEE of Harwich      91329**
Built by Vaux at Harwich, 1887. 121 x 26.4 x 9.4, 174 tons. Three-masted schooner, 'built out of a wreck'. Owned by John Mann Poole of Mistley and (1905) by Thomas Howard of London. Out of register by 1919.

**JUSTICE of Harwich      99459**
Built by Fellowes at Yarmouth, 1895. 88 x 21 x 7.8, 90 tons. Owned by W. T. Whitmore of Harwich and (1919) by Walter Waugh, London, and (1934) by Mrs E. M. Dines, Grays. In 1920 skippered by Captain P. Fulcher. Converted to motor barge. Owned (1938) by S. Pollock, Colchester.

**KATE of Ipswich      50390**
Built by Lambert at Ipswich, 1867. 84.7 x 21.7 x 7, 88 tons. Seven years A1 at Lloyd's. Square topsail. Owned (1873) by C. Andrews and E. Dale, master, and (1881) by E. Hayward, Chelmondiston. In 1869 rebuilt ten feet longer at Whitby, Ipswich being considered too

expensive. In February 1888 sunk in Thames by ss *Luteria* of Newcastle. Repaired and sold to C. Marshall of Faversham. Broken up 1909.

**KATE AND EMILY of Lowestoft      415**
Built at Lowestoft, 1851. 75 tons. Owned by Flory and (1881-90) by T. Lucas, Lowestoft, and (1919) by W. Fames, Gravesend. A clumsy barge with square stern and round bilge. Originally set square topsail.

**KATE POWELL of Rochester      2007**
Built at Maidstone, 1854 or 1857. 61 tons. Boomsail. Owned (1881-90) by T. Weekes, Halling, and (1919) by Fielder Hickman & Co., London.

**KINDLY LIGHT of Ipswich      120780**
Built by Harvey at Littlehampton, 1905. 90.3 x 22.2 x 7.8, 90 tons. Ten years A1 at Lloyd's. Owned (1910) by J. Ward and (1919) by J. Sawyer, Brightlingsea. Sailed out to West Indies, 1926, making the voyage Plymouth to Demerara in forty days. Owned there (1938) by Booker Brothers, London. Out of register 1954.

**LANDERMERE of Harwich      81165**
Built by Vaux at Harwich, 1879. 34 tons. Owned by builder till at least 1893.

**LAURA of Harwich      67259**
Built by Vaux at Harwich, 1873. 86 tons. Schooner with knee at bow and figurehead of Laura Stocks, daughter of a shareholder. Altered to ketch with standing bowsprit about 1880. Skippers included James Lewis of Woodbridge and J. H. Waters of Faversham, who converted her to wheel steering and left her about 1903 to take the *Goldfinch*. Owned (1910) by A. Middleton, then by Tom Rigden, diver. Then sold to Edward Saunders, who put in a boiler and used her for pile-driving. Then to London and Rochester Trading Company, which converted her to

motor barge, while in the First World War she was mined on her first cross-Channel freight.

**LAURA SHELBOURNE**
Built at Carnes Yard, Nine Elms, Vauxhall, 1854. 145 x 26.6 x 12.6. Barque-rigged, loading 560 tons. Named after builder's daughter. The first known big square-rigged barge. Built for Baltic trade, London to St Petersburg.

**LEADING LIGHT of**
**Ipswich      122973**
Built by Harvey at Littlehampton, 1906. 92.3 x 22.6 x 7.8, 95 tons. Ten years A1 at Lloyd's. Owned (1910) by W. Hawkes, Ipswich, and (1927) by her skipper A. Vince. Sailed to West Indies 1933. Owned there (1938 and 1944) by Booker Brothers, London. Register closed 1952.

**LEADING STAR of**
**Colchester      12194**
Built by P. M. Sainty at Fingringhoe, 1856. 130 x 23.6 x 13, 210 tons. Eight years A1 at Lloyd's. Three-masted barque with elliptical stern and full-length figurehead. Built for William Cross of Colchester, corn and coal merchant. Re-rigged at Folkestone 1864, owned by R. O. Page, and converted to brig. Out of register 1877.

**LILLY of Ipswich      86621**
Built by Robertson at Ipswich, 1884. 77 x 19 x 6, 64 tons. Built as sprittie, loading about 130 tons. Converted to ketch. Skippered by builder's son. Foundered with wheat off the Isle of Wight on 10 March 1891.

**LILY of Harwich (later of Rye and of Faversham)      67256**
Built at Millwall, 1873. 89 tons. Owned (1893) by G. Underwood at Southend and (1909 and 1914) by Colebrooke at Rye. Converted to sprittie, and in 1926 registered at Faversham.

**LLAMA of Harwich      67265**
Built by Vaux at Harwich, 1875. 106 x 25.5 x 9.4, 166 tons. A large ketch 'like *Pearl* but with sliding

bowsprit'. Only set one jib, but carried four sizes. Owned (1881) by W. T. Griffiths, Ipswich, and (1890) by A. Layzell, Upton, Essex, also by Thomas Howard, London. Sunk in collision down-Channel, December 1912.

**LORD ALCESTER of**
**London      98888**
Built by Harvey at Littlehampton, 1891. 132 tons. Owned by English and Continental Shipping Company, and later by R. Skinner, Woodbridge. Lost entering Poole, November 1914; crew of four rescued by Poole lifeboat.

**LORD BEACONSFIELD of**
**Faversham (later of**
**Grimsby)      75279**
Built by R. Shrubsall at Sittingbourne, 1878. 84 x 18 x 6, 58 tons. Built as sprittie (40 tons), and rebuilt as ketch (58 tons) between 1881 and 1890. Owned (1881) by W. Randall, Faversham, and (by 1890) by T. Bassett, Sittingbourne, and (1893) by Osborn Dan, Faversham. Converted back to sprittie and owned (1907) by R. & W. Paul, Ipswich. Sold to Grimsby (1917), and to Aldous of Arlesford (1918). Out of register 1921.

**LORD BEACONSFIELD of**
**London      95437**
Built by Harvey at Littlehampton, 1889. 75 tons. Owned (1890) by Herbert Hawkins, then by English and Continental Shipping Co Ltd and (1919) by W. Coppack, London. Crew saved by Margate lifeboat, 1897. Wrecked 1923.

**LORD BERESFORD of**
**London      96633**
Built by Harvey at Littlehampton, 1889. 75 tons. Owned (1890) by Herbert Hawkins, then by English and Continental Shipping Co. Ltd and (1919) by W. Coppack, London. Crew saved by Margate lifeboat, 1897. Wrecked 1923.

**LORD CHURCHILL of London (later of Faversham)      94389**
Built by Harvey at Littlehampton, 1888. 84.5 x 20.1 x 6.8, 76 tons. Owned (1887-91) by Herbert Hawkins. In 1900 sunk in

Gravesend Reach by ss *Batavia I*. Raised and sold to Whitstable Shipping Co., which converted her to sprittie, removing counter. Owned (1919 to 1948) by Daniels Bros., Whitstable. In June 1933 again sunk at Beckton by ss *Ruihini*. Sold as yacht 1948. Became houseboat at Wouldham, Medway, and taken as hulk to Whitewall Creek, where she now lies.

**LORD DUFFERIN of**
**London      93083**
Built by Harvey at Littlehampton, 1890. 132 tons. Owned by English and Continental Shipping Co. Out of register by 1919.

**LORD HAMILTON of London (later of Maldon)      96637**
Built by Harvey at Littlehampton, 1889. 81 tons. Owned (1890) by Herbert Hawkins, then by English and Continental Shipping Co. and (by 1919) by G. W. Frost, Tollesbury (m.o. Horace Shrubsall, Greenwich). Sold to Sarah Shrubsall, Cranbrook, Kent, in 1921, and lost on Goodwins, 12 February 1924. Wreck unseen by Goodwin lightship and by Ramsgate lifeboat till two survivors, Walter Farnes (skipper) and David Davies (deckhand), seen by passing motor-boat and saved after sixty hours in rigging. Inquiry refused by Board of Trade.

**LORD HARTINGTON of**
**London      94343**
Built by Gildea at Ipswich, 1887. 85.6 x 20.8 x 6.8, 87 tons. Owned (1890) by Herbert Hawkins and (1892) by English and Continental Shipping Co. and (by 1919) by J. H. Sankey and Son, London, and later by R. Skinner, Woodbridge. Sunk in collision in river Scheldt, 1928.

**LORD IDDESLEIGH of**
**London      95441**
Built by Gildea at Ipswich, 1888. 84.4 x 20.4 x 6.8, 75 tons. Owned (1890) by Herbert Hawkins, and (1906) by Walker and Howard and (1919) by Harwich Port Sanitary Authority. Broken up at Harwich.

**LORD LANSDOWNE of London    98099**
Built by Harvey at Littlehampton, 1890. 109 tons. The only one of the 'Lord' barges to have a square topsail. Owned (1893) by English and Continental Shipping Co. Sunk in Swin in collision with ketch *Kate* of Ipswich, January 1900, but evidently raised, as owned (1910) by A. Pittock and (1938) by Everet Llewellyn & Merritt Ltd, Cardiff. Abandoned in Panshards Creek, Penryn river, Cornwall.

**LORD NAPIER of London    98200**
Built by Harvey at Littlehampton, 1891. 132 tons. Owned (1893) by English and Continental Shipping Co. Out of register by 1919.

**LORD NELSON of London    96572**
Built by Harvey at Littlehampton, 1889. 86.9 x 21.5 x 6.9, 79 tons. Owned (1890) by Herbert Hawkins and (1893) by Walker and Howard and (1919) by Adolphus Parker, Bradwell, and (1927) by her skipper, W. H. Easter. Out of register by 1934.

**LORD ROSEBERY of Rochester    99922**
Built at Upnor, 1893. 72 tons. Owned (1919) by William Ellis, Stanford-le-Hope, and by W. Burkill, Grimsby. Converted to sprittie. Sank at anchor in gale off Britannia Pier, Yarmouth, 19 November 1937. Crew saved by lifeboat.

**LORD SALISBURY of London    91989**
Built by Harvey at Littlehampton, 1887. 78 tons. Owned (1890) by Herbert Hawkins and (1893) by English and Continental Shipping Co. Out of register by 1919.

**LORD SHAFTESBURY of London    91911**
Built by Gildea at Ipswich, 1886. 84 x 21.5 x 6.9, 78 tons. Owned (1890) by Herbert Hawkins and (1893) by English and Continental Shipping Co. Out of register by 1919.

**LORD TENNYSON of London    98889**
Built by Orvis and Fuller at Ipswich, 1891. 82 x 19.8 x 6.9, 78 tons. Owned (1893 and 1906) by Walker and Howard.

**LORD WOLSELEY of London    95545**
Built by Harvey at Littlehampton, 1889. 74 tons. Owned (1890) by Herbert Hawkins and (1893) by English and Continental Shipping Co. Out of register by 1919.

**LOTHAIR of Harwich (later of Rochester and of Rye)    67249**
Built by Robertson at Ipswich, 1872. 101.8 x 23.2 x 7.5, 129 tons. Schooner similar to *Alice Watts,* but ketch by 1881. Owned by John Watts, Harwich, and (1890) by George Gill, Rochester, and (1906) by J. Vidler, Rye, and (1919) by Walter Waugh, London. After the great gale of November 1880 was picked up abandoned with only a dog aboard. Nothing more ever heard of Captain Taylor of Trimley and the crew. Later lost on West Rocks, Harwich, through error by her skipper, who had not been into Harwich for forty years.

**LUCY RICHMOND of Maldon (later of London)    68313**
Built by Robertson at Ipswich, 1875. 106.7 x 24.4 x 8.6, 137 tons. Nine years A1 at Lloyd's. Schooner like *Alice Watts* and *Lothair,* with figurehead representing Lucy Richmond, mizzen topmast and stay between this and main topmast head. Owned by Peter Richmond, Burnham (after 1882 W. T. Richmond & Co; no connection with the Richmonds of Harwich), and (1906) by Marshall, Maldon, and (1919) by R. Burbage-Clarke, London, and (1934 and 1944) by T. Scholey & Co Ltd, E. Greenwich (m.o. T. Piper) and (1938) by T. Piper, Greenwich. Hulked at Greenwich, and broken up in 1940s.

**LYMINGTON of Harwich    81175**
Built by Vaux at Harwich, 1880. 116.4 x 24.8 x 9, 163 tons. Three-masted schooner with double topsails on foremast, loading 350 tons. 'Built out of a wreck.' Owned by Vaux. Wrecked on Holm Sands with coals, Sunderland to Eling, October 1889.

**MAGGIE of Littlehampton    81981**
Built by Harvey at Littlehampton, 1880. 46 tons. Owned by J. Harvey. Lost 1898.

**MAGNET of Colchester    87287**
Built by Taylor at Sittingbourne, 1884. 91 x 22.6 x 8.8, 117 tons. Owned by J. Smith, Burnham. Foundered in North Sea, 1897.

**MAJOR of Harwich    105427**
Built by McLearon at Harwich, 1897. 67 tons. Square stern. Converted into sprittie. Owned (1919) by J. H. Chaplin, Brightlingsea, and (1921 and 1934, still as ketch) by Mrs S. Chaplin, and (1938) by Anderson, Whitstable. Rebuilt at Whitstable. Later (1947) motor barge.

**MALVOISIN of London    87176**
Built by Howard at Maldon, 1883. 101 x 22.8 x 8.5, 113 tons. Owned (1890) by W. Meeson, Rochford, and (1893) by Marshall, Faversham, and (1919 and 1937) by Abbie Anderson, Whitstable. In 1905 ashore on Kentish Knock in south-east gale, but salvaged and ultimately lost off Calais on passage Gravelines to Goole with phosphates, 7 December 1929. Crew saved.

**MARGARET of Rochester**
Built at Maidstone, 1843. 126 new/ 85 old register tons. Eight years A1 at Lloyd's. Schooner. First owner T. Pybus, first master Captain Foreman. Not in Lloyd's Register 1852. Perhaps the earliest recorded schooner barge.

**MARIA of Faversham (I)    50301**
Built by Taylor at Sittingbourne, 1864. 35 tons. Ketch converted by 1881 to sprittie. Owned (1880 and 1890) by C. Wood, Milton, and (1919) by Walter Webb, Strood. Out of register by 1934.

**MARIA (II)**
Built by Taylor at Sittingbourne, 1866. 150 tons. Owned by Burleys. Wrecked on Goodwins laden with 137 tons pitch, January 1878.

**MARTINET of Goole    128880**
Built by Smith at Rye, 1912. 95.2 x 22.8 x 8, 99 tons. Built with oversized stern-post for possible propeller shaft. Set only one bowsprit jib after 1938. Owned (1919) by Frederick Fish, Goole, and (1935) by F. T. Everard, Greenhithe. Lost off Orford Ness, 1941. The last of the boomies.

**MARY of Ipswich    11864**
Built by Colchester at Ipswich, 1848. 77.9 x 17.5 x 6.6. Registered as ketch and, if this is correct, one of the first with this rig.

**MARY CAROLINE of Rochester**
Built at Rochester, 1848. 228 tons. Schooner, oak and red pine, iron-fastened. Six years A1 at Lloyd's. Owned by Reinhardt. 'London coaster.'

**MARY LYNE of Harwich    78973**
Built by Vaux at Harwich, 1878. 99 x 21 x 8, 110 tons. Owned by C. Redwood (skipper), Middleton and Fulcher of Harwich. Given Mrs Fulcher's maiden name. Lost with all hands at Filey Bay when she drove ashore at anchor, October 1881.

**MASONIC of Colchester (later of Ipswich)    68605**
Built by Aldous at Brightlingsea, 1876. 117 tons. The last boomie built at Brightlingsea. Under her owner-master W. Dove, sunk on Blyth Sand in collision with ss *Thetford*, 23 November 1881. Raised, registered at Ipswich and owned (1890) by Henry Smith, London. Capsized off Saltburn, 18 November 1893, and lost with all hands, including Captain H. Angier of Brightlingsea.

**MATILDA UPTON of Ipswich    95302**
Built by Orvis and Fuller at Ipswich, 1887. 86.2 x 21.5 x 7.4, 90 tons. Built as sprittie, but after

being run down in Ipswich river bought as a wreck by Cann and rebuilt as ketch. Owned (1887 - 1903) by W. H. Orvis and (1910 and 1919) by W. Dove, Brightlingsea, and (1923) by Leek. Ended on the mud at Harwich rigged as mulie.

**MAY FLOWER of Ipswich**
Built by Colchester at Ipswich, 1870. 69 x 18 x 7, 60 tons. Owned (1881 and 1890) by John May, Ipswich. Dandy. Out of register by 1919.

**MAY HAWTHORN of Rochester    78502**
Built at Teynham, 1877. 75 tons. Owned by Philander Garrod, Ipswich. Lost 1893.

**MAY QUEEN of Harwich    56438**
Built by Mills at Yarmouth, 1870. 92 x 21 x 7.7, 94 tons. Schooner with double topsails. Owned (1873 and 1881) by John Watts, Harwich, and (by 1890) by G. W. Walker and T. W. Howard, London, and (1919) by Charles V. Hardy, Hull. Register closed 1920.

**MAYLAND of Lowestoft (later of Lynn)    58308**
Built by Taylor at Sittingbourne, 1868. 59 tons. Owned by E. Dix and (1881) by R. W. Burleigh, Halesworth, and (1893) by J. L. Marriott, Swaffham. Lost in collision with brig off Haisborough, 7 November 1897. Crew saved.

**MAYOR OF ROCHESTER of Rochester    45510**
Built at Strood, 1863, 73 tons. Owned by R. M. Shrubsall, Milton. Out of register by 1890.

**MAZEPPA of Harwich    91330**
Built by Cann at Harwich, 1887. 88.8 x 20.9 x 7, 79 tons. Owned by John Wells, Harwich, and (1919) by Mrs M. Ward, Ipswich, and (1925) by Horlock, Mistley, who sold her to William Easter, Hastings. Round counter stern. Run down by steamer in Thames estuary about 1930.

**MECHANIC of Harwich    67252**
Built by Parsons and Cann at Harwich, 1872. 117 tons. Schooner 'of about 205 tons burthen'. Owned (1881) by John Wells, Harwich, but ketch by 1881. Wrecked at Withernsea, 28 October 1881.

**MEDINA of London    123787**
Built by White at Sittingbourne, 1906. 79 tons. Owned (1907) by Alfred White and (1910) by J. Sawyer, Brightlingsea.

**METEOR    45783**
Conversion of sprittie *Eclipse* into schooner by R. M. Shrubsall at Sittingbourne, 1863. Owned by G. Adams, Isleworth. Collier to Milton. Out of register by 1893.

**METEOR of London    87120**
Built at Blackwall, 1883. 77 tons. Ketch owned by Meteor Sailing Barge Co. Ltd, Poplar. Out of register by 1919.

**MOSS ROSE of Weymouth (later of London)    82553**
Built by Bayley at Ipswich, 1884. 94.9 x 22.5 x 9.3, 127 tons. Owned (1893) by Richard Cox, Weymouth, then by J. Smith, Burnham, and (1919) by W. Fagg, coal merchant, Sandwich. Standing bowsprit and counter stern. Lost with all hands on Kentish Knock.

**MOULTONIAN of London    131979**
Built by Harvey at Littlehampton, 1919. 99.6 x 23.3 x 8.5, 94 tons. The last of this builder's thirty-four boomies. Never rigged a topmast. Fitted with 90 h.p. oil engine 1928, when owned by Vectis Shipping Co., Newport, Isle of Wight (m.o. Thomas Price, her skipper from 1923 until at least 1944). By 1941 twin-screw motor barge, 132 hp. Laid up in river Itchen in 1960s, and became derelict there.

**MOUNTSFIELD of Rye (later of London)    80257**
Built by Smith at Rye, 1890. 99.3 x 23.5 x 8.3, 126 tons. Owned (1893) by W. G. Rubie of Rye. Fitted with auxiliary engine and registered in London 1918. Owned (1919) by Hansen Shipping Co. Ltd, Cardiff.

**MYSTERY of
Faversham      73253**
Built by Shrubsall at Milton, 1875.
61 tons. Built as sprittie for Robert
Dodds of Faversham, who owned
her till at least 1890. Converted
into ketch for Apollinaris Water
trade from the Rhine by 1919,
owned by Frank Webb, Ipswich.
Converted back to sprittie after
1934. Owned (1938) by H. Last,
Ipswich. Ceased trading 1939, and
later houseboat on river Deben.

**MYSTERY of Harwich      67262**
Built by Curtis at Ipswich, 1874. 90
x 22 x 7, 106 tons. Built of
secondhand materials as dandy,
and converted into ketch after 1890
with sliding bowsprit and tiller,
replaced by fixed bowsprit and
wheel. Owned (1881) by John and
Robert Lewis, Harwich, and (1910)
by R. L. Gooch. Her skipper,
Dudley Ward, died in Seaham
Hospital, and his body was brought
home aboard her to Pin Mill. Then
(1908) taken over by Captain H.
Porter, who bought her in 1914 and
skippered her till her loss in Dover
Harbour in December 1929.

**NANCY of Ramsgate      94600**
Built by Goldfinch at Faversham,
1890. 117 tons. Schooner. Owned
(1893) by J. J. Greenstreet, and
later by her skipper, J. Smith,
Sandwich. Run down and sunk at
anchor near Clayhole, 10
December 1909. Crew saved.

**NELL JESS of Ipswich      113754**
Built by Harvey at Littlehampton,
1902. 91.4 x 22 x 7.7, 115 tons.
Owned (1910) by F. B. Garnham,
Chelmondiston, and (1919) by
Samuel West and (1927 and 1934)
by Fraser and White Ltd,
Portsmouth. Took record freight of
80,000 bricks from Butterfly
Wharf, Conyer, 1928. Instead of a
headstick in her topsail she had an
extra tall topmast and jib-headed
topsail. Ended as coal hulk at
Portsmouth.

**NELLIE of
Littlehampton      81983**
Built by Harvey at Littlehampton.
1882. 70 tons. Owned by J. Harvey

and (1919) by William Watson,
Grangemouth.

**NELLIE S of Faversham (later of
London)      75271**
Built by Gann at Whitstable, 1876.
130 x 26 x 12.6, 262 tons. A1 at
Lloyd's. Reputedly named after
Nellie Smeed. Round-bilged
barquentine. Carried 500 tons.
Owned (1881) by G. H. Gann and
(1882) by Thorburn Bros and
(1890) by Col. N. B. Thoyts,
Cheltenham (m.o. J. E. Matthews,
London). Sold to Brazilian owners
1896. Lost on passage, Rio de
Janeiro to Rio Grande, 1905.

**NELLY of Maldon      58307**
Built by Lambert at Ipswich, 1868.
84 x 21 x 6, 81 tons. Eight years A1
at Lloyd's. Owned (1879) by J.
Green, Maldon. Out of register by
1881.

**NEW TRADER of Deal      22124**
Built at Ramsgate, 1865. 54 tons.
Sloop or dandy with lug mizzen.
Worked as Sandwich-to-London
goods hoy. Converted to sprittie by
1881, and owned (1881 and 1890)
by Samuel Groom, Harwich, and
(1919) by J. B. Groom.

**NINITA      91986**
Built by E. J. Robertson at
Ipswich, 1880. 67 tons. Named
after a Spanish dancer, and owned
by her builder. Built as a sprittie,
and converted to boomie in 1887
for trading down-Channel.
Foundered in English Channel
when a deep-sea skipper recklessly
tried to bring her home in a gale
after her regular skipper had been
lost overboard in Zuyder Zee. Out
of register by 1890.

**NORMANHURST of
Rochester      113691**
Built at Upnor, 1900. 68
tons.Owned (1919 and 1938) by W.
R. Cunis Ltd, London. Converted
to mulie, then sprittie. After 1945
became a boys' club on the
Thames. Still afloat as houseboat at
Kew.

**NORTHERN BELLE of
London      91837**
Built by Gildea at Ipswich, 1885.

84.9 x 20.2 x 6.8, 76 tons. Owned
(1893) by English and Continental
Shipping Company. Wrecked at
Sandgate, bound from Saint-
Valéry to Ipswich with phosphate,
January 1895.

**OLIVE of London      99054**
Built by Hartnell and Surridge at
Millwall, 1892. 93 tons. Owned
(1893) by Bushell, Dover. Out of
register by 1919.

**OLYMPIA of
Faversham      114453**
Built by White at Conyer, 1902.
Owned (1910) by J. F. Honeyball
and insured for £1,800. According
to one account burned out on
passage to France with coal in First
World War. According to another
account, run down in fog by a War
Department Inland Water
Transport ammunition lighter
while at anchor inside the Brake
Sand light vessel, 13 March 1918.

**ONWARD of Ipswich      79053**
Built by Bayley at Ipswich, 1878.
77 tons. Mast in keelson. Owned
by E. J. Passiful, Woodbridge.
Sunk by ss *Hawthorn* off Cross
Sand, Yarmouth, 7 July 1887.
Crew of four and owner's wife
landed by Aldeburgh fishing-boat.

**ORNATE of Harwich (later of
Bridgwater)      74443**
Built by Vaux at Harwich, 1875.
101.3 x 24.1 x 8.2, 122 tons. Owned
by J. Holmes, Harwich, and (1893)
by J. G. Sully of Bridgwater, and
registered there. Named after
barque *Ornate* built by Vaux in
1865, but commonly known as 'The
Hornet'. Out of register by 1919.

**OSPREY of Harwich      67263**
Built by Colchester at Ipswich,
1874. 94 x 21 x 6, 100 tons. The first
boomie with standing bowsprit, she
lay on the builder's ways a year till
John Holmes of Harwich bought
her for his son. Out of register by
1890.

**PARKEND of Bridgwater (later of
North Shields)      67228**
Built by Bayley at Ipswich, 1873.

101.7 x 24 x 8, 127 tons. Iron-fastened. Six years A1 at Lloyd's. Registered as a schooner, but in the 1890s a ketch. Built for and owned by J. G. Sully, Bridgwater. By 1919 registered as a ketch at North Shields, owned by Theodor Shipping Co. Ltd, Newcastle.

**PEARL of Ipswich     95309**
Built by Orvis & Fuller at Ipswich, 1889. 85.4 x 21.4 x 7.2, 88 tons. First skipper W. Harvey, but best known for her long association with Captain George Mynheer, who bought her before 1910, and still cared for her in Ipswich Dock in the 1930s. Then towed from Ipswich to London by ss *Shamrock*, and served as a powder hulk at Gravesend before ending her days at Hoo under the name *Pearl Wood*.

**PEARL of Portsmouth     76916**
Built at Portsmouth, 1878. 42 tons. Owned by J. T. Crampton, Portsmouth, and (by 1919) by W. T. Crampton.

**PHOENIX of Harwich     11219**
Built at Southwark, 1819. 81 tons. Owned by Johnson Richmond of Harwich. (The tonnage is so great for the early date that she was probably a small sloop rebuilt.) Out of register by 1890.

**PIONEER of Faversham     75273**
Built by Goldfinch at Faversham, 1876. 67 tons. Owned (1881 and 1890) by W. G. Dawson, Faversham. Sunk 27 May 1895.

**PIONEER of Maldon     62785**
Built by Curtis at Ipswich, 1874. 84 x 22 x 8, 92 tons. Counter stern 'like *Pearl*'. Built for John Rogers, Maldon. Owned (1890) by H. G. Warwicker, Maldon, and (1901) by Sadd of Maldon. Sailed from Hull Roads for London, and disappeared with all hands, February 1906.

**PIONEER of Rochester     10850**
Built at Rochester, 1897. 68 tons. Owned (1914) by Medway Barge Builders and Carriers Ltd, Rochester, and (1919) by

Wynnfield Shipping Co., Ltd, Grimsby.

**PRIDE of London     20476**
Built at Sandwich, 1857. 59 tons. Eleven years A1 at Lloyd's. Built for Pordage & Co., Ramsgate, as a yawl, but by 1881 a schooner. Owned (1891) by W. Beeson, London, and (1893) by G. W. Dane, Faversham. Out of register by 1919.

**PRIMUS of Harwich     11804**
Built by Colchester at Ipswich, 1841. 70 ft, 36 tons. Probably a sloop. The first vessel built at the Dock End yard. Top-up bowsprit, square stern. Owned (1881 and 1893) by J. H. Pattrick, Dovercourt, but not used after failure of Pattrick's Cement Works.

**PRINCESS MAY of Littlehampton     8825**
Built by Harvey at Littlehampton, 1893. Owned by J. Harvey.

**PRINCESS MAY of Poole     95658**
Built by J. Allen & Co at Poole, 1894. 89 tons. Owned (1900) by F. Griffin, Salisbury, and (1910) by W. T. Whitmore, Harwich.

**PROBLEM of Ipswich     29853**
Built by Bayley at Ipswich, 1861. 92.1 x 22 x 7.7, 128 tons. Nine years A1 at Lloyd's. Owned by builders, W. & J. R. Bayley. Schooner with three 'keels' instead of leeboards. The only example of the type. Zinc-sheathed. Foundered 26 February 1886, after hitting a rock between Start Point and Prawle Point.

**QUARRY of Rochester     90958**
Built at Frindsbury, 1886. 54 tons. Owned (1890 and 1893) by A. C. Hooker, Rochester. Converted to sprittie and owned (1919 and 1938) by London and Rochester Trading Co. (now Crescent Shipping).

**QUEEN MAB of London     99346**
Built by Taylor at Sittingbourne, 1888. 78 tons. Launched by Mabel Smith, captain's daughter. Owned

(1890) by J. Seagrave, Heathfield, Sussex, and (1910) by J. Harvey of Littlehampton.

**QUINTUS of Ipswich**
Built by Colchester at Ipswich, 1847. 71 x 16 x 5, 59 tons. Foundered off Sandgate, 3 January 1866.

**RAIMA**
Built in British Guiana between 1930 and 1933 as an exact copy of *Goldfinch*. Built of greenheart.

**RECORD REIGN of Maldon     10594**
Built by Howard at Maldon, 1890. 112.2 x 24.5 x 9.5, 139 tons. Schooner built to use Heybridge lock, but when she was fully loaded with 275-300 tons the gate would not close under her clipper bow. In the First World War a Q-boat with two 40 h.p. Bolinder oil engines and gun covered by dummy boat. In 1926 owned by Sadd of Maldon, with 40 h.p. auxiliary. Managing owner (1934) Harold Bates, Hertford. On 9 February 1935 as motor-ketch ashore at Keadby, and finally lost at Branscombe, east of Sidmouth, with a rock through her bottom.

**REINDEER of Harwich     21362**
Built at Ipswich, 1864. 63 tons. Among the earliest transom-stern boomies. Under Captain Osborne of Ipswich worked cement from Waldringfield to Southampton for the building of the new docks. (*May Queen* was also in this trade.) Owned (1881) by W. T. Griffiths, Ipswich, and (by 1890) by H. Keep, London. Converted to lighter 1892. Later H. Solly of Whitstable bought her from Everard as a lighter, and converted her to sprittie. In 1914 was an Admiralty lighter. Out of register by 1919.

**REINDEER of Ipswich     79056**
Built by Curtis at Ipswich, 1879. 77 x 22 x 8, 113 tons. Owned for over thirty years by A. Beaumont, Ipswich. Round stern and standing bowsprit. Had three hatches, including a small 'booby hatch' aft. Lost off Yarmouth on the Gudgeon

in 1911 through her coal cargo exploding when homeward bound from Seaham. Crew saved by trawler *Pegasus*. The *Reindeer* of Harwich was at this time loaded with explosives, and Trinity House had to be satisfied she had nothing more lethal than coal in her before they blew her up.

**ROCHESTER CASTLE of London      96580**
Built by Taylor at Sittingbourne, 1889. 90 tons. Built for J. Smith of Burnham, but owned (1890 and 1893) by G. W. Walker and T. W. Howard, London. 'Had round stern and painted ports.'

**ROSE BUD of Harwich      74432**
Built as sprittie by Orvis at Ipswich, 1875. 60 tons. Converted to small square-stern ketch. Owned (1881 and 1890) by W. H. Orvis and (1919) by Thomas Langford, London, then by her skipper H. Wright. Wrecked on Brighton Beach, December 1922. Owner-skipper, C. Dickinson of Sittingbourne, his son and a boy saved.

**ROSIE of Littlehampton      88823**
Built by Harvey at Littlehampton, 1886. 78 tons. Owned (1910) by J. Harvey and (1919) by Albert E. Scholey, London. Lost in English Channel.

**ROYAL OAK of Maldon      905**
Built at Limehouse, 1798. 71 x 20 x 5.1, 59 tons. Owned (1881 and 1893) by Vandervoord of Southend. Boomsail, running weekly service London to Southend, Wakering and Rochford. Condemned and dismantled, 1894.

**RUBY of Portsmouth      76905**
Built at Landport, 1877. 36 tons. Owned by J. T. Crampton of Portsmouth and (by 1919) by H. T. Crampton and (1934) by Henry Gilbert, Portsmouth.

**RUSSELL of Rochester      21799**
Built at Rochester 1865. 84 x 19 x 7, 94 tons. Schooner, owned by E. G. Watson, Rochester, presumably her builder. Sold (1877) to John

Smith, Burnham. Lost by stranding 1879.

**SD of London      114831**
Built by Smeed Dean at Murston, 1902. 97 x 23.4 x 8.1, 99 tons. Named after Smeed Dean, but commonly known as 'Sudden Death'. 'A big ugly square-stern ketch.' Owned (1900) by T. W. Howard and (1903) by Smeed Dean.

**SJB of Rochester      94562**
Built by R. M. Shrubsall at Sittingbourne, 1888. 46 tons. Ketch for S. J. Brice of Rainham, who owned her for over fifty years.

**ST ALBANS of London      68512**
Built by Castle, London, 1873. 90.8 x 21.7 x 7.7, 95 tons. Twelve years A1 at Lloyd's. 'London coaster.' Owned by H. Castle & Son. Out of register by 1881.

**SALLIE of Littlehampton      75235**
Built by Harvey at Littlehampton, 1879. 65 tons. Owned by Harvey. Out of register by 1890.

**SAPPHIRE of Colchester      22314**
Built 1867. 107 tons. Owned (1875) by William Sinnott, Nayland, Suffolk. Out of register by 1893.

**SAPPHIRE of Portsmouth      84226**
Built by J. T. Crampton at Landport, Hants, 1880. 51 tons. Owned by builder, and (1893) by John Bazley White and Bros., London.

**SARAH COLEBROOKE of Rye      128952**
Built by Smith at Rye, 1913. 102.6 x 24.6 x 8, 114 tons. Served as Q-ship *Bolham* in First World War, fitted with 90 h.p. auxiliary. Owned (1919) by G. Coote, and (1922) by J. Sawyer, Brightlingsea, and (1931) by her skipper, H. J. Polsford and (1934) as mb *Bolham* by Mrs M. Marshall-Hole, Emsworth, and Lt Cdr W. G. Gerard RN, London, and (1938) by John Coppack of Connah's Quay.

**SARAH SMEED of Rochester      67078**
Built by G. Smeed at Murston, 1874. 125.7 x 25.7 x 11, 241 tons. Three-masted schooner. Owned by George Smeed. Lost in 1882.

**SECUNDUS of Ipswich**
Built by Colchester at Ipswich, 1842. 59 x 12 x 5, 45 tons. Probably a sloop. Sold to London owners 1847.

**SEPTIMUS of Ipswich      27826**
Built by W. Read at Ipswich, 1860. 80.7 x 20 x 6. 75 tons. Sloop with lug mizzen converted to ketch in 1886. 'Similar to *Garson*.' Owned (1881 and 1890) by Mrs Mary Hayward, Pin Mill. Sunk in Hull Roads while lying at anchor with timber waiting for a tug, 1893.

**SEVEN SISTERS of Faversham (later of Rochester).      44093.**
Built by Frederick Sollitt at Smeed's yard at Sittingbourne, 1862. 116 x 23.2 x 9.1, 174 tons. Three-masted schooner, elliptical stern, converted to barquentine about 1881. Re-registered at Rochester 1882. Could load 300 tons. Out of register 1883.

**SEXTUS of Harwich      11866**
Built at Harwich, 1849. 80 x 20 x 6, 49 tons. Owned (1881) by John Watts, Harwich, and (1890) by W. Groom, Harwich, and (1919) by J. B. Groom and (1934) by London and Rochester Trading Co.

**SHAMROCK of Faversham**
See note at end of section.

**SOLENT of London      118476**
Built at Sittingbourne, 1904. 80 tons. Owned (1921) by E. Potton, Grays.

**SOUTHERN BELLE of London      89661**
Built by Gildea at Ipswich, 1885. 85 x 20.6 x 7, 80 tons. Owned by Herbert Hawkins, London, and English and Continental Shipping Co. Converted by 1890 to mulie. Owned by R. & W. Paul, Ipswich. Damaged in collision 1930, and hull presented to Ipswich Sea Scouts (renamed *Quest 1*).

**SPEEDWELL of
Colchester    87280**
Built by Taylor at Sittingbourne,
1883. 117 tons. Built for J. Smith of
Burnham. Traded regularly with
coal to Rigden's Faversham
brewery.

**SPY of Faversham (later of
Colchester)    11204**
Built by Goldfinch at Faversham,
1854. 75.7 x 18.5 x 7. Loaded 120
tons. 'Single-masted flat.' Nine
years A1 at Lloyd's. Sank twice
and unrigged and sold to J. H.
Beckwith, Colchester, as lighter,
1861. Perhaps the precursor of the
Kentish boomie. Out of register by
1890.

**STAR of Colchester    58160**
Built by Aldous at Brightlingsea,
1868. 80.5 x 20, 53 tons. Sprittie
converted to ketch before 1880.
Owned (1881 and 1893) by T.
Goddard, jun., Brightlingsea, and
(1901) at Lowestoft and (1906) at
Yarmouth (1935) jointly between
Capt Zabe Manners and MGS
Cargoes Ltd, Ryde, Isle of Wight.

**STARTLED FAWN of
Harwich    56431**
Built by Aldous at Brightlingsea,
1868. 100 x 23.2 x 8, 118 tons.
Owned (1881) by W. T. Griffith,
Ipswich, and (1890) by L.
Richmond, Harwich, and (by 1893)
by her skipper, James Meachen.
Run down in the Thames,
February 1916.

**STOUR of Harwich    18093**
Built by Vaux at Harwich, 1857. 99
tons. One of the pioneer schooner
barges. Doubled in 1887. Owned
by builder for over thirty years, and
on his death sold to A. S. Walton
of Newcastle, her skipper Captain
Day staying. Later sold to Matthew
and Luff, London. During the
illness of her last skipper, Captain
Layzell (who also had *Llama*),
stranded off Dungeness, 1904.
Crew saved.

**SUCCESS of London    118336**
Built by J. Kierits and Van Reede
Czn at Papendrecht, Holland,
1903. 90 x 23 x 9, 116 tons.
Steel-built as *Cymric*, sister to

spritties *Britannic, Celtic* and
*Oceanic*. Converted to boomie and
renamed after stranding in Isle of
Wight. Then reconverted to
sprittie, and (1932) to motor barge
with 100 h.p. engine. Owned by E.
J. and W. Goldsmith, Grays and
(1951 to 1964 as motor barge) by
London and Rochester Trading
Co.

**SUNBEAM of Harwich    91333**
Built by Vaux at Harwich, 1889.
101 x 22.5 x 8.5, 124 tons. One of
the most expensive boomies ever
built, she was lost on 2 October,
1892, bound from Sunderland to
Poole, when she was run down and
sunk by ss *Ariosto*. The crew were
saved. It was proved in the
Admiralty High Court that the
*Sunbeam* was not showing a stern
light. The expense and anxiety of
the case coming on top of the loss
caused her owner, William Gane of
Harwich, to commit suicide.

**SUNRISE of Rye    80256**
Built by Smith at Rye, 1890. 125
tons. Owned (1890 and 1893) by
W. G. Rubie of Rye. Sunk by
steamer, 1902.

**SURPRISE of Ipswich (later of
Maldon)    22187**
Built by W. Bayley at Ipswich,
1859. 84.6 x 21.5 x 7.3. Seven years
A1 at Lloyd's. Owned (1862) by
Bayley & Co. and Drummond,
Ipswich. Worked Ipswich to
Amsterdam in 1860s under C.
Harmer, followed by C. Osborn.
Registered at Maldon, 1866.

**SURPRISE of Rye    80255**
Built by Smith at Rye, 1889. 142
tons. Owned (1890 and 1893) by
W. G. Rubie, Rye. Out of register
by 1919.

**SUSIE of Littlehampton    75233**
Built by Harvey at Littlehampton,
1878. 88.6 x 18.8 x 6.1, 68 tons.
Found at sea, bottom up, 1892, but
still owned by her builders in 1893.
Out of register by 1919.

**SUSSEX BELLE of
London    99038**
Built by Smith at Rye, 1892. 80
tons. Built of Sussex oak, she was

often at Woodbridge, and was
much admired. Owned (1910 and
1919) by E. Garnham, Ipswich. In
1927, bound from Keadby to
Orford with coal, she anchored in
Yarmouth Roads, drove ashore in
an easterly gale and broke up.

**SYLPH of Harwich    78977**
Built by Vaux at Harwich, 1878. 95
tons. Owned (1881) by Robert
Gooch, Harwich, and (later) by
Robert Lewis of Harwich. Run
down in the Scheldt when only a
few years old. Lewis would not pay
for the salvage, for which reason
her sister ship *Active* could never
again go to Belgium.

**TEN BROTHERS of
Rochester    27618**
Built by E. G. Watson at
Rochester, 1860. 87 x 22 x 8.5, 122
tons. Five years A1 at Lloyd's.
Owned (1862) by builder, then by
J. Smith of Burnham. Sunk in fog
off North Shields by ss
*Northumbria*, May 1879. Captain
Ryder and crew picked up by
steamer.

**TERESA of London    10193**
Built by Alfred White at
Sittingbourne, 1892. 93 tons. Built
for owner, and owned (1893) by H.
White, London. Owned (1910) by
W. T. Howard and (1919 as ketch,
1938 as sprittie) by Samuel West,
taking ballast off Brightlingsea
beach. Then owned by Woods,
Gravesend, as *Teresa Wood*,
powder hulk. Sold 1957 for
houseboat at Oxford, but did not
get there. Owned (1958) by Sadd,
Maldon, as timber lighter. Ended
as houseboat *Teresa Wood* at
Woolverstone, Suffolk. Broken up
there 1978.

**TERTIUS of Ipswich    26547**
Built by Colchester at Ipswich,
1844. 60 x 15 x 5, 59 tons. Sloop
with lug mizzen, converted by 1881
to sprittie. Owned (1881 and 1890)
by J. Hooker, Ipswich. Out of
register by 1919.

**THALATTA of
Harwich    116179**
Built by McLearon at Harwich,

1906. 88.9 x 20.6 x 7, 72 tons. Transom-stern sprittie, converted to ketch by Horlock, Mistley. Sold (1917) to Wynnfield Shipping Co., Grimsby, who installed 70 h.p. engine. Rerigged as mulie (1923), and engine removed by Captain Body of Southend. Sold (1933) to R. & W. Paul, Ipswich. Traded as motor barge till 1966, when sold to East Coast Sail Trust, which rerigged her as a mulie, using mainmast and topmast from sb *Memory*. Still afloat.

**THE DARNET**
See *Darnet, The*.

**THE FRANCIS**
See *Francis, The*.

**THISTLE of Colchester    93971**
Built by Taylor at Sittingbourne, 1887. 103 x 23.5 x 8.9, 137 tons. Loaded 260 tons. One of the big colliers owned by J. Smith, Burnham. Sold (1916) to A. Moore, London, and finished as coal hulk *Jacques* at Le Havre.

**THISTLE of London    105727**
Built at Port Glasgow, 1895. 79 tons. Converted to sprittie about 1930. Probably the only Scottish-built boomie, and one of the few built of iron. Owned (1919 and 1938) by H. A. Covington, London, and later by London and Rochester Trading Co. Restored at Woodbridge 1980.

**THOMAS ETHERDEN of Harwich    65421**
Built 1862. Boomsail. Owned by C. Forster, Harwich. Out of register by 1893.

**THORNEY ISLAND of Portsmouth    62185**
Built by Foster at Emsworth, 1870. 185 tons. Brigantine owned by builder, then by Ash, coal merchant, Portsmouth. Unique in having raised quarterdeck. A hulk at Emsworth till end of First World War.

**THREE BROTHERS of Rochester    29436**
Built at Aylesford, 1861. 72 tons. Sloop later converted into ketch.

Transom stern 'like *Eustace*'. Owned (1881 and 1890) by J. Stone, Strood. Out of register by 1919.

**TRALY of London (later of Barnstaple)    128846**
Built at Millwall, 1912. 79.7 x 20.1 x 9, 70 tons. Pioneer attempt to combine sail and power, with engine and without leeboards. Owned (1922) by Wynnfield Shipping Co., and (1923 and 1940) by W. W. Petherick & Sons Ltd, Bude, Cornwall.

**TRIM of Harwich    84026**
Built by Vaux at Harwich, 1881. 95.3 x 22.1 x 8.3, 119 tons. Owned by William Christie, Ipswich. Left Ipswich, 27 February 1907, for Gateshead with timber. Damaged in collision with ketch *Aquila* and repaired at Yarmouth. Sailed again, and found lying off Sunderland flying distress signals by trawler *Doreen*. Sank, and crew rescued exhausted from their boat.

**TRIUMPH of Maldon    17813**
Built at Stow Creek, Burnham, 1842. 68.2 x 21.7 x 5.8, 57 tons. Owned by Green, Stowmaries, Essex. Involved in sinking of schooner *Fanny* off Scarborough in February 1873. Rebuilt at Greenwich (1887) as sprittie *Coombdale*.

**TYNEMOUTH CASTLE of London    98074**
Built by W. Dobson & Co at Newcastle, 1890. 100 x 24.1 x 9.9, 173 tons. 'One bulkhead, cemented, one deck, part steel, part iron.' Owned by Walker and Howard of London. One of the very few iron (or steel?) built boomies. Lost November 1893.

**UNITY of Ipswich    86627**
Built by Curtis at Ipswich, 1885. 85.4 x 20.6 x 6.8, 79 tons. Owned (1890 and 1893) by George Hayward, Pin Mill, and (1927) by Walter and Robert Rands. Later sold to Sadd of Maldon as a lighter. Out of register by 1934. Her hulk now lies in Samson's Creek, West Mersea.

**UNITY of Rye    80259**
Built by Smith at Rye, 1892. 126 tons. Owned (1893) by James Ward at Rye, and known as 'the big *Unity*'. She proved cranky, and was the only boomie requiring ballast. Out of register by 1919.

**VANGUARD of Colchester    87290**
Built by Taylor at Sittingbourne, 1885. 113 tons. A big collier ketch owned by J. Smith, Burnham. 'Similar to *Thistle*.' Lost in 1916.

**VICTORIA of London**
See note at end of section.

**WANDLE**
See *Dolgwandle*.

**WARWICK CASTLE of London    99174**
Built by Harvey at Littlehampton, 1892. 76 tons. Owned by Walker and Howard, London. Lost off Flamborough.

**WELLHOLME of Littlehampton    131976**
Built by Harvey at Littlehampton, 1916. 88 tons. Owned by Wynnfield Shipping Co., Grimsby. Out of register by 1934.

**WESSEX of Littlehampton    131977**
Built by Harvey at Littlehampton, 1918. 100.7 x 24.2 x 8.4, 84 tons. Pole-masted auxiliary ketch. Owned by Vectis Shipping Co. (m.o. Charles Price, Newport), trading to Isle of Wight, before Second World War. Last owned by Williams Steamship Co., Southampton. 96 h.p. engine installed by 1934. Broken up at Woolston, 1958.

**WESTERN BELLE of Exeter (later of Poole and of Guernsey)    69573**
Built by Holman at Topsham, Devon, 1879. 80 tons. Sprittie converted to ketch. Owned by John Holman, London, and his family and (1880s) by Herbert Hawkins and (by 1890) by English and Continental Shipping Co.

159

Then (1909) sold to George Paton, London, bargemaster, and after his death (1912) his widow. Owned (1912) by Reginald Renard, London, bargemaster, and (1917) by Thomas Ward of Gravesend and (1919) by Charles Leech, Guernsey. Lost by fire at sea, 31 May 1922.

### WILLIAM of Ipswich          79052
Built by Curtis at Ipswich, 1878. 87 x 21 x 7, 78 tons. 'Like *Empress of India*.' Owned (1881) by W. J. Curtis, Ipswich, and (1890) by Edmund Smith, Brightlingsea, then by her skipper, William Douse. On 2 October 1895 on passage Swansea to Wells, with coal, parted her cable and became total loss on Trebethcock Rock, Padstow. Captain Douse and crew saved by lifeboat.

### WILLIAM LEVITT
See *Emily Lloyd*

### WILLIAM PORTER of Rochester          58529
Built by Nash at Battersea, 1871. 83.7 x 20 x 6.5, 83 tons. Built under a roof, and given thirteen years A1 at Lloyd's. Owned by Webster & Co. 'London coaster.' Converted to sprittie by 1881, and owned by Burham Brick, Lime and Cement Co.

### WILLIAM VARNEY of Rochester          67028
Built by Burham Brick Co. at Aylesford, 1871. 95.2 x 21 x 7, 93 tons. 'More or less like *Pearl*.' Still in builders' ownership 1890. Out of register by 1919.

### WINIFRED MARY of Faversham          89863
Built at Whitstable, 1890. 109 tons. 'Like *Pearl* but bigger.' Owned by C. Marshall, Faversham. Lost November 1893.

### WORRYNOT of Littlehampton          131971
Built by Harvey at Littlehampton, 1910. 93 tons. Owned by J. Harvey and (1919) by Wynnfield Shipping Co., Grimsby.

### YULAN of Harwich          78980
Built by Parsons and Cann at Harwich, 1879. 73 tons. Owned (1881) by George Cann, Harwich, and (1890) by James Chaplin, Brightlingsea, and (1910) by W. Groom, Harwich. Captain Lewis of Woodbridge once took three months in her, taking a freight of chalk to Scotland and returning. In 1902 towed into Newhaven disabled off Portland, bound from Hull to Salcombe with coals under Captain Whinney of Ipswich. Lost on Goodwins, 30 January 1911, bound from Belgium to London with paper pulp.

### ZEBRINA of Faversham          60245
Built by Gann at Whitstable, 1873. 109.1 x 24.5 x 9.9, 169 tons. Eleven years A1 at Lloyd's. Nicknamed 'The Three-legged Stool'. Three-masted schooner or barquentine, with square chine but without leeboards, for river Plate trade. After eight years returned to home coasting. Owned (1873) by Holden and Gann Bros, Whitstable, and (1881) by Thomas Gann junr and (1890) by Whitstable Shipping Co and (1927) by Ajax Shipping Co., London. In 1932 coal cargo caught fire, and she put into Cowes badly burned. In 1937 sold for £50 to a Portsmouth firm of metal merchants who stated an intention to rename her *Mary Celeste*, to commemorate the fact that both vessels were found abandoned at sea, with no subsequent trace of their crews. But owned (1938 and 1944) by her owner-master David Morgan, Bedminster, Bristol, fitted with 55 h.p. engine.

### ZENOBIA of London          91903
Built by Bayley at Ipswich, 1886. 85.6 x 20.6 x 6.9, 78 tons. Owned (1890-3) by F. and A. Claydon, London, and (1912) by Bushell of Dover and (1918-21) by Claydon and (1926) by Mrs A. Howlett, Gravesend, and (1927) by F. Howlett and (1938) by William Howlett. Broken up at Gravesend by 1947, probably in early 1940s.

### ZEPHYR
See note at end of section.

The foregoing summary leaves a few questions unanswered.

The *Victoria* of London was burned out in the West Swin in November 1887 through her captain upsetting an oil lamp when turning in. The crew of four landed on Clacton pier. Only spr<sup></sup>itties of this name are in the register, and it seems likely she was converted from one of these without correction of this record. The likeliest (based on tonnage, and the fact she had a flag signal) was one built at Brightlingsea in 1862, of 63 tons, owned by J. Hooker, London. She was, however, still registered as a sprittie in 1881.

The *Zephyr* was described as 'a big square-stern boomie owned by Richmond at Harwich and at one time skippered by Captain Layzell'. Again she is not to be found in the register. (*Zephyr* of Ipswich was an old Whitby-built brig, and a ketch built at Rye in 1894 was only 29 tons, and so presumably a fisherman.)

We have also unconfirmed references to *Express* of Ipswich (lost in 1881), *Hetty* of Harwich and *Shamrock* of Faversham.

The first of these we have failed to trace.

The *Hetty* of Harwich, built at Krimpen in 1903, had a klipper's fiddle bow, standing bowsprit and counter stern, which probably suggested a boomie origin. She was, however, always a sprittie.

The sprittie *Shamrock* of Faversham (104943) built at Milton in 1899, may also have started as a boomie, but again we have no evidence.

# APPENDIX 2
# Some Principal Builders

**JOHN VAUX, Harwich**

| | |
|---|---|
| *Stour* | 1857 |
| *Gloriana* | 1871 |
| *Laura* | 1873 |
| *Enterprise* | 1874 |

**JOHN HENRY VAUX, Harwich**

| | |
|---|---|
| *Llama* | 1875 |
| *Ornate* | 1875 |
| *Empress* | 1876 |
| *Active* | 1877 |
| *Mary Lyne* | 1878 |
| *Sylph* | 1878 |
| *Carlbury* | 1879 |
| *Hesper* | 1879 |
| *Landermere* | 1879 |
| *Lymington* | 1880 |
| *Eliza H* | 1881 |
| *Trim* | 1881 |
| *Ada Gane* | 1882 |
| *Alcyone* | 1884 |
| *Genesta* | 1886 |
| *Jubilee* | 1887 |
| *Sunbeam* | 1889 |
| *Doric* | 1892 |
| *Britannia* | 1893 |

**W. B. McLEARON, Harwich**

| | |
|---|---|
| *Major* | 1897 |
| *Alice May* | 1899 |
| *Dannebrog* | 1901 |

**W. B. McLEARON JNR, Harwich**

| | |
|---|---|
| *Thalatta* | 1906 |

**PARSONS & CANN, Harwich**

| | |
|---|---|
| *Mechanic* | 1872 |
| *Amy* | 1873 |
| *Cyllene* | 1873 |
| *Francis* | 1877 |

| | |
|---|---|
| *Yulan* | 1879 |
| *Glenrosa* | 1884 |

**GEORGE CANN, Harwich**

| | |
|---|---|
| *Mazeppa* | 1887 |

**JOHN CANN, Harwich**

| | |
|---|---|
| *Carisbrooke Castle* | 1890 |

**ALDOUS, Brightlingsea**

| | |
|---|---|
| *Victoria* (?) | 1862 |
| *Jabez* | 1863 |
| *Dovercourt* | 1865 |
| *James Bowles* | 1865 |
| *Era* | 1867 |
| *Harwich* | 1867 |
| *Star* | 1868 |
| *Startled Fawn* | 1868 |
| *Antelope* | 1869 |
| *Masonic* | 1876 |

**W. J. CURTIS, Ipswich**

| | |
|---|---|
| *Mystery* | 1874 |
| *Gazelle* | 1877 |
| *William* | 1878 |
| *Reindeer* | 1879 |
| *James Garfield* | 1881 |
| *Unity* | 1885 |

**G. P. GILDEA & Co, Ipswich**

| | |
|---|---|
| *Northern Belle* | 1885 |
| *Southern Belle* | 1885 |
| *Lord Shaftesbury* | 1886 |
| *Lord Hartington* | 1887 |
| *Lord Iddesleigh* | 1888 |

**E. J. ROBERTSON, Ipswich**

| | |
|---|---|
| *Lothair* | 1872 |
| *Alice Watts* | 1875 |
| *Lucy Richmond* | 1875 |

| | |
|---|---|
| *Hudson* | 1878 |
| *Ninita* | 1880 |
| *Lilly* | 1884 |

**W. (later V. D.) COLCHESTER of Ipswich**

| | |
|---|---|
| *Primus* | 1841 |
| *Secundus* | 1842 |
| *Tertius* | 1844 |
| *Quintus* | 1847 |
| *Mary* | 1848 |
| *May Flower* | 1870 |
| *Osprey* | 1874 |
| *Fearless* | 1876 |
| *Davenport* | 1877 |
| *Eastern Belle* | 1883 |

**W. BAYLEY & Co. Ipswich**

| | |
|---|---|
| *Alpha* | 1858 |
| *Surprise* | 1859 |
| *Problem* | 1861 |
| *Parkend* | 1873 |
| *Azariah* | 1878 |
| *Onward* | 1878 |
| *Ida* | 1881 |
| *Blanche* | 1884 |
| *Moss Rose* | 1884 |
| *Zenobia* | 1886 |
| *Byculla* | 1887 |
| *Alert* | 1888 |

**ORVIS & FULLER, Ipswich**

| | |
|---|---|
| *Eliza Patience* | 1883 |
| *Matilda Upton* | 1887 |
| *Pearl* | 1889 |
| *Lord Tennyson* | 1891 |

**R. PECK, Ipswich**

| | |
|---|---|
| *Ethel Edith* | 1892 |
| *Ivy P* | 1893 |

### J. M. GOLDFINCH, Faversham

| | |
|---|---|
| *Garibaldi* | 1861 |
| *Ann Goodhugh* | 1872 |
| *Pioneer* | 1876 |
| *Bessie Hiller* | 1881 |
| *Cock of the Walk* | 1882 |
| *Nancy* | 1890 |
| *Goldfinch* | 1894 |

### SMEED, Sittingbourne
(under foremanship of Mr F. Sollitt)

| | |
|---|---|
| *Garibaldi* | 1862 |
| *Seven Sisters* | 1862 |
| *Invicta* | 1863 |
| *Eliza Smeed* | 1865 |
| *George Smeed* | 1866 |
| *Esther Smeed* | 1868 |
| *John Ward* | 1871 |
| *Ellen Smeed* | 1872 |
| *Emily Smeed* | 1872 |
| *Sarah Smeed* | 1874 |

(Under foremanship of Mr Denham)

| | |
|---|---|
| *SD* | 1902 |

### ALFRED WHITE, Sittingbourne

| | |
|---|---|
| *Teresa* | 1892 |
| *Harold* | 1900 |
| *Medina* | 1906 |

### ROBERT MARK SHRUBSALL, Sittingbourne (Milton)

| | |
|---|---|
| *Meteor* | 1863 |
|   (ex *Eclipse*) | |
| *Alpha* | 1865 |
| *Agnes* | 1874 |
| *Mystery* | 1875 |
| *Lord Beaconsfield* | 1878 |
|   (built as sprittie) | |

| | |
|---|---|
| *Genesta* | 1887 |
| *SJB* | 1888 |

### JOHN AND STEPHEN TAYLOR, Sittingbourne

| | |
|---|---|
| *Adsey* | 1863 |
| *Maria* (I) | 1864 |
| *Edith Wood* | 1865 |
| *Fanny Rapson* | 1866 |
| *Maria* (II) | 1866 |
| Schooner barge name unknown | |
| | 1867 |
| *Mayland* | 1868 |
| *Europa* | 1871 |
| *William Levitt* | 1872 |
|   (later *Emily Lloyd*) | |

### ALFRED AND JOHN TAYLOR, Sittingbourne

| | |
|---|---|
| *Speedwell* | 1883 |
| *Magnet* | 1884 |
| *Vanguard* | 1885 |
| *Thistle* | 1887 |
| *Queen Mab* | 1888 |
| *Rochester Castle* | 1889 |
| *Friendship* | 1890 |

### J. & W. B. HARVEY, Littlehampton

| | |
|---|---|
| *Forerunner* | 1862 |
| *Annie* | 1877 |
| *Susie* | 1878 |
| *Sallie* | 1879 |
| *Maggie* | 1880 |
| *Nellie* | 1882 |
| *General Gordon* | 1885 |
| *Rosie* | 1886 |
| *Lord Salisbury* | 1887 |
| *Arundel Castle* | 1888 |
| *Lord Churchill* | 1888 |

| | |
|---|---|
| *Lord Beaconsfield* | 1889 |
| *Lord Beresford* | 1889 |
| *Lord Hamilton* | 1889 |
| *Lord Nelson* | 1889 |
| *Lord Wolseley* | 1889 |
| *Lord Dufferin* | 1890 |
| *Dolgwandle* | 1891 |
|   (later *Gravelines III*) | |
| *Lord Alcester* | 1891 |
| *Lord Napier* | 1891 |
| *Athole* | 1892 |
| *Eric* | 1892 |
| *Warwick Castle* | 1892 |
| *Princess May* | 1893 |
| *Bona* | 1898 |
| *Nell Jess* | 1902 |
| *Kindly Light* | 1905 |
| *Leading Light* | 1906 |
| *Boaz* | 1908 |
| *Clymping* | 1909 |
| *Worrynot* | 1910 |
| *Gippeswic* | 1912 |
| *Wellholme* | 1916 |
| *Wessex* | 1918 |
| *Moultonian* | 1919 |

### G. AND T. SMITH, Rye

| | |
|---|---|
| *Enterprise* | 1888 |
| *Surprise* | 1889 |
| *Mountsfield* | 1890 |
| *Sunrise* | 1890 |
| *Diana* | 1891 |
| *Sussex Belle* | 1892 |
| *Unity* | 1892 |
| *Evelyn* | 1900 |
| *Martinet* | 1912 |
| *Sarah Colebrooke* | 1913 |

# Rigging Plans
## *Justice* and *Pearl*

The prudent skipper kept a note of his spar lengths in case he needed it to order a replacement. The notes kept by Captain Pollock for the *Justice* (88 ft long, 90 tons) and by Captain Mynheer for the *Pearl* (85 ft long, 88 tons) have survived.

|  | **JUSTICE** | **PEARL** |
|---|---|---|
| **Mainmast** | 63 ft (truck to keelson, 8 ft below deck) | 57 ft (truck to deck) |
| **Topmast** | 46 ft (including 8 ft doubling, so topmast truck was 101 feet above keelson) | 38 ft |
| **Mizzen** | 42 ft | 54 ft |
| **Main boom** | 40 ft | 35 ft 2 in |
| **Bowsprit** | 30 ft 6 in (overall) | 26 ft (to stem) |
| **Mizzen gaff** | 20 ft 6 in (excluding jaws) | 15 ft 6 in |
| **Main gaff** |  | 27 ft |
| **Mizzen boom** |  | 35 ft 2 in |
| ***Masthead** |  | 11 ft 6 in |
| ***Mizzen masthead** |  | 17 ft 6 in |

*Presumably the part above the hounds.

On another occasion, however, Mynheer said, 'The *Pearl's* mizzen was the same length as her main mast above deck. It was 56 feet. The main mast was longer because it went through to the keelson whereas the mizzen mast was in a tabernacle. I cut four feet off both.' Since this does not tally, I assume he means he cut down both masts till they were approximately the same length, as above.

# APPENDIX 4
# Values

The Harwich Barge Alliance Insurance Association list of 1910 includes the value of craft insured. These were presumably owner's valuations, and doubtless some owners preferred a high figure and some a low one. With this reservation, they give some indication of the quality of the fleet at this time, with an average value around £900. *Olympia* was the highest valued, at £1800, with *Boaz, Clymping, Leading Light* and *Nell Jess* at £1600 or over. At the other extreme, *Hudson* and *Mystery* (of Faversham) are valued at £500 or under. This list reads:

| | |
|---|---|
| *Ada Gane* | £975 |
| *Alice Watts* | £900 |
| *Athole* | £1500 |
| *Azariah* | £600 |
| *Birthday* | £600 |
| *Blanche* | £450 |
| *Boaz* | £1600 |
| *Britannia* | £1050 |
| *Britannic* | £1200 |
| *Cock o' the Walk* | £750 |
| *Clymping* | £1600 |
| *Dannebrog* | £1350 |
| *Davenport* | £675 |
| *Diana* | £1200 |
| *Dovercourt* | £750 |
| *Eastern Belle* | £600 |
| *Enterprise* (of Harwich) | £600 |
| *Evelyn* | £1275 |
| *Fearless* | £675 |
| *Flower of Essex* | £750 |
| *Gazelle* | £675 |
| *Genesta* (of Harwich) | £1050 |
| *Goldfinch* | £1200 |
| *Gravelines III* | £500 |
| *Harold* | £1350 |
| *Harwich* | £600 |
| *Hesper* | £900 |
| *Hudson* | £500 |
| *Ivy P* | £900 |
| *James Garfield* | £750 |
| *Justice* | £1050 |
| *Kindly Light* | £1500 |
| *Laura* | £900 |
| *Leading Light* | £1650 |
| *Lily* (of Rye) | £750 |
| *Lord Lansdowne* | £900 |
| *Maggie* | £900 |
| *Matilda Upton* | £900 |
| *May Queen* | £600 |
| *Mazeppa* | £600 |
| *Medina* | £1125 |
| *Mystery* (of Faversham) | £450 |
| *Mystery* (of Harwich) | £825 |
| *Nell Jess* | £1650 |
| *Nellie* | £675 |
| *Olympia* | £1800 |
| *Pearl* (of Ipswich) | £700 |
| *Princess May* (of Littlehampton) | £900 |
| *Princess May* (of Poole) | £900 |
| *Queen Mab* | £750 |
| *Rose Bud* | £600 |
| *Rosie* | £900 |
| *Startled Fawn* | £825 |
| *Susie* | £600 |
| *Sussex Belle* | £1050 |
| *Teresa* | £1200 |
| *Unity* (of Ipswich) | £825 |
| *Yulan* | £600 |

The list for 1927, which also survives, shows the following craft still in membership:

| | |
|---|---|
| *Azariah* | £600 |
| *Britannia* | £1050 |
| *Davenport* | £900 |
| *Flower of Essex* | £750 |
| *Goldfinch* | £1500 |
| *Matilda Upton* | £1500 |
| *Mystery* (of Faversham) | £900 |
| *Mystery* (of Harwich) | £1500 |
| *Pearl* | £675 |
| *Sussex Belle* | £900 |

At this date the best spritties, including *Olive May* and *Raybel*, were valued as high as £3200.

# Index of Ships' Names

# General Index

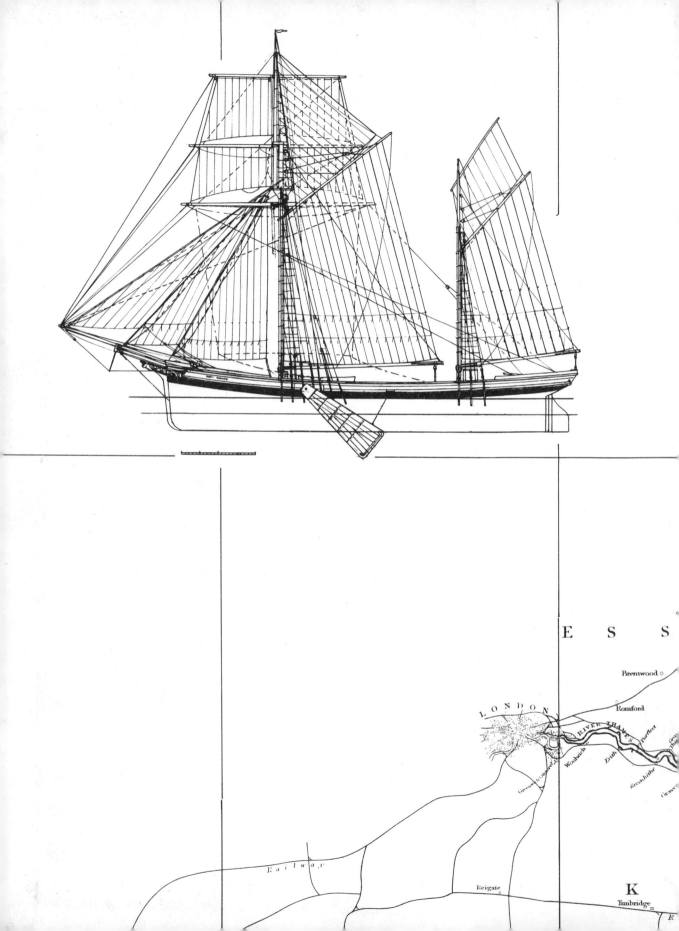